MERCEDES LADIES

MERCEDES LADIES

Sheri Sher

VIBE STREET LIT
is a division of VIBE Media Group, LLC.
215 Lexington Avenue
New York, NY 10016
Rob Kenner, Editorial Director

KENSINGTON BOOKS are published by
Kensington Publishing Corp.
850 Third Avenue
New York, NY 10022

All Kensington titles, imprints, and distributed lines are available at special quantity discounts for bulk purchases for sales promotion, premiums, fund-raising, educational or institutional use.

Special book excerpts or customized printings can also be created to fit specific needs. For details, write or phone the office of the Kensington Special Sales Manager: Attn: Special Sales Department. Kensington Publishing Corp., 850 Third Avenue, New York, NY 10022. Phone: 1-800-221-2647.

Kensington Books Reg. U.S. Pat. & TM Off.

ISBN-13: 978-1-60183-003-6
ISBN-10: 1-60183-003-3

First Printing: March 2008

10 9 8 7 6 5 4 3 2 1

Printed in the United States of America

Acknowledgments

To my Lord and Savior Jesus Christ, thank you for blessing me with favor. To my wonderful husband, my lovely in-laws Johnny and Lilly, and my whole family—all thirty-five nieces and nephews, twenty-two great-nieces and -nephews, six sisters, four brothers, and especially my moms, still hanging in there strong. Thanks for your strength, your grace, your patience, your unconditional love, your godliness, independence, resilience . . . and thanks for not letting me give up when I wanted to die at times, and helping me to prosper in all respects. Love you so much.

Thanks and praise to you, Heavenly Father.
Please watch over the loved ones, friends, and hip-hop brothers who've passed away:
Gordon, a/k/a Paul, my brother. Miss you sooo much.
Willie, a/k/a Cooley, my brother. Miss you sooo much.
My nephew Terry
My nephew Chris
Great-grandma, who taught me that spirituality helps one get through it all
Sarroya
Byrd
Keith Cowboy
My hip-hop family
Ol' Dirty Bastard
Big Pun
Big L
Jam Master Jay
Donald Dee
Angela Graham
Rest in Peace

Shout-outs:
To my husband, partner, and friend, **BMDubb**.
I could not have done it without you. You're the greatest!
Love ya, Will.
You're the next awesome talent, that Real Harlem Kat, and
that's solving that!
They need not sleep!

To **Gloria, Janet, Valerie, Pamela, Styrus, Calvin, Jerome,**
and adopted brother **Roberto**: love y'all.
To **Rob Kenner** for seeing and believing in my vision and
taking the chance.
To **Kenard Gibbs, Mimi Valdés, Cristina Veran**, and **Rob
Marriott**
for recognizing The Mercedes Ladies.

To Official Kustomz; Ali Brook, Lefty (Rob), and Sketch;
thanks for the awesome cover.
To The Mercedes Young Ladies—my sisters for life. I love
you all.
To all my True-School Pioneers—love y'all too.
Pebblee Poo: My girl. Hang in there, Mama.
Brooklyn is definitely in the house.
Hannah: Thanks for getting me through crazy days on the
job. You're one of a kind.
My OPD peeps from Harlem Hospital.
Janet Taylor, MD: You're truly a gem. Love ya!
Guy Fisher: Thanks for everything. You truly touched my life.
David Winfield: Thank you.

My Academy brothers and sisters—"D" squad for life.
My new friends at Bronx Supreme Court.
My locker room girls, Suite 9—you know who you are!
Wilson Projects; Marty and Hesse & 1199 / my hood.
Mike & Natalie
V12: Vance, keep doing ya thing.

Sha Rock
Bambaataa & Zulu Nation

Much props to the success of:
Russell Simmons
Andre Harrell
Alonzo Brown
Sean "Puffy" Combs
Nelson George

To **Danyel Smith** and everybody at *VIBE*, *VIBE Vixen*, and Kensington Publishing.
Thank you from the bottom of my heart.

I've got to send shout-outs to my favorite ladies of today:
Lil' Kim: I always love your tone and the way you attack the tracks.
Remy Ma: Keep filling the void of female rappers for today. Keep ya head up.
Missy Elliott: When I met you, you kept it real. Much respect.
Mary J. Blige: Words can't describe. You're truly a hip-hop queen.
Foxy: Loved your rugged sound from day one.
Eve: You've got your own style. And you remind me so much of Lina.
Keyshia Cole: I can just feel the realness.

And last but not least, my favorite male hit list:
Snoop Dogg: Only one of a kind.
50 Cent: Who can't love 50?
Jay-Z: Can't get enough.
Biggie Smalls: Classic.
Tupac: Prophet.
Dr. Dre: Wow, if he would produce The Mercedes Ladies . . . a dream.

Kanye West: Ain't mad at ya.
The whole Dirty South: Can't get enough of those Dirty South boys . . . fa real!
Diplomats: They're from around the way.
KRS-One: Thanks for the encouragement.

To my hip-hop generation: Please recognize the true soldiers you're meant to be . . . God bless!

P.S. If there is anyone I missed, sorry . . .

Preface

For the past twenty-five years, I've been approached by all types of journalists, historians, filmmakers, and fans from all over the world who are curious about hip-hop's founding females. Some people have the notion that Salt 'N' Pepa were the first women to make a mark in "the rap game." Well, just for the record, Sequence was the first group of female rappers to record a single in 1979. They were three young ladies from down South—including Angie B, who would become the soon-to-be-famous Angie Stone—who could sing and rap. Sylvia Robinson, the same woman who released rap's first true hit single, "Rapper's Delight" by The Sugar Hill Gang, was the label executive responsible for Sequence's breakthrough hit "Gonna Funk You Right On Up." After the era of Sequence, Sha Rock, and Roxanne Shante, the floodgates were opened and out poured a stream of bold soul sisters from Salt 'N' Pepa and Queen Latifah all the way to Lauryn Hill and Lil' Kim. Forget what ya heard about rap being a man's world. Women have been a part of hip-hop from the very beginning. And The Mercedes Ladies were hip-hop's first all-female DJ and MC crew.

Whenever I'm invited to colleges, radio shows, or panel discussions, I hear the same questions over and over. How did

The Mercedes Ladies start? What kind of obstacles did you face? Why did y'all not make it? It is so pleasing to see how many people of all ages are interested to learn about the female pioneers who did their thing back in the days. Time after time, after the many conventions and award shows that I've participated in, people always ask, Why don't you write a book? I believe that it's important to tell the whole truth about the first all-female DJ and MC crew—how we paid our dues while going through the trials and tribulations of broken homes, poverty, heartbreaks, drugs, alcohol, violence—all the elements of life the way it was dealt to us. I wanted to capture the realness of how we were living and what we went through, and our states of mind during that time without all the stereotypes society perpetuates about young women of color—you know, how we're all supposed to be hood rats with bad attitudes, no goals or ambitions, getting pregnant at early ages, selling our bodies, hooked on drugs, on our way to jail. I decided to write this book after years and years of doubt, not wanting to ruin anybody's reputation or make someone look bad. You see, I have crossed paths with some of the biggest movers and shakers in the hip-hop industry, back when they were just starting out. So I decided that the best way to tell the whole truth was to write a novel based on a true story. You know what they say—the truth is stranger than fiction. Many names in this book have been changed, but that just means the story is that much more real.

Through it all, my aim is to show that we were as strong and determined as our brothers in hip-hop. And no matter what the cultural critics say about rap degrading females and damaging their self-respect, that's not what hip-hop culture is all about. And The Mercedes Ladies are the living proof. Against all odds, our all-female crew made hip-hop history—without having to exploit our bodies. Whether we were doing it in the parks, the rec centers, or on the street corners, The Mercedes Ladies presented nothing more or less than our raw talents. Even though we never got the monetary reward, or in some cases the recognition we worked so hard for, we still paved the way for other women who followed in our footsteps. Let it be known that hip-hop was not just a man's world, but females helped mold it too.

Some people call us the "Dream Girls" of hip-hop. But this is not the Hollywood version of that story. Unlike Beyoncé or Jennifer Hudson, we didn't have record deals or even *American Idol*. But we held on to our dreams. And for us, that was enough.

So here it is, at last—the first female hip-hop story, as told through the eyes of one who never lost sight of the dream. One who ran the streets of the Bronx—along with the rest of my all-female DJ and MC crew—and lived to tell the tale.

Now, you may ask yourself, why did we do it? Well, we sure didn't start rapping so we could be rich and famous. If that was our only motivation, then we were definitely wasting our time. Hold up! Wait a minute! Isn't hip-hop supposed to be "All About the Benjamins"? Well, not for us. Don't get me wrong— money and fame are cool. But we were after something else. Like Aretha Franklin, we just wanted a little respect. Actually, let me rephrase that—we wanted maximum respect. And as young women of color trying to make our way in this male-dominated arena called hip-hop, we deserved it.

This is the tale of seven teenage girls from different areas of the Bronx whose paths came together during the late 1970s to create an everlasting bond. We had so much in common. Being raised in single-parent homes in a poverty-stricken environment without father figures made life a constant struggle. Of course we were all unique individuals with our own personalities and family backgrounds. But nevertheless, our neighborhood, and especially hip-hop culture, helped to mold us into independent, strong, and feisty young females who were more than able to handle the challenges we would face as we found our way through life.

Being females made the odds long and the stakes high, but we were determined to gain respect from our male competitors while struggling with our individual demons and surviving all the pressures of the streets. We stayed steady on the grind to build our street reputation as Mercedes Ladies. But in time, betrayal, drugs, homelessness, and just being victims of our environment began taking a toll. Our hopes were constantly being crushed, our drive began slowly fading, we started turning against one another. All the negativity that surrounded us eventually ate away at our dreams of just wanting to be respected for our talents. But hip-hop itself was never the problem. It was our solution, a mental escape from it all.

Hip-hop culture stems from the way we were brought up, our neighborhood and the things we experienced there. It's the way we played the hand that was dealt to us. It's the way we struggled with the pain of young lives lost, of not knowing where tomorrow's meal was coming from or even whether there would be a roof over our head. It's crying for a moment, then standing like a trooper. It's the ass beatings, the junkies, the crackheads, the drug dealers, the churchgoers, the stickup kids, the number runners, the baby daddies, the down-low hos, and all the fatherless children. It's the hustlers, the hoochies, the players, the strippers, and the wannabe balers. It's the noisy tenant patrol, the nosy neighbors, the bodegas, the Chinese spots, the corner liquor stores, the park benches, and the basketball courts. It's the gangbangers and the banging systems riding by, whether in a hoopty or an SUV on chrome. Hip-hop makes you feel *that* vibe. It makes you hear our cry for long overdue salvation. Hip-hop is the sound of the so-called "ghetto children," who have not yet discovered their worth; the real soldiers, children of God. Hip-hop generates so much raw power that it totally contradicts what the rest of the world was brainwashed to believe by media, politicians, music industry bigwigs, and all those who underestimated our true potential—even ourselves. Upscale society used to hide our world from their children. Now their children want to be just like these ghetto children. But with all the glamour and glitter, let's not forget those true values of hip-hop. Its true essence lies in how society left us out there with nothing to look forward to but welfare, broken homes, drugs, alcohol, violence, and all the negativity that life can bring—right down to feeling ashamed of our own skin. But like the Bible says, "the first shall be last and the last shall be first." And yes, roses do grow in the cracks of the concrete.

So get ready to learn the truth about your hip-hop heritage. The Mercedes Ladies may not have reaped monetary benefits or the glitz that "the game" soon delivered. But one thing we do have is the title of being the first all-female DJ and MC crew from the Bronx. Nobody can ever take that away from us. We will forever be a part of history. Wait a minute—let me rephrase that. Not just "His" story. This is "Her" story. *Our* story.

Prologue

The Mind-Frame of a Young Black Girl

I have a dream, I guess. Wait a minute—let me rephrase that. I have an urge to *become* somebody. I want to be an actress, but I live in the hood. Nobody gets discovered here. Who the hell is going to come to my part of the Bronx and risk getting shot or mugged to find talent? I want to be a lawyer, somebody important, but who am I kidding? You need good grades and money for college, unless you have a special talent and you're fortunate enough to get a scholarship. Moms can't afford to send me to college. She has ten mouths to feed all by herself. She's working day and night just to put meals on the table and keep that roof over our heads. She's stressed out all the time. She has no time to discuss my dreams. I understand. So all I can do is imagine.

It's hard to concentrate in school. There's too many problems at home, and besides, even the teachers don't seem to give a shit. They never reached out to me. Just once, one of them could have said, "Hey, Shelly, why do you keep cutting classes? You need to study." But no. They don't understand nor care about my struggle anyway. The streets are calling me; the urge to be out there just keeps growing and growing. I am searching for something. I just don't know what it is yet. One thing I do know is that I don't want to be a junkie. I don't want to sell drugs or steal either. I can't stand the thought of my freedom being taken away. What other choices do I have? I have something special, but what . . . ? I am a young black female. My body is all I have that's mine. I can freely give it away or cherish it, demanding respect from the male species. I choose to cherish my body, so selling it is out of the question.

I'm out here in the streets no matter what my moms says. I don't mean to stress her out, but what else is there for me to do? I just can't sit at home watching her struggle. That shit hurts my heart. I have to go out there and search! I am going to take my chances. Any worries about the dangers out there will just have to be buried inside. I can't and won't show fear, no matter what. Plus I got my girls with me. They have just as much heart as I do. Who the hell is going to mess with us?

I always vowed that I would not join a gang, but when you're hanging in the hood with the same crew every day, I guess you are a gang, so to speak—or that's how you're going to be perceived. We have the same mentality as a gang. If one fights, we all fight. If one gets in trouble, we all go down. We wear the same colors. I guess (looking from the outside) we are a gang. I vowed never to do drugs, but when you're out there and it's being passed . . . *Girl, you ain't gonna get hooked, just try it!* Aw, what the hell? I don't want to look like a punk. I vowed never to become an alcoholic, but then it's . . . *Girl, let's get some pink Champale. Oh, hell, I got some vodka. Let's get drunk.* Damn, that shit gives you courage. And so it goes. . . .

But I still want to be somebody. I don't know where the streets are going to lead me, but trust they're leading me somewhere. I'm just going to have to discover it when I get there. Um, hold up—what's this on the corner? A DJ cutting records and someone MC'ing on the mic? Now, that's kinda fly. The music makes you forget about any worries, and the shit homeboy is kicking on the mic, damn! Life may be rough, but you can still have a good time.

I want to follow this hip-hop journey. Let's give this a try and see where it leads. It's got to be better than what we're doing now.

Chapter 1

Mom, Don't Go Now!

New York City, 2005

Early one Saturday morning I'm cleaning up my apartment when the phone rings. I look at the caller ID box, and a number appears with a 770 area code. Atlanta—Oh, it must be my sister Camela.

"Hey, girl, what's up?" I say as I anxiously answer the phone. See, Moms lives in Atlanta too and these days I'm always worrying about my mother's health. Funny, after all the stress I put her through as a kid, running the streets. I probably would be the last one of my siblings she would expect to worry about her. Truth is I always worried in silence.

"Well," she replies in a casually playful tone, "guess who's coming for dinner?"

"Who?" I ask impatiently.

"Guess," she continues in a devilish manner.

"Stop playing, girl," I tell her. I worked a double shift yesterday and I'm in no mood for games right now.

"Me and the kids are coming up to New York next week, and we're bringing Ma."

"You're kidding, right?" I reply in disbelief. I pause for a moment. Suddenly I forget all about cleaning.

She then responded, "No, Mom is going to come with us." I am shocked but excited at the same time, at a loss for words. It's a long story—where should I begin?

See, Moms had left New York in 1990 after winning a lawsuit from a car accident. She'd been awarded enough money to put a down payment on a house in Atlanta. Since all of my sisters had basically hung on my mother's apron strings from an early age, they were right behind her with their children in tow. Camela had moved down the same day my mother did; then the other three sisters and two brothers had followed soon after. Next thing I knew, they'd all left me behind in New York. That was okay. I wasn't ready for that country-bama lifestyle anyway—I'm strictly a city girl. Besides, out of all my sisters, I was always the one who went against the grain, no matter the consequences.

I'll never forget the day my mom moved away. You could see the excitement in her eyes as the moving company was packing her stuff in the truck. Finally, she could have a house of her own. After a lifetime spent bouncing from apartment to apartment, this had always been her dream. She picked Atlanta because Tallahassee, Florida, where she was born and raised, was a little too laid-back for her. I did feel a sense of sadness because I knew I was going to miss her and my sisters, but I was happy for them too. When she left, she vowed that she would never step on New York City turf again. According to her, the only thing she was going to miss about New York was the illegal number spots.

Exactly one week after my sister's phone call, at about 5:00 p.m. on a beautiful Saturday, I hear a loud knock at the door. My adrenaline starts flowing and I can feel the blood rushing through my veins. I open the door, and there she is, fussing like always.

"I can't stand that Carlton!" are the first words out of her mouth. "He would not listen to nothing I was saying, and his driving was horrible."

Carlton is my sister Camela's husband. His family is from

Jamaica, and he's got that rebel spirit. He and my mother never see eye to eye. He enjoys challenging her controlling ways, and it's funny to hear them go at it, especially with his Jamaican accent and her high-pitched voice. I'm happy to see her, but before I can help her in, she pushes right past me, running for the bathroom, still fussing all the while.

I have no idea how this week with my mother is going to go, but my husband, Junior, and I feel like we're ready. Nobody comes to our home and tries to take over. We're both strong-headed individuals—you have to be if you're dealing with my mother. You see, Moms and I have the typical mother and daughter relationship; we love each other dearly but we can't be in the same house for long without certain little disagreements coming up. Okay, sometimes big disagreements. Anyway, my sister and her family were going to stay uptown in the Bronx at her in-laws' house, but Moms was bunking with us. It was no threat, just an adventure! When I told my husband the news, he gave me this look and said, "I know it's going to be a hell of a week."

"Mom, relax," I say. "You're on vacation. Sit and let us serve you, all right?"

"Please, Ma," says Junior. "Relax. It's gonna be okay."

But it's no use. Here she goes, getting up off the couch. "I just want to start the dinner," she says. "You know I can't keep still."

"No, Mom," I insist. "I got it." But my mother has to control whatever domain she's in. Always has. That's just Mom.

"Junior, honey, could you go to the store?" she says in that good ol' manipulative tone.

"Yeah, what you want, Moms?"

"I need a Pepsi and a B.C. powder," she says. "How long you gonna be, Junior?" B.C. powder was a headache pill in powdered form sold in every bodega. This was my mom's cocktail whenever she was stressed out. "Cause you *know* after 16 hours with Carlton I have a headache," she adds dramatically.

"Don't start questioning me, Ma," he replies, looking her dead in the eyes and trying not to laugh. "You know I'm not going for that. Now come on, Ma."

"I just want to know how long," she comes back at him.

I jump in. "Mom, he's going to come back, okay?" I interrupt, while fighting to keep my composure. "Please relax."

About fifteen minutes pass, and I see she's starting to get restless. Oh, here she goes:

"Shelly, what store did he go to?" Then, before I can answer: "He *always* stay that long at the store?"

Damn, Mom, I think to myself.

"Mom, he's a grown man," I tell her. "I don't time his trips to the store."

With the ready-to-start-some-shit look, she goes on. "He reminds me of Steve," says Mom, reminiscing about an ex-boyfriend. "He used to say he's going to the store, and I'd go look for him and come to find out, he was messing with some chick down the block."

"Okay, Mom," I say, trying to change the subject. "That's enough."

"I beat the living shit out of him."

I have to stop this discussion with a quickness. I raise my voice just a little.

"Junior is not Steve and I am not worried about nothing like that, so *please*, Mom," I say.

It's bad enough that this same conversation takes place every time my husband goes out for the next week. But oh Lord, don't let the phone ring and someone hang up when you answer. You cannot tell her it isn't another woman calling. Meanwhile, my husband gets a kick out of messing with my mother.

"Ma, this is my house," he says with a twinkle in his eye, "and I'm in control, *woman*." Then she starts fussing and hitting him. I actually think she likes when he does that, but she'll never admit it.

Even though I do get frustrated during Mom's stay, it sure brings back memories of when I was growing up. I wonder why I never thought of my mother as a person with humor back when we lived under one roof. In my mind she was always "Mom," with a street type of demeanor.

Before we know it, it's already Friday, the day before Mom heads back to Atlanta. Junior and I feel like celebrating, so we decide to go all-out and show her a good time.

"We'll take her out to eat at Red Lobster," he suggests. "Then take her to Forty-second Street so she can see the changes on the Deuce since she left New York."

That morning I get up early and take her shopping. I want to buy her a dress and some new shoes so she can really feel special and enjoy herself tonight. At about 4:00 p.m. we head up to Co-op City Mall in the Bronx to get to Red Lobster in time for the early bird special. Mom's looking beautiful in her new outfit, and she let me make up her face, which she knows I enjoy doing. As a little girl I felt everybody should look glamorous, like Barbie. I would always want to dress my friends and family up and put makeup on their faces.

"Shelly, you were always the independent one," Mom says as I'm getting her ready today. "You know, it looks like you've made a pretty good life for yourself."

"Thank you, Ma," I say, while applying blush to her pale skin.

At Red Lobster we tell her to order anything she can see.

"I'll have the jumbo shrimp," she tells the waitress.

"That doesn't make any sense," says Junior with a grin. "How can it be jumbo if it's a shrimp?"

"You're so crazy," says Moms, smiling as she sips a glass of white wine. "Shelly, do he ever shut up?" We're having more fun together than we ever expected.

After dinner we head downtown.

"Wow," says Mom. "Look at all these bright lights! But Forty-second Street sure has changed since I was in New York."

"Yeah, no more kung fu or peep shows," jokes Junior with a disappointed tone in his voice. Mom and I laugh as we play-fight with him in the streetlights' colorful glow.

Mom notices a crowd gathering and she gets girlishly excited. "Why all those people standing over there?" she asks, clasping her hands together. We walk her over to where some guys are break-dancing for money on the corner. It's one of the most beautiful nights of the whole summer. The busy New York street is full of light and laughter. The buzzing electric glow of the billboards and marquees transforms the whole scene into some sort of showbiz wonderland. It's simply stunning. Then suddenly Mom's getting tired, and we decide to call it a night.

At five o'clock Saturday morning, I am awakened by a familiar voice that sounds strange somehow.

"Shelly, Shelly!"

I rush into the room to find my mother sitting up in bed and looking gray.

"Mom, you all right?"

"No," she says, sounding weak. "I think it was something I ate. Call the ambulance quick."

By this time my husband is awake. "I'll drive you to the hospital," he says.

I refuse to panic. "Mom wants us to call the ambulance," I say as I dial 911. Then I call my sister Camela to let her know what's going on.

The paramedics arrive in about ten minutes. As they rush into the room, I tell them it was probably something she ate. Of course she's already fussing with them—sick and all—when, to my surprise, she blurts out, "I am having a heart attack."

"If you're having a heart attack, you would not be fussing," the paramedics reply in a joking manner.

What the hell did they say that for? I ask myself, crinkling my eyebrows.

Mom's letting them have it as they put her on the stretcher.

"Don't tell me what's wrong with me! I know my body. I am having a heart attack."

My husband and I walk behind my mother's stretcher and we climb into the ambulance with her. They rush us all to the emergency room and the doctors start working on her right away. After fifteen minutes in the harsh, fluorescent-lit waiting room, my sister arrives and we hug for what seems like a long time. They finally let us into the room with Mom. She's wearing an oxygen mask, but it seems like she's having problems breathing. All of a sudden her face turns blue and the machine next to her bed starts beeping loudly. I am frantic, losing my speech in shock while my sister starts crying. My husband takes us out of the room while the doctors rush in to work on her.

The truth hits me all at once. Moms was right. She is suffering a massive heart attack. The surroundings just seem to freeze as my husband pulls me away from the room. All I can think of is the idea of losing her. No, this is *not* happening. Could never be. Maybe I shouldn't have taken her out last night. Maybe I shouldn't have been fussing back and forth with her all week. How could she come to visit me after all these years, and then just die on me?

Thoughts and fears of guilt and anger take control of my mind. All my years spent fatherless, homeless, struggling with addictions to drugs and alcohol—all my own demons for which I had silently blamed my mother for so long—they rush out of my mind in an instant. I want my mother. I want to show her how much I love and respect her. I want her to know I'm sorry for running the streets, for not understanding how hard it was for her to raise eleven kids by herself. She was our mother and my father, our parent and provider. She never gave us up for adoption. She hung in there no matter what. "My children always come first," she would say. And her actions spoke louder than words.

All of a sudden, as she lies in her ER bed connected to all types of sophisticated medical equipment, I gain a newfound appreciation for my mother. I want to hear her voice fussing right now—but I can't. I want her to know the strong, independent woman I've become through all my struggles, our struggles. I just want her to really see me, the same one who put her through so many worries when I was out roaming the streets in the name of hip-hop. I want her to know it was all for a purpose: I was trying to find that drive inside of me for something, but never to hurt her.

"Mom, if you can feel me right now," I pray silently, "I just wanted to *be* somebody. I was just searching to find myself as a young black woman. Do you know what it means to feel empty inside? I just wanted to be somebody so you could be proud of me."

There is so much we have left unsaid, and so much left to do. I want her to see the person her daughter has become. I want her to know that her work was not in vain. I want to pay off that house that she's always dreamed of. I want to make it comfortable for her. If only I could just tell her about my journey. Just explain the whole thing to her. Maybe then she'd understand.

"No, Mom. You can't leave me," I pray as the tears flow. "Not *now*. Not until I tell you my story. . . ."

Chapter 2

Dreams

New York City, 1971

I was the kind of child who daydreamed a lot. My mind was always wandering, wondering what life would be like if I were a beautiful movie star who could get anything she wanted. I could just see it now—lights, camera, action—an army of assistants catering to my every whim, all the hype centered on me. I would stand in front of the mirror and talk to myself, making funny expressions to see which one was most convincing. I would picture myself with long blond hair, cherry-red lips, diamonds around my neck, and a hot mink coat on. . . . The limo would be waiting for me outside. Maybe it had something to do with the lack of attention from my mother, who had too many kids to give much attention to any one of us. Mom worked nights at the post office while my older brothers and sisters babysat, but most of the time I would stay in my own little world. At this time we were living across from the Bronx Zoo.

I wanted nothing to do with the images of black women I saw on TV—always struggling and stressed out. Of course when the theme song from *Good Times* would play—"Keeping your head above water / Making a wave when you can"—I would smile and maybe dance a little. Just like with our African ancestors before us, no matter what we were going through, music would help to ease the pressure. But most of the black women I saw on TV reminded me of problems at home. Mom, Grandma, and the women around the way always seemed to be struggling. I guess that's why I did not want to see them. Those images constantly smacked me in the face and brought me back to the reality I saw when I looked in the mirror. Well, what do you expect when you're one of eleven siblings raised by a single mom?

I always considered myself the middle child, although it wasn't really as simple as that. My mother had her first set of children (Devon, Cooley, Ronnie, and Tori) by her first husband, before I was even on the scene. She was living in Florida at the time, but she left when her husband became physically abusive. She ended up moving to New York in this building located on 145th Street and Seventh Avenue in Harlem where she met this man named Larry, and ended up having the next set of kids, Paul, Angel, and Lavern. Things did not work out with Larry either—she found out he was seeing another woman in Queens who had kids from him too.

I was born after the older children were already out of the house and she decided to move to the Bronx. Here she met my father, the player. I heard he was a very handsome man who had a lot of women. They said he used to drive a cherry-red convertible and always had a different woman in it. He used to give all kinds of boat rides and parties, where the women used to fight over him. He said his mother was this white woman from London who ran a prostitution house in Virginia along with her sister. He never knew who his father was, but he always regretted what his mother did. That's all the history I know about his family and him, the Berchettis. Nevertheless out of their affair came me.

I never met my father. Whenever I asked about him, all I would hear is "look in the mirror." Apparently, I looked just like him. But that fact alone didn't satisfy my hunger for answers. Was he still alive out there, somewhere? And if he was, then why wasn't my father a part of my life?

One Saturday morning while sitting on the edge of my mom's bed, I decided I couldn't wait any longer. "Ma, I need to ask you something."

"What, Shelly?" she answered abruptly. I could see she was tired from working last night, but I had questions that needed to be answered.

"What happened, Mom?" I said in a quiet voice. "Why isn't my father here?"

She hesitated for a moment; then she took a deep breath and started talking.

"When you was born," she said, "I called him up to the house to see you. You were just two days old. I thought I would surprise him. The doorbell rang, and he came into the house. I had you dressed up and wrapped in a beautiful baby blanket. I said, 'Here, Alex, she's yours,' and I handed you to him. He was nervous. Sweat was running down his face. It looked like he was about to have a heart attack," she said. "He quickly handed you back, and he ran out the door. All I could see was the back of his shoes, hauling ass. And I never heard from him again."

I looked at her with my mouth wide open, unable to speak for an instant.

"Wow, Mom!" I said as my emotions welled up. "He left just like that?"

"Yeah, that's the same thing I said—Wow!"

I could only imagine what I might have done if I were in her shoes. It would not have gone down that easy.

"Damn, Mom," I said. "At least you could've thrown a pot or glass at his ass while he was running."

I wish child support was in effect back then. This man never even brought me a pacifier, and I did not like that shit. Was he running from me or was he running from my mother? I did not know how to feel after listening to my mom's tale. But she was finished telling her story and that was that. She almost seemed like it didn't affect her, but my mom was never one for wearing her emotions on her sleeve.

As I grew older these strange feelings about my father started making me mad. His no-good ass had run away from responsibility. Then on top of that, she hit me with the bomb: she said he was married with a daughter that she never met. Maybe I did not need to hear that story after all.

My mom then met Richie. The affair was short, because he was scared to commit, but she had a baby girl, Camela, by him. After that she met Melvin. He was a good man, but he liked to use drugs a lot. She stayed with him for a while, but she just could not deal with the drugs. Then he got real sick and was on the respirator in the hospital for a while, and he eventually died. I guess putting all that poison in his system over the years caught up with him. Out of that relationship she had another girl named Lizzy. She was about five when her father passed, but you could see the sadness in her eyes. Part of me actually envied her. At least she had known her father for a little while. No matter what else he was doing, Melvin always made it his business to be around his child while he was alive.

Besides the older children that were out of the house, there were two sisters, a brother in front of me, and two sisters behind me. Then came Rudy, our adopted brother. My mother adopted him later on.

I often felt left out, because my two younger sisters always did things together, and my two older sisters were really close. This left me playing by myself a lot. My mother would pay more attention to the two younger girls; I guess this was because they were the babies of the family. Looking back on it now, I only had a second to be the baby. I think that was some of the reason I always was a dreamer.

At this time we were living at 900 Park South in the Boogie Down Bronx. It was a huge apartment with a big living room, three bedrooms, and one long-ass hallway. When my mom was working at the post office downtown on Thirty-seventh Street, my older brothers and sisters pretty much had the run of the place. Around the corner from us was Daily Avenue, one of the busiest stretches of road in the Bronx. There was never a dull moment, whether it was a street fight or a simple argument—the block was alive. Here you had every kind of action—the drug dealers, the drug addicts, the stickup kids, the number spots, and the number runners—all in one convenient location. But it wasn't all bad. You would be sure to find a church on every block along with the liquor store and the numbers spot.

Back in those days everybody who lived on the block was related or at least knew one another. Everybody used to watch out for each other. There was a sort of a hood bond throughout the neighborhood. For instance, if you needed something like clothes, food, car parts, or just about anything else, the addicts could always get it, and you would pay half price. And if they liked you, sometimes they would go out of their way to get you what you wanted free of charge. Even though you knew the stuff was hot—hey, it was considered a blessing, especially when times were so hard. And if you had beef, you could be sure it was handled. There was a certain respect everybody had for one another—no matter who you were or what you did.

Summertime was the best. It was too hot to stay inside with no air-conditioning, so it seemed like everybody would be out on the block. Everybody always knew what the other one was doing, and you can bet that nothing was missed. Talk about snitching—those old ladies on the block watched everything and somehow they always told your mother everything you were up to before you even got back home. Moms would have her belt ready and waiting for you as you came through the door.

"What the hell did I do?" you'd protest.

"Don't even act like you don't know," she'd say as she started whaling. "Miss Mary said she seen you stealing candy out of the corner store." *Pow!* "Ya ass know better than to be embarrassing me like that." *Pow!* Her sentences were punctuated by the sounds of that belt hitting your jeans or ass. You were lucky if you had jeans on; the material softened the impact of the belt.

I preferred the other sounds of summer, like the melody of the Mr. Softee ice cream truck rolling through the block. From the window in our living room, I could see kids running up to the truck. Whether they had money to buy ice cream or not, they were just drawn to Mr. Softee like the Pied Piper. Some kids were hoping that a grown-up would see that they had no money and buy them an ice cream cone. The unfortunate ones just stood there looking all sad and shit, watching the other kids happily lick at their push-ups and Popsicles.

During the dog days of summer, the fire hydrant was everybody's favorite recreation, just like kids in the suburbs love their backyard sprinkler or swimming pool. The boys in our neighborhood would get a wrench and open the hydrant full blast; then they'd dance in its waters or try to wet up passing girls by grabbing them and throwing them in front of the pump. It was so funny to see the girls just running. Oh my God, don't let them have a cute outfit on, or be on their way home from having their hair permed or pressed with the straightening comb. The boys would use an empty tin can opened up on both sides so they could direct the stream of water wherever they wanted it to go—whether on a passing car or some unsuspecting victim walking by. This went on until the cops came and shut it off. They said it was unsafe. But we figured, why not? If your building was burning, the fire department wouldn't show up on time anyway.

At night you would hear people outside laughing, talking, arguing, and fighting. The air was filled with the sounds of sirens—ambulances, fire engines, and police cars—mixed with the boom box banging songs by Shalamar or The Jackson Five. "Dancing, dancing, dancing, she's a dancing machine," they'd sing, "Aw, babe—do it, baby!"

Basketball courts stayed busy, with the guys running up and down the courts while somehow keeping their Afros intact.

The girly girls would stroll by being cute for the fellas. They had the big loop earrings on in colors that matched their outfits and their hairstyles were always correct, whether it was a curly Afro or Afro puffs with the straight bang in the front. Yeah, that was summertime on Daily Avenue. You may not have had much or felt like you came from much, but you just made the best out of what life gave you. The irony of it all was that no one ever seemed unhappy.

My brother Cooley was one of the drug dealers who ran the block. He was in his early twenties and his street name was Cadillac. Cooley was known all up and down Daily Avenue for cracking a few heads. If someone tested him, he would knock their ass out. He was always into some static, usually over somebody owing him money. Cooley was the coolest out of my brothers. I always thought he was a big businessman, because he used to be dressed like the Mac—all of his clothes would match, from the socks to the underwear, and he would just stand on the block profiling like that was his place of employment. Even when he got into fights, the outfit stayed intact. That's how nice his knuckle game was. He was tall, dark, and handsome with curly silky hair. All the women from the block wanted to get with him. They figured if they had his baby, the baby would come out with "good hair"—another crazy ghetto mentality. He had that sort of pimp attitude, and it didn't hurt that he kept his pockets full of money.

When my sisters and I would be outside playing or going to the store for my moms, we would see him on the Ave and go running to him like he was the long-lost sixth member of The Jackson Five.

"There goes Cooley," we'd yell with excitement in our voices. Cooley would see us coming and put a grin on his face. Oftentimes he'd be surrounded by some strange guys we didn't recognize.

Usually, I'd be the one to ask, "Cooley, who is those men?"

"Ah, these are my business associates," he would quickly respond in a mind-your-business attitude. "Stop asking questions. Anyway, where are y'all going out here by yourselves?" This was his way of changing the subject in an authoritative big brother way.

"Mom sent us to the store," Lavern and Camela would answer at the same time like a pair of hummingbirds.

"Okay, y'all got some money?" he'd ask.

We would all say, "Noooo." We knew the routine. Whenever he had people around him, he loved to show off. He'd go in his pocket and pull out a knot with a rubberband around it, then peel off a couple of bills.

"Here's some money," he'd say, and hit us off with anywhere from a single to three dollars. Back then three dollars was considered a lot of money. Once we got the money, he'd send us back up the street.

"Ya'll go home now," he'd scold.

We'd be, like, "Bye, Cooley," in our little innocent girl voices. And we knew he'd watch us all the way until we were out of his sight, then he was in the clear to start his business again.

One of Cooley's biggest problems was that he often got high on his own supply. Because of his passion for the latest fashions, it was hard to tell if he was an addict or not—and he always denied it, so you might question yourself. Cooley joined the Navy when he was in his teens and used to box overseas. From my understanding, he got discharged because he started using drugs. I remember when I used to think that my brother had magical powers. I thought it was amazing the way he could sleep standing up. Eventually I realized he was really nodding off from shooting heroin. He used to come live with us from time to time and tell us his business was going slow. He almost overdosed a couple of times in our apartment, and Mom would have to call the ambulance. Mom used to kick him out the house when she would find his stash in the house. He was always getting arrested but he never admitted his guilt. He'd always swear that the police planted the drugs on him.

Because he was always getting locked up, Moms used to

take us to see him in prison. The Bronx Detention Complex was close by, right there on River Avenue. My sisters and I were too young to go inside for the visit, but we would stand outside the prison gates to wave at him. I used to cry, because I wanted my brother to come home. I did not like seeing him caged like an animal. That's how I viewed prison at an early age. In my eyes, my brother was never wrong.

My brother Alvin was the oldest of all of us. He was in his late twenties and he had a military background too, but unlike Cooley he was the serious type. Alvin always walked with his hands behind his back and his head in an upright position. Being the oldest, he felt like he had to carry himself in an authoritative way all of the time. He was married and lived across town, but he was always ready to go deep cover and investigate something for no reason. He thought he was a family detective, always trying to find out something wrong we did. Even though he didn't live with us, he tried to act like he was our father. Actually, he was more like a dictator. And we had to listen to everything he said. And sometimes he was very harsh toward us.

Whenever he came to visit, before he would say hi, his first comment would be something like, "Why are there dishes in the sink?" Then, before you could answer, he'd ask, "Where is ya'll homework? Isn't it report card time?"

Oh, this man would go on and on with the bass in his voice. The house would stay silent; everyone would be scared to speak or answer back. He always demanded respect and usually got it. I used to think he was the meanest person that ever walked the earth. But I guess he felt he had to play the role, because there was no other father figure around.

Then came my big sister Toria. She was the next oldest, in her mid-twenties. Toria was a very attractive light-skinned young lady with green eyes. Mom said Tori used to run away from home a lot when she was a teenager. Eventually Toria left our home and got married at an early age, just like Moms, looking for a way out. She married a man from Honduras who used to beat the crap out of her. Every time my mother and my other brothers would try to intervene, she would stand by her man and flip on the family. One time he beat her so bad, Moms went gunning for him and gave him a choice of the window or the pistol. Toria started screaming and crying. She went into such a panic that she called the police—not on the man who just beat the shit out of her, but on her own mother.

"Yes, please send the police," she said. "My family is trying to kill my husband. Come quick." By the time the police came, my mom had left and vowed to never get involved again. After a while, everyone got frustrated with the whole situation and left it alone.

Toria would drink a lot. It was her way of drowning out the pain. Every time there was a family function, my mom would not want her to come, because she would act out after a few rounds. When she got wasted she would either start cursing everybody out or start dancing in the middle of the floor. Her and her husband had two little boys who were around the same age as us younger kids. We would have to babysit whenever she and her husband went through a crisis.

Toria had dreams of being a part of the fashion world, and she used to give her own fashion shows. She would make and design every outfit that was modeled. She had an unbelievable talent for sewing, but her husband would find ways to stop her every time she wanted to go after a career. He just wanted to keep her home to cook and clean and cater to him like he was some type of king in his castle. When we would go to her house, she worked like a slave to make sure the table was prepared, his slippers were out, and the newspaper was ready for him to read. But when he came home from work, he was so mean to her. He'd have this mad mean mug on his face and talk to her in a blunt manner all the time, like, "Tori, I'm ready to eat."

Oh, I used to hate hearing his voice. I wasn't into boys yet, but I used to think, *Damn, is this what it's all about?*

"I guess men are mean and evil," I told myself. But I made

myself a promise. "I will never be some man's slave." I might have been young, but I just knew something was wrong with that picture.

My next brother, Ronnie, was right under Tori. He was also in his mid-twenties. He was a very quiet person who would never bother anyone. He usually stayed to himself and liked to listen to the blues or James Brown. He loved to imitate JB and make my sisters and me laugh. Ronnie was all right until he drank, and then he would get violent if someone messed with him. He wouldn't care who it was. Just leave him alone when he has his 40 ounce and his music. According to mom when he was little, he fell out of his crib and hit his head hard—this might have explained some of his more outrageous actions.

At times my brothers would get into serious fights at home over stupid things like clothes, food, and other dumb shit. My mom did whatever she had to do to get them to stop, by any means necessary. She was a little woman, and my brothers were big, but she did not care. Her motto was, "I brought you into this world, and I can surely take you out."

One time Cooley tried to fight my mother. He was about six feet three inches tall, and she took a brick and knocked his ass out, then called the police to come take him out of her house. Mom didn't play. When Ronnie finished off a 40 ounce, anything would trigger him off, and he was ready to go buck-wild. My mother was the only one who could really control his rage.

One day Paul and Rudy kept teasing Ronnie, and he got mad. He said he was going to shoot them if they didn't stop. They just laughed and kept on messing with him, so Ronnie went to his room. When he came out he started shooting everywhere. Everyone in the house was trying to run for cover. Luckily, it was just an air gun. But by the time my mother got home, Ronnie was gone, on the run. He knew my mother was going to flip. Another time he got so mad from arguing with my other brothers that he threatened to shoot them with a real gun. Sure enough, he went outside, and then the next thing you know, the ambulance was coming. Ronnie had shot himself in the foot.

Next in line was Paul, the devilish one of the family. Paul was a prankster who always played jokes on us. He was always the main one to instigate Ronnie's outrage. He would do things like turn out all the lights in the house to scare us or just pick and pick at Ronnie until he went off. He used to get a kick out of stuff like that. Paul liked to instigate arguments between us sisters too. He'd spread rumors and get us fighting over silly things. He thought he had game when it came to the girls. He always tried to juggle more than one girlfriend at a time. Even though she denied it, my mother spoiled him—he was a brat who got away with everything. So naturally, Paul and I used to fight a lot.

Now came my sister Angel and Lavern. I say their names together because they were always together. Angel would get beatings because she used to wet the bed a lot, and Lavern got beat just because. Now that I think of it, Lavern was the slickest one of us girls. She was the snitch of the group. If you did not want something revealed, you didn't do it around her.

And then there was me, the stressed-out daydreamer and big time movie star in her own mind. After that came Lizzy and Camela; they were the youngest. They were cute, adorable little girls who were basically good kids, but whenever Lizzy did something wrong, both she and Camela would get beaten. You know the saying "Peter pays for Paul"? That's how it worked with these two. There was no time to figure out who did what, so the safest thing was to spank them both.

Lizzy's father, Melvin, would come around and he treated Camela like she was his too. He worked for a kids' clothing factory and used to bring them clothes—that was a blessing for my mom. Camela's father, Richie, only came around once in a blue moon, and when he did, he would do absolutely nothing. He would come over to our apartment and just sit in a chair, literally just smiling. I didn't get it; I would just stare back at him. He never said a thing to me, so I said nothing to him. I would get a little jealous, because of all the clothes Lizzy's father would bring over, none of them was ever for me.

My brother Rudy wasn't our biological brother. He was Paul's best friend from school. He hung around our apartment so much everyone thought he was family. His real family was from Puerto Rico, but one day there was a terrible fire and his mother, father, cousin, three nephews, and a niece were killed. My mother eventually adopted Rudy, not by going through the courts or anything.

"We're your family now," she said one day. "Call me Ma." And that was that.

Since my mother was raising ten kids of her own, I have the utmost respect for her adopting Rudy. She refused to let him get lost in the system. I often wondered if I had been in Rudy's place, whether I could have handled losing practically my whole family. That would have been too much for me to deal with so young. But he was incredibly strong. He never showed any weak emotions, but I knew he was hurting. My brother Alvin made sure his family had a decent burial. It was crazy seeing all those caskets lined up at the one funeral. Even though Rudy was Spanish, he seemed to fit into my family like he was our own flesh and blood. For better or worse, we were all he had. God gave him another family.

Chapter 3

The Gunshot

Across the hall from us lived a couple named Pearl and Sam, who were in their early fifties. They were not very social to anyone else in the building but my family. I guess it was because they did not have any kids, so in a way, my siblings and I filled that void. They used to buy us junk food now and then, and on Christmas they would knock on the door with arms full of toys for us. When Mom was working nights, they would check on us from time to time to see if we were all right. Sam was this big-ass man who was very quiet at times. Then other times we would run into him and he'd be very talkative.

"I think Sam be sippin' on that whiskey," Moms would say. "I know I smell alcohol on his breath."

He was surely the biggest man I'd ever come across, especially as a little kid. His wife Pearl was a quiet, mild-mannered type of lady. She always wore wigs that looked like they were about to fall off her head. She seemed to have one in every color. She had a very small frame and spoke slowly in a soft, high-pitched tone of voice.

She'd see us and say, "How ya'll doin'?" smiling big. "Y'all some nice kids. Anything you need, just ask Aunt Pearl . . . okay?"

Over time Sam started showing more of his talkative side,

replacing the laid-back side. The alcohol smell started coming out more strongly too, along with the stagger. He started approaching my mother, saying crazier shit every time she ran into him.

"Hey, Vergie," he told her one day. "Ya know, I keep hearing some voices at night telling me to kill your kids."

He could barely stand up as he spoke, and his breath smelled like a liquor store. After a few more of these threats, Mom told his wife. But she was in denial.

"Oh, Vergie," she said. "Don't pay him no mind. Sam just talking nonsense, especially when he drinks." Then she would add, in that soft, innocent tone of hers, "Sam won't hurt a fly." It seemed like her husband could have been choking her, and she would still be like, "Oh, Sam is just playing."

One night, while Mom was at work, one of my sisters was braiding another sister's hair while the other two were playing records. They kept playing this one song over and over called "Zodiac Signs." It was a popular song at the time. My sisters were nodding their heads to the beat and singing the lyrics. I was in my room talking into the mirror, playing movie star as usual. The only brother at home was Ronnie, who was in the hallway playing with our dog, Queenie. She was a beautiful golden German shepherd that acted like she was one of the kids. Someone had given her to my mother two years ago, and even though Mom was allergic to dogs, she just could not get rid of Queenie.

The doorbell rang.

"I got it!" Ronnie yelled while walking toward the door. My nosy butt decided to run right behind him to the door. Usually, when the doorbell rang, Queenie ran under the sewing machine located in the hallway. But this time Queenie started to growl before Ronnie even opened the door. I was standing behind Ronnie, all curious, as he looked through the peephole asking, "Who is it?"

"Ah, Sam," said a familiar voice in a stern manner.

Ronnie said, "Oh, it's Sam," and unlocked the door to see

what he wanted. Ronnie opened the door ready to greet our neighbor, but as soon as he opened it, all we heard was a loud popping sound along with smoke.

"Run!" Ronnie screamed. "Sam's got a gun!"

Ronnie tried to grab me as he ran into the next room where there was a fire escape, but he didn't have time because Sam was already coming in our front doorway firing. All I had time to do was hide next to a closet in the first bedroom before Sam burst through that door. Imagine that shit—this big-ass burly man who looked like he weighed three hundred pounds or more, coming at me with a gun in his hand. He was the real bogeyman. All I could do was freeze. My vision went all blurry and everything seemed to be stuck in suspended animation. All I could see through the smoke was Sam's huge silhouette standing over me and the barrel of the gun. The sounds from the gun were loud. *Pop! Pop!* the shots echoed and the bullets just kept coming, but I felt nothing hitting me as he fired away. His face became clear through the cloud of smoke and I could see his killer eyes, his mouth dribbling with saliva, and sweat running down his face. He wasn't staggering this time. It seemed to me, at that moment, that he was making sure to stand still. I could see in his eyes that he thought I was dead as he kept walking and firing.

There was nobody to save us. Even our dog Queenie was under the sewing machine, trying to hide just like we were. All I could hear were gunshots and the sound of his heavy-ass footsteps thumping through our apartment. As the shots rang out, I kept thinking about my family being killed. Then I heard the thumping sounds coming back toward my direction, but they passed me as he walked out of the house. I guess he figured his mission was accomplished or the voices were done speaking to him for the night. All I could see was that big-ass silhouette disappearing in that cloud of smoke, and the door slamming behind him.

When the cops came, I was still standing there, too scared to move. They called my mother and told her that a neighbor came into her house and shot at her kids. She damn near fainted when she got the call. I later learned that her coworkers had to help her gain composure. The next thing I knew, she was home. By the grace of God, we all survived without a single bullet wound. Two of my sisters ran up the fire escape along with Ronnie. The other two sisters hid under the bed. And that left me, standing there alone. I always felt as though I had been spiritually protected, because he was shooting right at me, but it seems the bullets never hit. God must have had other plans for me, or else Sam must have been staggering. I just didn't understand how his shots were off.

They put Sam away in a mental institution for a long time. Looking back on it now, my family and I should have received some type of therapy too, because that was an extremely traumatic situation to go through at any age. But back then nobody ever talked about mental illness, not in my neighborhood anyway. You were just considered crazy, and that was it. A lot of curable mental problems were left untreated because people were reluctant to admit that they or any of their family members even had a problem. Nobody wanted to be the talk of the neighborhood. Maybe they did not know that things like depression or anxiety attacks could be controlled through medication or therapy. There really wasn't any usable information about mental illness in the hood. If someone acted psycho, everybody figured it was due to drugs or alcohol and they'd be all right when they sobered up.

As for me, my nerves were never really the same after that night. I would get edgy whenever I heard a doorbell, like I needed to be ready to take action. One thing was for sure—I would not let anyone invade me again ever. If I didn't expect you to come over, the door was not getting opened. I harbored a deep-seated fear that one day Sam would get out of the mental institution and come back to finish the job. The nightmares didn't help either. I never wanted to listen to that "Zodiac" song again.

Chapter 4

Mom's Roots

My mother was a strong woman who stood by her own principles. Whatever she asked, you did without hesitation. She was born and raised in Tallahassee, Florida, along with her brother Clarence. She had seven other brothers and a sister by her father's other wife. Mom said that back then in the South, that sort of situation was never questioned. Her grandmother raised her and her brother, which I think she resents her mother for. She would often say, with anger in her voice, that her mother would rather chase after men and run the streets than raise them. My great-grandmother was a strong-statured woman, still very strict and stern even at her advanced age. She was still singing on a gospel radio show in Atlantic City when she was ninety-four. It was clear to see where Mom's strength came from.

Growing up, my sisters and cousins would be scared of our great-grandmother. She used to sit at the top of the steps in her house, and if any kids dared to venture up there, she would start preaching to them about the world coming to an end. She had this way of looking you dead in the eye without a squint, one hand on her hip and the other hand pointing at you as her index finger shook up and down for emphasis. My other siblings were terrified, but I used to love going up the stairs to see her. There was something about the way she told stories that amazed me as a little girl. I could sit there and listen for hours.

Mom told us how they used to get chased from school by black and white kids alike. She and her brother were called "mulattos," because Mom had a pale complexion with reddish hair and her brother was light-skinned with freckles, curly brown hair, and a pointy nose. Her father's mother had been a black slave who got pregnant by her master, a prominent white man in Tallahassee who had no kids by his wife. After giving birth, my great-grandmother was sent off into the woods, along with her son (my grandfather). Of course it was a disgrace for a prominent white man to have a baby by a black slave.

"Can you believe that shit?" I'd say every time I heard the story. "Our great-grandfather was a senator, and here we are living in the hood—broke as hell."

My mother and her siblings always swore that this big white hospital in Florida belonged to them. They claimed that when their great-grandfather died, he had no other children, so the hospital went to the state. I guess that's just another good ol' "Roots" story. But who would believe it coming from some ghetto dwellers in the Bronx?

Since neither the blacks nor the whites would accept Mom, Great-grandmother taught her and her brother how to stand up for themselves. They were not allowed to cry or act weak; in other words, there were few emotions involved in their upbringing. Instead, Great-grandma taught Mom how to shoot a rifle, how to fight and fend for her brother and herself. Whenever strangers came on their property, Great-grandma had no problem shooting at them. Otherwise the kids had to work in the yard and peel potatoes all day in the scorching heat. Mom still hates the smell, even the sight of potatoes.

But that was just the tip of the iceberg. Mom had lots of built-up issues because of her upbringing. She didn't tell us until we got older, but she hinted that an uncle of hers had molested her when she was very young. That would explain her overprotectiveness when it came to her daughters. But I never asked about that subject, because I knew she didn't like talking about it.

Chapter 5

Gang Territory

Our days in Bronx Park South came to an abrupt end when the landlord raised the rent and Mom could no longer make ends meet with her job at the post office. They gave her a date by which we had to pay the increased rent or be out. Getting evicted wasn't so bad; the bad part was figuring out where to stay next.

About a month later she found an apartment in a complex over on Garden Street. Garden Street was a somewhat hard neighborhood. You had different gangs like the Black Spades and the Five Percenters. I had always heard about gangs, but now we were living in gang territory. It was easy to recognize the Black Spades with their leather vests that had the gang's name written across the back in black letters. The Black Spades were known for getting into beef wherever they went, whether at house parties, block parties, or just everyday stuff on the block. When they walked down the street, you knew not to mess with them. Their forboding presence spoke for itself.

The Five Percenters were easily mistaken for being Black Muslims. In practice, their beliefs were similar: they would change their names, stop eating pork, and start preaching knowledge. I can't say what they were giving five percent of—either it was the truth or a breakdown of five percent of the truth.

They would talk really fast, and some of the fake ones could make you believe they were really saying something.

"You know you're the earth, my queen," they would say. "And I am a God."

Five Percenters would adopt names like Born, Divine, or Rakim, and every name had a meaning to it. They would drop their birth names, because they said those were slave names. They would break down the stars, and how they related to you, your sister, your mother, and so on. One day my brothers Paul and Rudy claimed they were Five Percenters. They even changed their names, but I think they just wanted to be down. They used to come in the house talking fast, claiming they were breaking down knowledge to us, but we never understood what the hell they were saying. As far as I was concerned, they were frontin'. On occasions there would be beef and then the Five Percenters acted a lot like the other gangs. At the end of the day, each group represented for their beliefs and respected each other's turf.

Our new neighborhood wasn't too far from our previous neighborhood, except that it was more like living inside the project buildings that used to be across the street. The layout was kind of tight. The complex consisted of six buildings with a huge courtyard in the middle where everybody hung out. The people from the complex, across the street and down the block, would all hang out there. The Black Spades dominated the block, mainly because this guy named Lonzo lived across the street along with his family. He was the leader of one of the Black Spades' branches. Every evening, they would be out there playing music and kicking the gang lingo. See, you could claim to be a Black Spade or part of any other gang, but if you weren't familiar with their lingo, they knew you were fake, which could be dangerous. But as long as you didn't try to perpetrate, you were okay. Parents and kids would be out there. Lonzo was almost like the protector of the neighborhood. He would handle any beef or situation on the block. You didn't see a lot of addicts around there, or at least it was more hidden. The neighborhood was based on gangs and their families.

A couple of blocks away was the neighborhood known as Little Italy, all along Arthur Avenue. There used to be beef between Arthur Avenue and Garden Street. I guess you could say it was between the Italians and blacks. One night people were chilling in the courtyard, listening to music and shooting the breeze as usual, when a car slowly cruised by, its window rolled down, and out came an arm that threw a cocktail bomb into the crowd. Cocktails were bottles filled with gasoline and capped with a dirty rag. Once you lit the rag you had a home-made bomb, but you'd better know what you were doing— they were crude weapons that could easily backfire. When this one hit the pavement a wall of fire spread all over the place. Everybody started running, grabbing their kids, and looking for cover. Fortunately, it didn't hurt anybody, but the word went out along Garden Street. Lonzo gathered his boys and started running up to Arthur Avenue to bring it to the Italian boys. This sort of back and forth was the norm for these neighboring territories.

I was about to start Junior High School 45 on Arthur Avenue in the Bronx, right next door to the White Castle hamburger joint. White Castle was the hangout place at lunchtime, and sometimes the after-school social spot too (plus hamburgers were only 16 cents). It was a mixed student body of blacks and Italian kids with Little Italy right around the corner. What this meant for us was that we used to have to run home because the Italian kids would chase us. Once in a while, when there weren't too many of them at once, we would fight back, but sometimes we just couldn't. Going to that school, you could not help but be in the middle of the ongoing beef between the two neighborhoods.

I didn't spend much time bothering with boys. Even though I did think one or two particular boys in my school were cute, my fear of rejection kept me away from them. You see, Mom used to shop for us in the basement of Alexander's on Fordham Road and the Grand Concourse. If you were poor and had a lot of kids, Alexander's Basement was the place to be, and we always made do with what she had. That meant we would get one pair of shoes, two dresses, and two pairs of slacks for the whole school year. I remember there were times when we had to eat corn bread and milk for dinner, but we never starved.

Every Christmas we were allowed to get one toy, but it wasn't bad. We would put up the Christmas tree while dancing and singing to The Jackson Five Christmas album. Moms would be in the kitchen cooking corn bread stuffing for the turkey; collard greens; candied yams; and oh my God, the mac and cheese—forget it. We always volunteered to help out in the kitchen just so we could lick the spoon and clean the bowl with our hands, smacking away. Afterward she would make us go to bed before midnight. She said if Santa caught us up, he'd put sand in our eyes. In my mind, I pictured this white man with a big belly, a long beard, and rosy cheeks coming through the fire escape while the reindeers waited on the roof. In my hood? *Yeah, right!* Anyway, the story worked for me. I ran my ass to bed, anxiously waiting to get up the next day to play with the toys under the tree. Though we got one toy apiece, it seemed like so many packages were under the tree—all perfectly wrapped with our names on them. Christmas was always a wonderful time for us, no matter what we had.

The only holiday that came close was when one of Mom's numbers hit. Then we all got to pick what we wanted and get another gift too. Mom claims that if it weren't for the numbers, many times we would have not seen Christmas. Grown-ups in the neighborhood would play their numbers based on the dreams they had the night before. Every morning Mom would ask, "Did you dream?" and translate the dream into numbers by looking it up in her mysterious number book. Most households in the hood had a number book for this very purpose. Once you translated your dreams into numbers, you had to go play the numbers for a dollar. Single numbers paid eight dollars. A whole number for a dollar pays six hundred dollars. Or you could play a be-leader (that's two numbers) or a combination. The old men and ladies would play a bunch of ten-cent numbers. There would be about a hundred numbers on the number slip—all for ten cents.

Let me tell you, as much as we went to the number spots for my mother, I could have run a number ring at an early age. No matter what else was going on, Mom's numbers had to go in. I remember one day she sent my sister Lavern and me to play her numbers. As soon as we walked into the spot, two guys came in after us.

"Okay, everybody lay on the floor!" they shouted. They both had on hoodies, trying to hide their faces. They were probably dudes from the neighborhood who knew somebody would identify them.

"You know what time it is!" the first guy yelled sarcastically, waving his gun around. "Don't make me blast anybody!"

They moved around the room, making people empty their pockets while snatching whatever jewelry they had on. Number spots got stuck up all the time, so everybody knew the routine. Basically, whatever you had, they took it. And whatever you were instructed to do, you did it.

But I had other ideas. Lying on the floor I held my mom's number money crumpled tightly in my fist. Even though it was just twenty dollars—two fives and a ten—I knew that was all the money she had left in the house. I could have gotten shot, but I held on to that cash and took the risk. I just closed my eyes and squeezed the bill inside my hands.

"God, please don't let them take the only money we got," I prayed silently as they made their threatening noises, telling people to hurry up. "*Please, please, please.*"

After what seemed like forever, they were finished robbing the spot.

"Nobody move for twenty minutes or else you're going to get shot," they said, and then they were gone.

It was not my first time seeing a gun, but a scary experience nonetheless. After it was all over, my sister and I had a good laugh.

"I can't believe they didn't see the money in my hand," I said as we walked home.

"Girl, you crazy," said Lavern with a grin. "I can't believe you took that risk."

Yeah, thinking about it I couldn't believe it myself.

The experience of playing numbers for my mom paid off for me as I got older and needed to earn money. Back then the Italians owned the number spots. To work in there, you had to be connected. But we were in because Joe liked us. He was this tall, heavy-set Italian man who wore glasses all the time. He always treated my sister and me nice. He'd buy us ice cream or have candy for us when we would play my mother's numbers. One day I had enough confidence to speak up when I was putting Mom's numbers in.

"Hey, Joe," I told him. "I need a job!"

"First, let me ask your mother," he said. But I already knew what she would say. Pretty soon my career in the numbers spots was on and poppin'.

Chapter 6

A Man in the House

This was my first year of school as a teenager, which is usually time when girls in class just want to talk about boys who they thought were cute. But to me, the topic was quite boring. Anytime my homegirls started talking about guys, I would change the subject or start snapping on the teacher just to cause some sort of commotion in class. It usually worked; they would forget all about the previous topic of conversation. Anyway, I had no time for boys. I was too busy planning how to become a movie star. That's what I concentrated on. I would sit there just daydreaming away until the bell rang for the next class.

One of my closest friends at school was a Jamaican girl named Vonnie. She and her mother lived down the hall from us. She was a tall, brown-skinned beauty with long hair and a somewhat shy nature. It was a neighborhood friendship type of thing—I'd hang out with her around the block, our mothers used to talk all the time, plus we went to the same school. We couldn't have been much closer.

There was one problem, though. I used to hear my mother complimenting Vonnie all the time about how pretty she was. Sometimes it used to bother me, because Moms never said anything to me to make me feel confident about myself. It seemed like all she would do was complain and fuss to me.

Although I was a bit hurt, I always kept it hidden inside. I used to start fights with Vonnie, over simple shit like barrettes, candy—anything I could think of. I guess it was a way of expressing my jealousy. Even though she was meek, when she got mad she'd let a couple of words come out from time to time, and that Jamaican accent would come out when she got mad. One day I was in one of my bitchy moods, and she decided to take a dollar out of my pocket, playing around. I worked too hard for my little chump change at the numbers spot. I was not having her nonsense today.

"Vonnie, give me my dollar," I said. "I'm not playing with you."

"No!" she said with a big grin on her face. "*Hell* no—what you gonna do?"

I was, like, *No, she ain't testing me!* And the next thing I knew, we were throwing down. Yep, right there in the apartment. Paul had to break us up, but he took his time though, enjoying the show with amusement. I don't know where her guts came from that day, but she went head-up with me. It was a good fight, though! And all for a dollar. But it seemed like much more at the time.

Whenever I was mad at Vonnie, I would hang out with this girl named Belinda and her friend Nadine. They used to live around the corner from us on Clinton Avenue. Belinda always seemed a little bit more mature than everyone else in school. She was a tall, brown-skinned chick with a strong type of demeanor about herself. On the other hand I always felt like Nadine didn't care for me too much. She always had somethin' to say about my hair and clothes—anything that came to her mind, but never anything pleasant. Sometimes it would get to me until I just started ignoring her trifling ass. Gossiping is a bad habit. And you best believe that the person you gossip about is talking about you when your back is turned. She was the Queen of Gossip. She knew everybody's business. Whenever we'd be talking with someone, Nadine would start her gossiping as soon as they walked away. "Did you see what she had on?" Or "Look at her hair!" Of course she always saved her comments until the person she was laughing at was halfway down the hall. Now, that was some real cowardly behavior. I liked hanging with Belinda, but when Nadine was around her, I went the opposite way. That girl just irritated me, and sometimes I felt like I was just seconds away from punching her ass out.

Lo and behold, Moms was making new friends too. She met this man named William at her job. She would come home and talk about him a lot.

"He's so nice to me at work," she would say with a glow all over her face. "He takes me out for lunch all the time." Whenever she talked about him, her voice would be so soft and gentle. It was nice to hear Mom sound like that instead of being so stressed out all the time. When she felt better, we felt better.

It got to the point where all you heard was "William this" and "William that" when she came home from work. He started calling her at night, and they'd talk for hours on end. Before long we got to meet this mystery man. He came home with her after work, "so we could get to know him."

I could see what Moms was talking about as soon as he arrived. *Mmm—Moms has taste now*, I said to myself with a smile. Here stood this tall, skinny man with an Afro, his shirt all buttoned to the top, bell-bottom polyester pants to match. The Afro was tight, you know—the shaped-up type, topped with the Afro-sheen spray. His voice was deep but smooth, and he had a real laid-back attitude. I was really happy for Moms. I barely heard her complaining about anything anymore. I finally saw why she had that glow.

Still we were a little bit surprised when Mom came home from work and said she had a big announcement to make. We gathered around, eyes full of curiosity.

"What is it, Mom?" we shouted excitedly, hoping it wasn't some eviction speech. But now she was smiling—a good sign!

"Ah, well . . ." she stammered, then blurted it out. "How do you all feel about William moving in with us?" We just stood there shocked. Nobody knew what to say. We never had a man live with us before, so this needed to marinate a little. But it didn't look like she was really going to wait for our decision anyway. The next thing we knew, William was at the door with bags and all, moving in.

We did not know what to expect having a strange man under our roof. Was he going to play the father role or what? Having him there did have its perks. He was helping Moms out with the bills. He kept her happy just being around. And he did not allow her to give whoopings anymore. Of course my illegal numbers career was on hold for a while. But I didn't mind. In fact, I was starting to think that having a stepdaddy around the house might not be so bad after all.

When we were bad, William would make us stand in the corner with a sign taped to our back, stating whatever crime we did. It wasn't funny then, but I look back now and that shit was hilarious. We used to look stupid walking around with a big old sign on our back. My problem was that I would not shut up, so my sign would read BIG MOUTH in huge black Magic Marker letters. If someone wet their bed, their sign would read I'M A BED WETTER. I guess it was better than an ass-whooping. If you were really bad you had to stand in the corner with one leg up and a sign on your back while the other siblings made fun of you.

William would take us on trips, which Mom never had time or money to do. We would get up on Saturday mornings to take long drives to Atlantic City to see my grandmother and great-grandmother. I used to love the fresh air, and just seeing the mountains, the trees, and beautiful waterfalls along the way. We would sing songs as we drove, then stop and eat. I used to look forward to those trips.

Sometimes when we went to Atlantic City we'd see our cousins, Uncle Larry's kids. Mom's baby brother Larry had married a woman from Germany who he met while he was in the war. Larry's wife, Marie, was always so nice to us. She showed us love whenever we came around. She had long black hair and a heavy German accent. They had three girls and a boy named after my uncle. Larry used to treat my cousins like they were in the military. And he didn't trust us around his kids. My cousins could only hang with us under Uncle Larry's supervision. Because we were from New York, he felt we would be a bad influence on them. Back then, if you had family in other states, they did not trust you because New York had a bad reputation. And guess what? Maybe that rep was well deserved. The Bronx *was* pretty wild.

We were kind of scared of Uncle Larry, because out of nowhere he would black out and start cursing, talking some commando shit and wanting to fight if you mentioned guns or even if he saw them on TV. Sometimes he would think his enemies were coming to get him, and I guess during his blackout moments in his head we were the enemies.

"Larry, just cut that shit out," my grandmother would yell at him with a cigarette hanging from the side of her mouth, especially when she was secretly sippin' on that happy juice. "You're not in the war no more!"

His wife would just sit there with a sad expression while all of us watched the drama unfold. Great-grandma would sit at the top of the steps shaking her head the whole time.

"Mm–hmm," you could hear her saying in a quiet voice while chewing gum with no teeth in her mouth. "He needs Jesus," she added as the gospel songs kept playing on the radio from her bedroom.

Moms told us her brother was shell-shocked—that's why he acted so crazy. Most of the time she would just shake her head at him, but you could see a look in her eyes that said, *He better not mess with my kids or me*, when he started his shit.

One night Uncle Larry decided to take all the kids out to eat at some diner. My sister Lizzy went outside with her cousin for air. Not a minute passed by and he comes running out in front of the restaurant yelling "What the heck y'all doing out here? I know y'all looking for them boys." My sister and cousin tried to say "What boys? What are you talking about?" But he kept coming up with some illusion shit. "I know they ran when they seen me coming. Get ya asses back inside of this restaurant!" They felt so embarrassed they tried to act like they didn't know him and walked away. His crazy ass got in the car mumbling something about, "Don't mess with me. I'll kill you all," and he acted like he was going to run them over. When my mother found out, she was heated.

"Larry, you crazy asshole," she said, going off on him like never before. "I'll take you out of your misery if you ever try that shit again." Yes me and my sisters snitched on his crazy ass, even though my cousins were scared to tell on their father.

He saw the look in her eyes, and decided not to play crazy. Instead he just took his kids and marched out of Grandma's house. William wouldn't say nothing to my uncle. I don't think he feared him, but he was more like, *Let me just stay away from this nut.*

Overall, the trips gave me a pleasant feeling. It just seemed like we were one big happy family, craziness and all. Sometimes I was like, "Wow, is this what it's like to have a father around? I could get used to this."

But just as soon as life began to look bright, I noticed William and Mom were acting sort of distant toward each other. On a few occasions I thought I heard arguing going on in the bedroom, but I wasn't sure. William felt children should not see or hear stuff of that nature, so we did not know exactly what was going on. That is until the morning I was awakened by two people talking in very stern tones. I went to check on Moms and she told me to "go back to sleep," in an angry tone. Then I heard bags being thumped on the floor, and then the front door slammed. The next sound I heard was my mother crying, and by the time everybody was awake, William was gone.

Mom never did speak on it, and we did not ask. All we knew was that William was not around anymore. According to the family gossip, Mom caught him cheating with this other woman that worked on her job. She ended the relationship with a quickness. She's not the type of woman to put up with that mess. I guess I inherited that from her.

Chapter 7

The Drama Unfolds

And so our Bronx version of *Little House on the Prairie* was over, and things mostly went back to normal. Or what we considered normal, anyway. Moms continued to work nights while my brothers turned the house into Studio 54, ghetto style. Any- and everybody from the neighborhood would come over to hang out in the house. My brother Paul used to play drums in a band named Express and Mom let him have rehearsals at the house.

The standard rehearsal schedule worked something like this: one hour of playing, the next hour of smoking marijuana, another hour of arguing, and then several hours of all different types of chicks in and out of the house. My sisters and I used to sit there watching the drama unfold each night.

Paul used to play with chicks' heads and cause all types of chaotic situations. One night this girl who was madly in love with Paul found out about another chick he was messing with. She started crying and ran into the bathroom. We thought she was trying to get her composure together, but the next thing we heard was a loud scream from the bathroom and then a boom, like somebody fell down. Cooley started banging on the door, and she would not answer, so he broke down the door and there she was, lying in a pool of blood on the floor with blood all over the bathroom.

"Aw, shit," Cooley called out. "This dumb-ass chick cut her wrist!" Just then she started screaming uncontrollably. Cooley tried calming her down, but it was no use. She just kept screaming and moving around.

"Shut the fuck up," Cooley yelled, "and hold still so I can wrap your wrist!"

But she kept screaming. He damn near had to knock her silly ass out just so he could get a rag around her wrist to stop the bleeding enough to call the ambulance. They had to clean that blood up and fix the bathroom door before Ma got home. It was a crazy scene, trust. I sat back making mental notes not to play myself like a lot of these girls did. Over some *man*? You're kidding me.

Despite their hectic rehearsals, the band got really good. They ended up recording an independent record that might have made some noise if it was pushed properly. It was a disco type of groove that got a little play in the clubs, but unfortunately they did not have the money to promote it, and the music business is strictly a money game.

As a result the band started arguing with one another a lot. Their personalities were clashing, and sometimes there was too much testosterone in one room. Having all those different women floating in and out did not help the situation either. One day the band members split up the equipment and went their separate ways.

Nevertheless, our house remained the party spot of the block. Being that we were one of the biggest families on the block, everybody knew us, the Henrys. We were like the real live grown-ass version of *BeBe's Kids*.

Then Paul would have his goofy-ass friends over to the house. They would sit there, high on marijuana joints, and try to make me the target of their jokes.

Somebody would say something dumb like, "Shelly look like she got a camel on her head," and they'd all bust out laughing at this stupid shit. This would go on until I got mad and started chasing him and his friends around the house with a shoe, a knife, or whatever I could get my hands on. Looking back, I'm amazed nobody ended up in the hospital. That's how heated I would get.

This sort of thing took place three to four times a week while my mother was at work. My older sister Toria was supposed to be helping watch over us, but she would just cause more havoc when she came over bossing people around. She would always try to make me go to bed early or make me wash the dishes when it wasn't my turn. Dumb, irritating shit like that.

"Shelly!" she'd yell, while I was trying to ignore her. "Shelly, I know you hear me."

Why doesn't she go home to her husband? I'd be thinking to myself, but I wouldn't dare to say it out loud for fear of repercussions.

One day I was fed up with the harassing.

"*Shelly*," she said, "go to bed. It's past your bedtime!" She started coming at me, and before I knew it, I pushed her. I didn't realize how hard the push was, and I ended up knocking her ass across the room. She fell straight on her ass, and of course everybody jumped in, hoping to instigate even more action.

"Oh, *shit*, did you see that?"

"Yo, Shelly, you better haul *ass*."

"Tori is going to *fuck* you up."

After pushing her I was so scared, I didn't know whether to run or deal with the consequences. As she was getting up from the floor, I froze. She gave me this look, like, *Girl, I'm gonna fuck you up.* I was going to run, but to my surprise, she just gritted her teeth and yelled, "Take your ass to bed now!" I guess she was showing the instigators she was still in control. I know it took a lot out of her not to kick my ass. Maybe it had something to do with Toria's abusive husband, like she didn't have the heart to do the same thing to her little sister. Anyway, I hauled my ass down the hallway to bed, and after that incident

I noticed she did not bother me too much anymore when she came over.

Cooley did not live with us, but I used to love when he came around. He would pay my sisters and me to go out so my other brothers and he could have girls over to do whatever. My younger sisters used to go upstairs to the neighbors' apartment to play with their friends. My older sisters, I guess, would go somewhere in the building's staircase on the down low with their boyfriends—according to the rumors. Me, I found my way to the fifty-cent house parties.

Somebody on the block was always throwing one at his or her house but Moms would forbid me to go. This was a way to have fun and take advantage of her work schedule. They'd charge two quarters at the door and a dollar for a cup of beer, usually Golden Champale. Once the word spread throughout the hood, it was standing room only. Either the champagne was flowing or they'd pop a forty-ounce of Olde English like it was champagne. Everybody chipped in a dollar for bottles of Golden Champale or forty ounces of malt liquor. Then you had the DJ, usually the older brother or someone in the family, playing the records. You did not need a lot of equipment, just a record player and some speakers. The music was so loud you could hear it from outside. Once you made it up in the spot, the lights would be out and all you could see was the flicker from a strobe light.

A party wasn't a party without those blinking white lights that made everything look like it was moving in slow motion. People always wanted to dance when the strobe light was on, because it made them look like they could really do the robot. In project house parties, the strobe light stayed on all night, because your Con Ed bill was included in the rent. In the tenement house parties, they would put the lights on randomly—so you knew they had to pay their electric bill separately. Everyone knew one another from the neighborhood. Fights might break out, but nothing major. If anything, whoever had a problem would just take it outside with their boys and settle the matter with their knuckles.

Oh no—don't let a slow song play. Then you had all types of grinding going on in the corners, on the walls, or right in the middle of the floor. Everybody would be sweating their Afros out, and wearing out their heavy Lee bell-bottom jeans with the starched crease in the middle, rubbing the tightly stretched denim together in a steady rhythm of motion against a partner who was pinned to the wall while Norman Connors sang "You Are My Starship." The real grinding was like sex without taking your pants off. I was really too young to be there, but no one knew or cared as long as you paid your fifty cents at the door. It never seemed like any adults were around. Maybe they were somewhere, but it never seemed that way.

My brothers would stress for me to be back in the house at least by 1:00 a.m., which wasn't a bad curfew for a girl my age. I was never afraid coming home that late, because everyone in the streets knew my family or were friends with Cooley. And besides, most of the parties were being held in our building anyway. Moms worked from ten at night until eight in the morning. By the time she got home, everything was cleaned up and back to normal. She would still find little things we did that weren't to her satisfaction, and when one got beat, we all got it. Like if the house was not spotless or the dishes were dirty, you had to answer to her—especially if it was your chore. But sometimes she seemed to let the boys off easier. One time she came home and found a hole in the wall with a sneaker in it. No one confessed to it, and Mom didn't bother with a Cinderella-style shoe check to see whose foot fit in the magic sneaker. All of the girls got a beating—no questions asked— and my brothers, who were probably the ones responsible, got away with no punishment whatsoever. How unfair was that?

Chapter 8

Grandma's Secret

For some reason, especially towards the end of junior high, I used to be so bored with school. I became very hype at times, couldn't focus. I would disrupt the class by starting fights or talking too much. The teacher would try to discipline me but I would yell back, which resulted in them calling my moms and marching me down to the principal's office. Mom would always say my mouth was what kept me in trouble. I just felt the need to always express myself, and nobody would give me that right. I thought it was a way of earning respect from the other kids in school, even though it kept me in a lot of problems. I always took my right to speak no matter what the consequences.

"Ms. Henry, I don't know what we're going to do with Shelly," the principal would say every time. "She just doesn't have a proper respect for authority." Then we'd go home and Mom would do her best to whoop a little respect for authority into me. Somehow it never did anything but make me feel worse. She always believed the teacher.

Then while she was at work one night, Moms had her first slight heart attack. An ambulance picked her up at the post office and rushed her to the hospital. Grandma had to move from Atlantic City to watch over us until Moms got better. Now, living with Grandma was no picnic first of all. She was very strict and had little tolerance for children since she had never really raised her own. I guess she meant well, but her patience was thin.

"Hey, you little stinker"—that's the nickname she called all of us—"get away from there! I will whoop that butt, you know I don't play." She would yell at us constantly in that high-pitched voice of hers, cigarette hanging from the side of her mouth. "Don't do this! Don't do that!"

We were used to it, because when we would visit her in Atlantic City, it was the same thing. Grandma loved to cook. All you would hear was pots and pans, then you'd smell the aroma of the food she was preparing. She made sure everybody ate. But she had one big rule—nobody was allowed with her in the kitchen. One day I eased into the kitchen while her back was turned and I discovered her hidden treasure. She kept a bottle of Southern Comfort tucked away under the sink cabinet. I could see her stirring away while humming one of her favorite gospel songs. Then she slid over to the cabinet and bent down to pull out a bottle with some brown liquid in it. After looking both ways to make sure the coast was clear, she cracked the top open and took a swig. *Aha!* I said to myself. *That's* why she didn't want anybody in the kitchen while she was cooking—Grandma was sippin' that happy juice. Then I had to sneeze. I tried to hold it but she turned around and saw me. I didn't know whether to run or to scream.

"Get in here, you little stinker," she said, hastily closing the cabinet door. "You better not tell anybody, especially ya mama." With one hand on her hip and the other one pointing the finger, she definitely meant business. "Now, if you do, I'm gonna spank ya butt."

"Okay, Grandma," I told her with a smile on my face. "I promise."

It made me feel special to have a secret about Grandma. This brought me V.I.P. status in the kitchen while she was cooking. Yep, I was the only one she let in there while she was cooking, as long as I didn't snitch. She had my word, and that bond between Grandma and me was special. It was something I would never violate, and never forget.

The difference between Grandma and Moms was that my mother would wait until we got home to whip us if we stayed out past curfew, but my grandmother would come and *get* us no matter where we tried to hide. We could be in someone's house, down the street, or around the corner. It didn't matter. She *would* come find us. It never failed. I couldn't understand how she always knew where to look for us. She wasn't even from N.Y. There must have been a snitch among us. Had to be.

Once Mom got better, Grandma went back to Atlantic City, so we didn't have to worry about living by her rules again until we made our summer visits to her. But I knew that next time I would have something on her in case I needed a little slack.

Chapter 9

Another Eviction

After two long years, I was finally graduating from junior high school. I was ready for the big leagues! Now I would be going to Evander Childs High School, uptown in the Bronx on Gunhill Road. I had heard it was a bad school, but I had no choice; this was the school my junior high school assigned me to. According to the word on the street, a lot of shit happened at Evander—mostly fights and drug selling. But you heard that about every school in the Bronx, so who cares?

Mom was proud of me for graduating. Even though we couldn't afford the school yearbook, the class ring, or a dress for the prom, she kept playing the numbers to get up some money so we could at least buy some copies of my school picture. But the right number just would not come out.

"I just *knew* that triple one was going to fall," I heard ma say with frustration. "I dreamt it twice this week." But I felt it wasn't that serious. Hell, graduation was still going to happen, and who cared about a ring, pictures, or a stinking yearbook anyway? I told myself that the prom was probably going to be wack as hell! Deep down inside, part of me was kind of curious, but I refused to let myself be sad. Besides, it would just be a bunch of fake boys and girls there anyway.

Who could be sad when school was out, and summer was finally here? I was about to start working for the summer youth corps. My mother signed my work papers so I was getting ready to work with little kids at day camp. Those summer youth corps jobs were cool, and the pay wasn't bad for a teenager. Lots of kids would use the extra income to buy a little gear or save up for school. I didn't get to keep my money because it went toward household bills, but that was cool—it just felt good being able to pitch in when I could.

I had to get up early in the morning to sign up for youth corps. I didn't feel like it, but the light from the sun was hitting me dead in the face—the best natural alarm clock. I knew today was going to be a scorcher; I could already feel the heat coming through the window. I lay in bed for a minute, staring up at the ceiling, wondering what type of day I was going to have. I knew I had a long walk ahead of me, because the youth corps office was all the way on Tremont and Webster Avenue. I finally got up, ran into the bathroom in time to beat my other sisters to it, took a shower, got dressed, and headed for the door.

As soon as I got outside I was glad I wore shorts and a T-shirt because it felt like this was going to be one of the hottest days of the summer. I kept on walking those sizzling sidewalks with a smile on my face and a spring in my step like there was nothing wrong in the world. But as soon as I approached the youth corps office my smile faded. There was an enormous line running out the front door.

Damn! I thought to myself. I got to stand on this long-ass line? All kinds of faces were staring at me as I slowly made my way to the back of the line. They looked like a bunch of hungry-ass teenagers, all eager to work. You could just read their facial expressions, standing there looking at me like, "I *know* you're not trying to jump in front of me!"

It seemed like we were standing there forever. The line was not moving, and I was starting to feel a little sick from the long walk and the sun beaming down on my head. Nevertheless, I had to deal with it. If I didn't bring in these papers, I had no summer job except for the numbers spot.

After an eternity in the hot sun, here came this big guy with his hair sticking straight up. In those days, if you rocked an Afro, it was supposed to be picked out with the Afro pick and shaped. An unkempt 'fro can mess your whole look up. Anyway, this man had the nerve to wear an unkempt 'fro along with a tight-ass dingy shirt, shiny shoes, and tight jeans with his belly hanging over his pants. He came out with a bullhorn just to let us all know who was in charge.

"If anyone leaves without turning in their papers," he boomed down the block, "they will automatically be dismissed." You could see the stressed-out looks on everyone's faces. People were tired from standing in the heat, and his loud, stern voice was not helping matters as he walked up and down the line eyeing us.

"Again, keep one line formed," he said as he strutted his big-ass self back into the air-conditioned building. He was acting like we were joining the Marines or somethin'. I figured this must've been an important role for him. I was tempted to blow my cool, and I saw a couple of kids who did say "Fuck it" and bounced. But whenever I got too tired, I just kept thinking about the feeling when Moms got that eviction notice. That made it easier. It was afternoon by the time I made it through the door. The dude with the busted 'fro looked surprised to see me as I dropped off my completed paperwork with a smile.

"Damn, this was a long-ass day," I told myself on the way home. "But mission accomplished." It made me proud to know I would be able to help my family. No more 72-hour notices.

Walking through the door, I was feeling good until I saw Moms sitting in the dining room like the weight of the world was on her shoulders. I was expecting her to ask me a whole lot of questions like, "Where have you been?" or "Why did that take so long?" But no. Instead she sat there with a worried expression on her face.

"Ma, what happened?" I said softly.

"We have to move," she replied, clearing her throat.

"Why?" I said, slowly slipping into the chair opposite from her. I was so puzzled, that's all that came to my mind to say.

"We owe back rent," she said simply.

"But I thought we was paying rent—"

She interrupted me to continue. "Remember the constant leak in the ceiling? The one I kept complaining about to the landlord?" She paused to let me catch up. "Since he did not fix it, I held the rent."

"So, we have the money to catch up, right, Ma?" I said in an agitated voice, trying to convince myself that there was a simple solution. My mind was racing, and before she could answer, I added: "All they have to do is fix the ceiling, right? That's no big—"

Ma interrupted me again and her voice was so calm it made me more upset.

"They won't accept what I have," she told me as she stood up to go to the bathroom. "They said we have seventy-two hours to be out."

My heart stopped for a moment. I had to catch my breath. I could not believe we were getting evicted again. Now all that paperwork I filled out would be useless with the wrong address. I just wished she could have told us another way or given us more warning. It hurt me, but deep down inside I was getting used to this sort of thing.

"Hey, this is part of life," I told myself. "Mom does the best she can." I knew the routine—start grabbing whatever is valuable to you before the eviction people take it.

It didn't take us long to find another apartment way up on Tiebout Avenue and 181st Street, not far from the Grand Concourse. The building stood by itself at the bottom of a hill. The neighborhood was decent, because of the police precinct being up the block. It was sort of like an upgrade from the projects with rent control. Ours was a nice duplex apartment with the living room and kitchen upstairs and the bedrooms downstairs. Only one question remained—what about the neighbors?

The first day we pulled up to the building with the moving truck, I noticed some boys in the lobby. Once they saw the truck rolling up to the entrance, they all came outside with curious expressions on their faces. They had jeans and T-shirts on, little nappy uncombed Afros, and puberty bumps all over their faces, trying to look tough. I figured this must be the greeting team for the building. You could clearly see they wanted their presence to be felt with the new tenants. While we were moving in, they changed positions to inside the lobby, especially when they saw there were some new girls moving in. My sisters and I just concentrated on carrying stuff from the truck, making sure there was no eye contact with these boys. I could tell they were a bunch of jerks, because they were acting silly, play-fighting and cursing at one another for attention. Then one of them tried to say something slick.

"Yo, you want me to carry that for you, baby?" he ventured, but we just ignored him. Then he proceeded with: "One of y'all gonna be my girl," in a fake wannabe tough-guy tone. We turned around to tell somebody off and—wait a minute! there were two boys standing there, looking exactly alike. *Oh no*, I said to myself. *Twins!*

Anyway, our hands were full, and we had no idea who had said what, so I kept it simple.

"*What* did you say?" I replied with the chicken neck motion along with the mean mug facial expression. I wanted to make sure they knew not to try us from day one.

"I was only kidding," one of them said, trying to play it off and laughing to make his brothers think he was joking because he knew he just got dissed.

"Ah, don't pay him no mind," the other twin butted in. "He's just crazy."

We were, like, "Yeah, *whatever*!"

Then they properly introduced themselves as the Johnsons

from the fourth floor. They were four brothers, two of them were twins. We soon came to learn that hanging in the lobby or in front of the building starting shit with everyone was sort of their thing. That was cool with me. They could continue bothering other people in the building, just not us. We nipped that shit right in the bud.

Chapter 10

The Death of a Friend

I barely slept the night before the first day of high school. I was so anxious for the next day to come. That morning I could not wait to get to the bathroom. With five girls in the house plus Moms, we were always fighting for the bathroom. You know that was ill; bathroom time was crucial. Moms literally timed us in there, and she would really stress us on school mornings.

"Everybody gets fifteen minutes," she'd say. But I wasn't trying to hear it today of all days.

"Shoot, fifteen minutes?" I said through the locked door. "Hell, I'm a girly girl. It takes half an hour just to stare at myself in the mirror." My sisters could pound on the door and complain all they wanted. I was gonna take my time and get ready today.

As I gazed on my reflection, my mind started wandering as usual. Starting high school was so special for me. I had to make the first impression count. My older sisters Lavern and Angel were in high school already. They attended Roosevelt High School on Fordham Road near the Bronx Botanical Gardens. That school was also considered a bad school, but my sisters had a laid-back demeanor that kept them out of trouble. Besides, they were both scared to do anything for fear of what

Moms might do to them that they ended up mostly hanging out with each other. To hell with that! I thought.

I spent my extra time in the bathroom looking at myself over and over and over. I couldn't change my look or my outfit, but at least I could make sure the expression on my face was tight. I was doing the actress thing, trying on different personalities, until I heard Moms yelling at me through the door.

"Shelly, get out of the bathroom," she roared. "You've been in there too long."

"All right, Ma," I replied nervously. "I'm almost finished."

"No," she said in her most stern, authoritative tone. "Come out now!" Once she put that bass in her voice, I knew it was time to step. I burst out of the bathroom door and out the front door without pausing to hear my sisters' complaints.

I had to run to the bus stop to catch the Webster Avenue bus line. It took you straight up to the corner of White Plains Road; then you only had to walk three blocks along Gunhill Road to get to Evander. Kids were all lined up at the bus stop with their new back-to-school outfits on. Their hair was all fresh, and their faces were all shiny from Vaseline petroleum jelly. That was the moisturizer back then. If your skin was ashy, your mother would say, "Go get that Vaseline, girl, and rub it on that ashy-ass face or legs! Then bring it here, so I can grease your scalp." The darker you were, the shinier your face would be.

The bus went to several schools in the Bronx so it was always crowded. When I got on board it was standing room only, and everybody was looking around curiously, wondering who was going to be in the same school as they were. When the bus finally reached our destination, we anxiously climbed down the steps. You could see everybody secretly checking each other out. There was no telling what the boys were thinking, but all the girls were hoping that any cute guys they spotted on the bus would be in the same class as they were.

As I was walking, getting closer and closer to the school building, I started feeling butterflies in my stomach. I truly could not believe I was in high school already. Was I really ready for this? Approaching the school, I noticed all these tall-ass kids hanging outside the entrance. Some of them looked just like grown-ups. They weren't dressed like teachers so they must've been the seniors. You could tell the school vets by the way they looked at everybody else entering the school, like they were sizing us up or just reminding us of our proper place in the school pecking order.

You could see the guys staring, laughing, and bragging, while the girls were gossiping or trying to take you apart with their eyes. Some of them tried to give you that intimidating look, like, *This is our school, our rules.* Even though I felt nervous walking up the school steps, I kept thinking over and over, *Whatever you do, please don't show any fear.*

Uh, I don't care if y'all was here first, I would tell myself. *I'm not scared. Just respect me—that's all I ask.* Thinking like that brought up enough confidence to hide my nervousness.

Once inside the school, while I was waiting for instructions from the monitors, I saw a familiar face that looked as intimidated as I felt.

Oh, shit, I said to myself, *it's Belinda from my old junior high!*

Yo, what more could you ask for on the first day of high school? Seeing somebody I knew made me feel much better. And even though Belinda always appeared to be the strong one back in junior high, I could see that she was relieved to see me too.

Belinda and I hung out together for the whole beginning of the school year. Her gossipy friend Nadine was not in the mix anymore—she had been sent to another high school—and that made it even more comfortable for me hanging out with her. We were becoming best friends.

One day we were having lunch in the noisy student cafeteria when she said she had something to tell me. She said it so casually that I didn't suspect there was anything wrong. But when I asked her what it was, she changed her mind.

"Never mind," she said, sipping on a carton of milk. Of

course I was too curious now. I wouldn't let her leave the cafeteria until she told me. Finally she just spit it out.

"Okay, I'm pregnant," she said, much to my astonishment. "I'm having a baby."

"Girl, I know your mother is going to kill you," was the only thing I could think to say.

Fortunately for her, that was not the case. She said her mother had told her to keep the child. She delivered this news with no fear in her eyes, not even a worried look. Somehow, she just seemed too calm for the situation. Hell, I had enough on my hands trying to cope with high school. But raising a baby—forget about it! I hoped to myself that she had a good man to help her.

In junior high Belinda always used to talk about her boyfriend. He was older than her, but that was no surprise since she always seemed so much more mature than the rest of us. She even talked about their plans of getting married. This was too heavy for me. Moms would have killed my ass for sure, and I don't think I could've handled so much responsibility. Besides, based on the past experiences with men in my life, I never would even think about anything like that.

Belinda wasn't even showing when we first heard her big news. But time passed so quickly that the next thing I knew, she was giving birth to a beautiful baby boy she named Daniel. Of course she had to leave school for a while, but she seemed cool about the whole thing. Between her mother and her man, maybe it was going to be all right after all. Of course I missed her company—that was my girl. But we were from the same neighborhood so it wasn't too hard to keep in touch. I would visit her and the baby occasionally, usually bringing little things I could afford.

She surprised me one day by asking me to be her son's godmother. I accepted her offer, not really understanding what it was all about. My godparents were a white couple that ran a church over on Saint Paul's Place across town. We used to go to their church on Sundays. Moms made us go to church and

Sunday school, even though she would only occasionally attend herself. I guess she figured, "Hey, maybe I don't go to God, but at least I make my kids go!" Father Elli and his wife, Dessa, were very mild-mannered people who had a child of their own. I would get a box of pencils and some nasty salted candy from them every Christmas. They became my godparents because when I got baptized at their church, my mother did not have anybody else—so they stood in. Then came John, whom Moms sometimes called my godfather. He drove a bus. Every once in a while he would come to visit us, and I would run under the bed and hide. I don't know why, but I was scared to death of this man. He was real dark with bumps all over his face and he always seemed to have this devilish grin every time he looked at me. Whenever I heard him coming, I would haul ass under the bed until he left the house. I don't even know how my mother met John. Looking back, he could have been an undercover lover. What made her pick him to be my godfather—*hmm?*

Bottom line, I really did not understand the true meaning of being someone's godmother. But I would soon find out.

I sure did miss Belinda. I couldn't wait for her to come back from her pregnancy leave. But when she finally came back to school, I noticed something different about her. Something just felt strange to me but I couldn't figure out what it was. At first I thought that maybe when people had kids, they grew up overnight. My friend just seemed even more mature than before, and a little bit distant. Our relationship was still cool, but she started missing a lot of days at school. I would look to see her in class or the cafeteria, but her seat would be empty. I wanted to know what was going on with her so much that I started showing up on her doorstep.

"Belinda home?" I'd ask.

"She is asleep," her mother would answer. "Come back later."

You know me—I came back later. Finally Belinda would come to the door looking very weak.

"Belinda, what is wrong?" I'd ask. "You okay? Is the baby making you tired?"

"No," she'd reply. "Just feeling a little sick."

Now I knew something was wrong with Belinda. She just did not have her usual strength in the way she carried herself. Was this what happened to people when they had babies? Belinda was barely showing up to school at all anymore. So, persistent me, I decided I was going to get to the bottom of this. Hell, the child was getting bigger, plus I was the boy's godmother!

I showed up at her door again and my friend finally told me the truth. With tears in her eyes, Belinda told me that the doctors discovered she had cervical cancer.

"Cervix cancer," I said. "What the hell is that?" Never having heard of this shit before, I had no idea how serious cancer of the cervix was. But that soon became very clear as I kept coming around and witnessed the toll it was taking on her. As the godmother, I wanted to help with her baby, but she told me not to worry about it. Her family was taking care of Daniel along with the baby's father. When she was hospitalized, I kept going to the hospital to visit her. It would bug me out just seeing her lying there connected to all those tubes, but helpless. There was nothing I, or anyone, could do for her.

Within a year Belinda lost her battle with cervical cancer and passed away. I was devastated. She was too young to go, and I had never witnessed anybody so close to me dying. I knew deep inside that her son would be all right. Even after she passed, she would visit me in my dreams.

With all the serious stuff I was going through, it was hard to care much about high school. It was nothing like I expected. I thought it was going to be all serious, but really it was one big hangout. It seemed like folks spent more time in the hallways or outside the building than they did in class. Guys would hang out on the front steps of the building trying to holla at whatever chick would respond. Girls mostly hung out in the hallways, and a few hung out on the front steps along with the fellas, trying to look cute, looking around to see which of the guys were staring at them.

By this time, guys were hitting on me left and right, which gave me a little more confidence in my appearance. But in truth, this was really false confidence—a fact you don't realize until you're older. It wasn't that I needed these boys' attention in order to feel confident, but it did give you that feeling. What girl *doesn't* like to be told that she looks good?

Even though the attention was flattering, I found no boys attractive to *me*. I'd always find something wrong with them, like a crooked nose or big lips. While they were kicking their game, I took them apart from head to toe.

Damn, look at his big-ass head, I'd say to myself. *Lips looking all ashy . . .* In order to appear popular, I would talk to them anyway. It was good for the reputation. I had always been curious about having a boyfriend, and now I had several guys to choose from, but wanted none of them. I'm not going to front; I enjoyed hanging with some of the guys—mostly the comedians. I'd get a good laugh at their silly-ass jokes in school. But that was it.

I was never one to make friends easily, especially with other females. Growing up, I mostly hung around my sisters, and we never lived in one place long enough to make lasting friendships with anyone. Since Belinda and I came from the same junior high school and the same neighborhood, our friendship came much easier.

It took a while getting over Belinda's death. I used to look forward to meeting up with her in the lunchroom. I missed the gossip, the girly girl talk, and her tough-ass demeanor. Sitting in the lunchroom reminiscing, I could almost hear her now.

"It ain't nothing, girl," she'd say with that tough stance of hers. "Ya know me—I'm no crybaby type of girl."

Damn, why did she have to go?

Chapter 11

My Twin and the Stalker

One afternoon, in the middle of changing classes, I saw this girl coming toward me with a big smile on her face. I used to see her hanging in the hallways all the time and I think she was in one of my classes.

"Hi, my name is Tina," she said as she approached me.

"What's up?" I said, but in my mind I was like, *What the hell does this girl want with that phony shit?*

"So, you're the one everybody says looks like me," she said in a happy high-pitched tone. I had noticed her checking me out before, but we'd never spoken until this moment. Everybody in school used to think we looked alike. I guess it was because we were both light-skinned, with long faces. But this wasn't just one of those *"all light-skinned people look alike"* or *"all dark-skinned people look alike"* kinda things. No, this was a bit more extreme. I was constantly hearing it in class and even outside school. People would come up to me and say, "Wow, you look just like this girl named Tina. Are y'all related?" Tina was my twin.

At first I wasn't eager to hang out with her, but I decided to play along and try to be friendly. We started out gradually, meeting in the lunchroom and talking in class, and before you knew it we'd slipped into a real friendship. In time she started showing her true colors. Tina created her own chaotic little world, which consisted of packing a Thermos full of vodka (from her parents' stash) in her bag and cutting school on a daily basis. She was also very controlling, which resulted in many arguments between us. It was her way or no way—or so she thought.

Tina came from a family of four that consisted of herself, one brother, and her mother and father. Her parents gave her anything she wanted. I didn't know many people who lived with their mom and dad. To me, they seemed like the Bronx version of *The Cosbys* or something. Tina had that spoiled ghetto type of attitude, but she was fun to hang out with because she made everything that was wrong to do seem cool. Tina brought out all those devilish ways inside me that were just dying to come out.

She had a boyfriend named Allan, and they were perfect for each other. They were from 224th Street, loved to party, and most importantly, he was just as caught up in her world as she was. He was a little dude with a very big head, dimples, big eyes, and a quiet, laid-back attitude. She truly ruled the relationship, no question about it. In fact, it seemed like he enjoyed having her control him.

"Allan," she would say in that demanding voice of hers. "When I come out of school, you better be there."

Sure enough, Allan would just hang outside the school all day smoking joints and waiting for Tina. There seemed to be no limit to what he would put up with.

"Allan, go get this," she'd say. "Allan, go get that!" And he would act just like a puppy dog, wagging his tail and obeying his master.

I began cutting class with Tina, except for my acting and communication classes. I liked my communication class because the teacher was kind of dizzy—she always seemed drunk or something. She was like a permanent substitute teacher; she never much knew or cared what was going on. And it seemed like she could fall asleep at any moment. Sometimes she would even fall asleep in the middle of class—yep, right in the middle of teaching! She wore a wig that looked crooked, and the makeup used to be scattered all over her face. She would draw on her eyebrows real thin and arched, like the Joker from *Batman*. She wore ruby-red lipstick, went heavy on the eyeliner, and had red blush all over her dark complexion. She wore so much cake on her face, the kids greeted her by saying, "Happy birthday, Mrs. Weldon," and she would just smile, not realizing the joke. Her class was too much fun to miss, especially with all the students cutting up and snapping on each other. "Uh, pleassse doooon't taaaalk," Mrs. Weldon would say, her speech all slurred and slow. "Okayyyy?" Meanwhile the whole class would be laughing and sneaking sips of the vodka Tina brought to school from her parents' stash. Later on we found out the teacher was diabetic, which explained why she appeared tired all the time.

Acting class, on the other hand, was fun because I just loved acting. Instead of homework, we did charades for extra credit. Charades are when you have to act out a part without saying anything—the teacher called that a pantomime—and the audience has to figure out what role you were playing. The teacher would call you up, and you did your pantomime in front of the whole class. It was funny watching other students make fools of themselves, acting out corny-ass plays by the teacher—if they could get through the whole thing without laughing. Acting had to be the most attended class in school. Even if you cut the other classes, you still showed up to that one because it was a time for everybody to clown around. Our teacher, Ms. Schwartz, reminded me of an old actress. She kept her hair in a bun and always spoke precisely, like she was auditioning for a part. "Good morning, children," she would say in such a proper way, holding her head up and her chest out. The class was of particular interest to me because, of course, I wanted to be an actress—but I kept that secret to myself. I didn't want the other kids to think I was corny.

Tina and I were becoming very popular in school. We were

almost inseparable until the end of the school day, when Tina would take the bus uptown, and I would take the bus downtown. Those buses used to be crowded, and most of the kids entered through the back. If your bus pass was expired, the back was the way to go. It also made you feel down because you dared to go through the back. There were too many kids doing it for the bus driver to stop us. He would yell at us, or threaten to put us off or call the cops, but all his efforts were just a waste of breath. Most of the time the kids would yell back. "Shut the fuck up and keep driving," some smart-ass would say, and then the others would join in. The bus drivers never won. The smarter ones knew we were too much for them to deal with. For the most part, they just left it alone.

I'd ride the bus with the guys who lived across town in the Bronx, on Webster Avenue—the Webster Avenue Projects to be exact. I would sit there watching with a grin as they terrorized the other students on the bus with their loud music and snapped on anybody who caught their attention. Whenever they got on the bus, older people would get off at the next stop—some wouldn't dare to get on the bus at all. All those rowdy kids, loud music, and cursing sometimes resulted in fights breaking out on the bus. You either went along with the program or took the chance of getting jumped.

It always started the same way—some guy with a huge boom box would pop the cassette tape in and start blasting that funk. Then it was on! The tape would usually be from a jam in one of our local parks, school yards, or block parties, where anyone from Afrika Bambaataa to Kool Herc, The L Brothers, or Grandmaster Flash and the Furious Five were playing every weekend. If you had a tape from one of those jams, you were the man. Most of the time it was the guy who hung outside the school all day who had the box. You never saw him with any schoolbooks, just that big ol' boom box in one hand and a forty-ounce of "Ol'E" in the other.

At this time the radio was playing a lot of disco music, like "Do the Hustle" by Van McKoy, or "Good Times" by Chic.

Rap music was not on wax yet, but all around the Bronx you had MCs rapping over all kind of beats—anywhere from disco to rock, soul, or jazz break beats while the DJ mixed and scratched. The bass was pounding extra-heavy and then you would hear a voice chanting in time—"Keep on / And ya don't stop / Party people in the house"—with the crazy echo effect. It was nothing too complicated, but that shit sounded so fly it could blow your mind. At the time I had no concept of ever being part of these outer-space audio antics. To me, it was just some after-school fun for when we were riding the bus or standing out on the school steps.

In those days there was this one guy named Boyd, from the basketball team. He was very popular because he was nice on the courts, he was from Webster projects, and he always walked around with a boom box. Even though he liked me, I had no interest in him, but he just did not get it. It seemed like every day, when it was time to get on the bus, he would be there, even if fifty other buses had passed by already. He was a big-ass goofy guy with bumps all over his face. The clothes he wore looked sloppy and outdated, and let's not talk about the short lopsided Afro. I purposely walked slowly to the bus, trying to avoid him, but every day after school, there he stood, waiting by the bus. "Hey, Shelly," he would said in a goofy-ass fake-surprised tone while holding the back of the bus door open. "Come on."

Boyd always found a way to end up next to me on the bus, tryin' to hold conversations but saying nothing. He would usually try to get my phone number in what he considered a "slick" way.

"Yo, let me call you," he'd say, "just as a friend."

I would always give the same answer: "No, Boyd, my moms will kill me if you call my house." But still he would keep trying.

Somehow, Boyd found out where I lived—maybe he wasn't as dumb as I thought. Anyway, he figured it out. One evening, as my family was about to have dinner, we heard a hip-hop tape playing.

I was like, "*Yeah*—somebody's playing the jams outside." Then I heard a voice from outside.

"Shelly, Shelly, are you home? Come to the window."

I tried to ignore it, 'cause I knew that voice. I whispered to one of my sisters, "I know that is not dumb-ass Boyd. I know he don't have the nerve." But yeah, it was him. My mom gave me this look. I read her eyes. Before I could say, *I don't know how* . . . she was at that window.

When she looked down she saw this overgrown boy standing in front of the building. She opened up the window and let him have it.

"Get the hell away from this building," my mother yelled. "I know you ain't calling for my daughter."

His stupid ass just stood there. Next thing you know, she was grabbing for a potted plant, a glass of water, anything she could find at that moment to throw at him. Moms used to tell us that if you kissed a boy, you would get pregnant, so you know she was not having any night visitors. Boyd hauled ass so fast, when my sisters and I ran to the window all we saw was his raggedy butt running up the hill. We were cracking up until Mom turned around. Our laughter had set her off all over again.

"I'm not playing," she said, her face turning red. "The next time a boy comes for you, you're gonna get it." We knew that meant an ass whupping. There was no way for her to know it, but she didn't have much to worry about with me anyway. I already felt all guys were jerks, based on the prime examples of men in my life—both seen (Boyd) and unseen (my father). I had watched my brothers cheating and treating women they were supposed to be with like dogs. And there wasn't even a father figure around long enough to teach me any different. On that note, relationships were the furthest thing from my mind.

Chapter 12

Sugar Daddy

High school put a lot of pressure on a young girl's head. The peer pressure of doing wrong wasn't the problem. Much worse was the fashion pressure. It wasn't about doing the wrong thing, but wearing the right thing. Especially if you were a female, you had to keep up with the latest clothes for reputation purposes. I could not get away with two outfits a year for high school like I did during junior high. Eyes in high school would definitely be on you, especially if you were popular and well known. Waiting for Moms wasn't gonna make it anymore. Money had to start coming in from somewhere, I just needed to figure out where.

There was this girl named Sharon, who I met through Tina at school. She was from up around Tina's neighborhood, and she hung out with us on occasion. Sharon was attractive and wore nothing but designer clothes. She was tall, light-skinned, and slim, with bowlegs and a lot of weave in her hair. Hair weave wasn't very popular back then. I used to think that was her real hair, until I noticed some thread coming from the back of her head.

"Sharon," I said, "you got a thread hanging from your hair."

I went to grab it, and she damn near died.

"Girl, don't *pull* it!" she cried. "Then the whole thing is going to come out. It's a weave!"

That was the very first weave I ever discovered.

Sharon was the girlfriend of this DJ from uptown named Kail. He used to spin at a big club called the T Connection and some after-hours spots in the Bronx. He was not known to be a street DJ; he mainly hit the uptown down-low club spots. But once you were a DJ at the T Connection, you were known. It was the hottest spot uptown. Every MC and DJ known played at the T Connection.

Sharon never had a job, so I assumed her boyfriend was taking good care of her. That's the way she made it seem in school.

She'd be, like, showing off new shoes or jewelry like, "*Girl,* look what Kail bought me!" Then she'd go on with a squeaky, irritating tone and a fake smile. "Next week I'm getting some shrimp earrings—the big ones." Shrimp earrings were in fashion then. If you had a pair of big gold shrimp earrings, you were considered a fly girl. Oh, and don't have on the Lee jean suit, heels, and the tight hair-do to go along with the shrimp earrings—all eyes would definitely be on you. For guys, if you had the big gold medallion around your neck, a brim hat, and a quarter field coat with big fake fur around the collar, you were a fly guy. You could have worn the same jeans all year long; all girls would see is that big-ass medallion around your neck and the quarter field coat. Keeping in style was harder for us females. Fly girls wore all the latest fashions in the hood that the other chicks couldn't afford.

We did not mind the weave diva Sharon hanging with us, but it seemed like all she would do is talk about herself—what she was getting, what she got, and how every man wanted her.

One morning before class, I ran into Sharon getting off the bus, and she came with that phony fly-girl talk right away.

"Hey, girl, where you going?"

"I *think* aah . . . to school Sharon," I responded in a sarcastic way.

"Stop playing," she said, still with that phony smile of hers.

"Okay, Sharon, what you want?"

"Well, I was thinking we should cut school today. Tina is absent." I paused for a moment. See, when I cut school with Tina, we would hang in the hallways or outside the school, drinking vodka and ducking the security guards. Tina knew where all the hooky parties were. But Sharon was boring. What the hell were we gonna do all day long! Talk about her weave?

"And do what?" I asked hesitantly.

"I got somewhere for us to hang out at," she said, adding mysteriously, "And don't worry, money is involved."

"Bet," I said. "Money—that's all you had to say."

We walked about five blocks away from the school to this private house. I figured it was a hooky party somebody was throwing, but then again, I wondered, *Where does the money come in?* Hooky parties were thrown at least twice a week, whenever somebody got access to an apartment that was free of adults during school hours. Everybody would chip in for alcohol and weed and then sit back and listen to music. Whatever happened after that was up to you.

When we got there, Sharon rang the bell three times, like some type of code.

"Who is it?" an old man with a heavy accent replied harshly through the intercom. I couldn't tell if he was Spanish or West Indian.

Sharon answered, "It's me."

He buzzed the door to let us in.

The old man had recognized her voice. *This must be a regular thing for her*, I thought. But it felt anything but regular to me. We walked up a long flight of narrow stairs lined with dirty carpet. At the top was a door that led to a living room. There stood an old man in his sixties with gray, nappy hair on his head and face. He had on a white tank top and old-man pants, those polyester trousers that they wear all the way up to the chest—the kind you see old men on the corners or in church wearing. As he came to greet us, I noticed that he walked with a limp. He was so bowlegged, his legs looked broken. Not only did he have a heavy accent, he had the killer eyes to match. He was a very mean-looking dude, and he was staring at me hard. I felt a little uncomfortable until Sharon broke up the stare and introduced us.

"Scoop," she said, "this is Shelly, my friend from school."

He continued to stare so I stared back, wondering, *What's up with him?* I knew I had heard his name before, but I couldn't figure out where. Then he said, "Sharon, did she ever come to the club before?"

"No," Sharon said, and I thought, *Club?* I looked at her puzzled.

"Oh, girl," she said, "Scoop owns the after-hours club around the corner."

It finally hit me. That was one of the clubs where her man DJ'd, I'd heard a lot about that place. Word on the streets was that you could get any drug you wanted out of there, and this man from Cuba owned the place. Everybody knew him from uptown. They said he didn't play when it came to his money. He was a ruthless type of cat.

What was the connection between these two? *Damn*, I thought to myself. *Sharon is a sneaky chick.* Scoop offered me something to drink, and I refused it.

"Don't be scared," he said. "I don't bite. Have a seat."

Yeah, right, I thought to myself.

Looking around, I noticed that the house was nice but it was cluttered with all types of things, from stereos to TVs to coats with tags still on them. It almost looked like a down-low department store, there was so much merchandise. Scoop stood and went into his room and Sharon followed saying, "Girl, I'll be right back."

I sat there being a bit naïve as to what was really going on. I waited for about fifteen minutes, and then Sharon came out alone with a silly grin on her face.

"Are you ready?" she said. "Let's go!"

As we were walking down the steps, she was counting her money. She stopped at the door and turned around to say, "He thinks you are pretty." That didn't flatter me. I wanted to know what her sneaky ass was doing, but she tried to avoid the topic.

"Here is twenty dollars for you," she said. "He told me to give it to you to buy some lunch." On the same breath she added, "By the way, he wants me to bring you back when I come again."

"For what?" I said.

"He has a lot of money," she replied. "He always gives me money, jewelry, practically anything I want. Maybe he wants to do the same for you."

What? I stopped walking and looked her dead in the eye.

"I know you're not just up there holding his hand," I said. "What's really going on, girl? Tell me something."

She did not answer me. All she did was smirk with that silly-ass phony grin, and I read the eyes. To my surprise, she had no shame in her game. Even though the offer sounded tempting, I still had some pride in what I did. Hell, selling your body is easy. Every girl born and raised in the hood struggled so she would not have to go out like that, even though society wants you to believe the opposite. Imagine me doing something with that old man! I didn't even want to picture him naked in my mind—*gross*! I wanted shrimp earrings too, but not that bad.

Chapter 13

Loose Joints

One morning as I was about to go into Evander, I spotted Tina and her lapdog of a boyfriend Allan standing in front of the school gates. They motioned for me to come over to where they were standing. As I approached them, I noticed that Tina looked anxious.

"We have a proposition for you," she said, "and we're gonna get paid, girl!"

I thought, *What the hell could they possibly be coming up with to make money?* Tina continued her spiel while Allan stood there with a big ol' smile on his face, watching his girl talk her bullshit. She started running her mouth about how we could start selling marijuana joints at school. *Hmm*—it wasn't a bad idea. I knew a lot of people who smoked joints at school. And financially, shit was hectic at home.

"Who's gonna supply it?" I asked.

"My man from uptown," Allan said. "All we do is sell it and collect the profits."

"Aw, what the hell?" I said, and decided to take them up on the offer. Loose joints were marijuana rolled up tight in Bambu paper. You could get one for a dollar and three for two. I knew Allan could get us the hookup as far as getting the product went; he knew all the drug dealers uptown. In fact, he had about forty of them skinny cigarettes in his pocket right now.

We started putting out the word in school. "We got loose joints. One for a dollar or three for two dollars." Customers started coming quick. Hell, this hustle looked promising. I thought we would have shit locked by the end of the month. I started calculating the money I was gonna have, and shopping in my mind. I visualized those shrimp earrings, some jean suits, a gold medallion—all the fly-girl shit. *Yeah*, I told myself, *I'm going to be the shit.*

Think again. When I went to Tina to check the status of our business venture, all I heard was, "We are out of product and there's no money to re-up cause we had to pay Allan's man off the top."

"So where's all our profits Tina?" I demanded. "Don't tell me you and Allan smoked up our profits!"

What? I wanted to kill their asses. Silly me, I let Tina and Allan take control of the money and the product—the biggest mistake ever. First of all, the product was wack. I know because the guys that we got to try the weed smoked a whole joint and didn't even get a buzz. The real heads were complaining, so they got discounts just to shut their mouths. Second, Tina and Allan were smoking up the product, which burned through our re-up money. Last but not least, what the hell was I thinking? I should have known better than to be business partners with that crazy couple. Within a week I cut off my business partnership with them before I ended up owing money to some drug dealers I didn't even know.

Chapter 14

Nettie and Stacey

In my acting class there was this brown-skinned, kind of tall and big-boned girl like myself, a girl with a round, sad face. I used to notice her because she would always sit quietly in the back of class with a blank expression on her face while the rest of us were clowning around. She was very serious all the time, and did not seem like the friendly type. I didn't know whether she was somewhat shy or just didn't want to be bothered. No one in class seemed like they were trying to socialize with her or even had a clue about how to approach her.

The bell rang signaling the end of class. On this particular day, Tina had not shown up to class, so I was rolling solo. As I closed my book and got up to head for the door, I felt someone staring at me. I slowly looked over my shoulder while picking up my books and noticed "the quiet girl" eyeing me. I could have sworn she was giving me the *want to start something?* grill face.

"What's up?" I said in a defensive way.

Her response was quick. "Nothing! What's up?"

I started to respond in a *what you wanna do?* tone, but then I realized that she wasn't aggressive at all. She had spoken in a friendly way. I calmed down and took another approach.

"What's up, girl?" I said. "My name is Shelly."

Then she smiled. Wow! I had never seen this girl show any emotions on her face. She said her name was Nettie, and she was not at all like I expected. She turned out to be mad cool—still real laid-back, but cool. I soon felt stupid for trying to come at her in such a defensive way, but that's what the streets will do to you.

Nettie was from Webster Projects on 165th Street and Webster Avenue. Her mom had her at a later age, so her brothers and sisters were much older than she was. We started meeting at the bus stop after school to ride the same bus home.

I introduced her to Tina one day in class, and I could see that she knew Tina was wild by the expression on her face. But Nettie didn't protest. Slowly but surely she started hanging out with us in the lunchroom or after school. She wasn't into cutting class yet, but the more she hung around me, the more her personality became at ease. Everybody couldn't adapt so quickly to that off-the-wall shit that Tina brought.

As time went on I started hanging out with Nettie more than I did with Tina, which was probably good for me anyway. On the weekends Nettie would come over to hang out around my block. She eventually got to know my family, and I got to know hers. Come to find out, her niece Beebe went to the same junior high school as me.

Nettie had another friend by the name of Stacey, who she grew up with. They were from the same projects. She would always mention how much fun they had hanging out. I was kind of eager to meet this cool-ass Stacey. Finally one weekend I snuck off of my block to go hang around Nettie's way. That's when I finally met Stacey, but from the looks of it, she really wasn't too enthusiastic about meeting me.

Nettie was waiting for me in front of her building. I noticed this other girl standing next to her. She did not look too friendly, kind of grilling me up and down from the side of her face. She had a mean look about her, like she was ready to beat my ass or something. I knew what time it was—I was the third wheel coming into their friendship. You know that girlfriend stuff. Y'all two been hanging around each other since child-hood—now here comes the "new friend." Your mind starts playing tricks on you, and you start to wonder, *Is she a double agent playing both sides? Is she talking about me to her? Telling her all my business and secrets that we share?* It sounds silly, but that's just the way it is when it comes to girlfriend relationships.

Nettie was like, "Stacey, this is Shelly. Shelly, this is Stacey." She was all happy and shit for her two friends to finally meet.

Stacey went, "Yeah, how ya doin'?" with a soft yet snappy voice and a hard-ass facial expression. Stacey was sort of chubby, short with a well-rounded face. Her hairdo was tight, with the fake baby hair gelled down to the sides of her face.

"Yeah, I'm all right," I responded without emotion, letting her know her reactions didn't even sting me.

Stacey went to Walton, an all-girl high school that was kind of rough. She had a somewhat cool, almost gangster attitude. She was the only girl of three brothers, and according to Nettie, her mom was real strict with her. Stacey also came from a single-parent home. We all had that in common. Even though they lived on Webster Avenue, they hung around 163rd and Boston Road, a busy corner of a bustling street that runs all the way through Bronx and on up to Boston. One of Stacey's brothers, Larry B, ran a crew over there named the Boston Road Crew. I started creeping off of my block to hang with them on Boston Road, even though I would hear much riffing from my mother whenever I came home.

Chapter 15

The Boston Road Crew

The Boston Road Crew was well known throughout the Bronx. If you were down with them, nobody would dare fuck with you. Larry B would treat us like we were all his little sisters. When we came around with Stacey, he and his crew would stand next to us with arms folded, as if to say, "Watch out for them while they're on this block." He kind of reminded me of the way my brother Cooley was when my sisters and I came around his turf. Larry was a big guy, so his presence alone used to intimidate a lot of people. He was mild-mannered, but if you fucked with him, he had no problem stepping to that ass, no matter who you were.

Boston Road was the place to be, especially during the summer months, because you always had different DJ crews playing music on the corner. The block was always rocking. Come on, with Grandmaster Flash and the Furious Five, Grand Wizard Theodore and the L Brothers, Kool Herc and the Herculords, DJ Breakout from uptown—and the list goes on—Boston Road in the Bronx was one of the original home bases for hip-hop. We'd just be rockin' on the street corners or in '63 Park, which was actually a concrete school yard down the block. Wherever the music was playing, everybody would be out there. The streets used to be packed, especially during the summer months. Speakers were big as hell with amps to match. They'd be plugged into the street lamppost, or the electric cord extension would be coming from somebody's house through the window. People danced in the streets or simply stood around posing while the music blasted. Every MC would be dying to get a shot at the mic, while the DJ scratched the hell out of records like *Good Times* by Chic, over and over, like "good / good / go-o-o-d times / times / times." Or they'd chop up *Rock Creek Park* by The Blackbyrds "Doing it in the park / park / park / doing it after dark / dark / dark." You name it, they played it. And whatever was playing, you can bet the MC ripped it. If you're a real hip-hop head, you can imagine the electricity that was in the atmosphere. This went on until either the power went out or you heard gunshots from somewhere. Then the cops would come shut shit down. All this action fell under the heading of street jams: they were like a free concert without any promoters or salaries involved, held purely for street rep and fun. It was always a carefree atmosphere.

Of course the crowd was full of all types of crews representing in sweatshirts bearing their crew's name on the back in iron-on letters. The females wore tight-fitting Sergio Valente or Jordache jeans while the fellas had the Lee bell-bottoms with the permanent crease ironed down the middle. In those days, to be down with a crew, you had to be at all the jams where your DJ crew was playing and be ready for whatever might go down on any given night—with a straight-up raw dog personality.

At this time there weren't many female crews out there, and they mainly served as an extension of the male crews. You had the Red Devils representing for the Boston Road Crew. Then there were the Sisters Disco, who represented for DJ Breakout. Female crews would hang tight, and they had their crew's back any time a fight broke out at the jams. When you think about it, these neighborhood hangout crews were just a transformation of gang life. They were no longer called "gangs," and they weren't into as much straight-up criminal activity—depending on the situation. But the girl crews were tough, just as tough as their male counterparts. They had no problem getting buck-wild if they had to.

Chapter 16

The Birth of Mercedes Ladies

DJ Breakout was one of the hottest DJs from the Edenwald Houses in the Bronx, which was saying a lot since there were several redbrick buildings in that enormous housing complex off of Gunhill Road. Out of all that competition, Breakout broke out as the one to watch.

I liked Breakout because he was the DJ for The Funky Four Plus One More, a rap crew with a female MC who went by the name of Sha Rock. The whole group consisted of Rodney C., Keith Keith, and Jazzy Jeff, but I loved Sha. She was a tiny little girl, but her heart was huge, and she could hold her own with any male MC. Sha was in one of my math classes at school. There were a lot of MCs and DJs at Evander Childs High School, but Sha was the only girl I knew. In fact, she was the first female MC I'd ever heard of back then. She was the quiet type, but she was real chill and pleasant at all times. I'd always see her in class with a notebook and a pen in her hand—not for class notes, but for writing rhymes.

I'd be like, "What's up, Sha?"

She would lift her head with that little girl smile, and say, "Just chillin', girl."

The next time I saw her she was rocking live at '63 Park off Boston Road. Sha was real cute, with a baby face, but when she got on that mic, there was no question who was in control. She had a unique voice that added a natural echo behind her lyrics. "Yes, Yes, y'all, y'all . . ." she'd rap in such a pretty but firm tone that it made the crowd stop and listen. Her delivery was so awesome, she commanded respect on the mic with no sweat. I don't think any female MC could ever match Sha Rock. She was truly in a class by herself.

Stacey, Nettie, and I started getting more and more popular on Boston Road. I found myself hanging out there a lot, but I would usually pay the price by the time I came home. My mom used to get heated she would literally kick my butt. When I started getting used to that, she would make threats of putting me in a group home. Her worry was understandable since she did not know or have a clue as to what I was doing out there in the streets. She had enough stress in her life already; she didn't need her daughter stressing her out too. Soon as I hit the door, if it wasn't a fist coming, then it was the yelling.

"I'm not playin'!" Mom would yell. "Your ass is going to be put away tomorrow." Somehow tomorrow always became next week, and eventually I realized that these were just idle threats. I never heard Nettie complain about having to go through beef for being out late. Her mother was more laid-back like her, a real nice lady who never said much. When I went to Nettie's house, her moms mainly stayed in her bedroom.

"Mom, I'm out," Nettie would say, and then you heard her mother answer from the bedroom, "Just lock the door behind you, okay?"

And that would be that. No riffing or yelling—it was a done deal.

I would leave the house to go to school, but I never went to classes anymore. I just really wasn't interested in school, not even acting class. With all the stresses at home, I couldn't concentrate anyway. Meanwhile mom was working so hard to keep a roof over our heads that she did not have the time to check on my schoolwork. I just felt like school was not my thing, and I didn't have anyone in my life to help me through these feelings or check me on my delinquent behavior.

Sometimes it felt like all we had was each other. So one day on Boston Road Stacey, Nettie, and I decided to start our own crew. Beebe, Nettie's niece, was hanging with us too. First thing we needed was a name.

"The Cowgirls," someone blurted out. *Nah*, we all said, laughing.

"The Boston Road Girls." Hell no—that name was taken already.

"Rodeo Girls!"

"No, no," I said. "Those sound too corny. We want something classy, something that represents money."

"Yeah," the group said. Then after a string of suggestions, followed by much heavy debating, one of us finally said it:

"How about Mercedes Ladies? It sounds classy, like the Mercedes-Benz."

Hmm, that had a nice ring to it. The room got quiet as we let it ring in our heads a moment.

"The Mercedes Young Ladies," we all said at once.

"Yeah," I said, "that name is *dope*." You would've thought we hit the numbers or something—that's how excited we were about our new crew name.

Now we were off and running. The next thing we did was to make plans on how to represent the crew. We met once or twice a week, meticulously planning every detail of The Mercedes Ladies philosophy. Our goal was to be an all-female crew with a reputation for being strong, serious, and classy with a street edge. Most of all we would be loyal to each other, sisters to the very end. Making music was not part of the plan, but we knew we wanted to build our own empire, not just be a backup for some male crew. We wanted to recruit other females, but they would have to go through some type of initiation to see where their head was at. We wanted dedicated soldiers. Everyone who was down had to pay weekly dues in order to get money up for our uniforms: different color sweatshirts with

MERCEDES YOUNG LADIES spelled out on the back. Those velvet letters that you could iron onto the back of your shirt cost about twenty cents per letter—for nineteen letters that was almost four dollars each.

When our first recruiting mission began, I started with crazy-ass Tina. I thought she would be perfect, because she was always down for whatever. I wasn't too sure about her dedication, but we could work on that. I ran into her at school and told her about the crew we were starting. She agreed to come to our meeting. We had our first meeting on Boston Road. Since there was a jam that day, the street was busy, so we went down where it was less noisy, sitting on the steps in front of this tenement building.

As soon as we got there we noticed that some of the Red Devil crew was peeking at us from the opposite side of the street. They knew not to fuck with us because we were connected to the Boston Road Crew. All they did was look and talk shit among themselves. I knew they were wondering what the hell we were up to—some girls meeting up on their turf . . . *Uhhh!* But we paid them no mind. The meeting went on, but we were still watching them on the down low just in case they were gathering to start some shit. Tina showed up as promised along with one of her friends, Arlene, from uptown. The girls seemed like they were clicking. The vibes were right. We had a pen, a notebook, and big plans.

Chapter 17

Recruitment

The Mercedes Ladies' recruiting campaign was still in full swing. Our latest candidate was this girl named Lina. I knew her because her mom was the number runner on Daily Avenue, the block where my brother Cooley sold drugs. I ran into Lina one day while visiting Cooley around the block, and kicked it to her about the crew we were starting, and she said she would check out the meeting to see what it was all about. Lina was light-skinned with chinky eyes, a small frame, and short curly hair. She was very cute and lived with her mother and younger brother. She was kind of wild, but not really rough—more of a sassy mouth than anything, but not totally convincing. I didn't know if she could fight or not, but she had all the motions down: rolling her eyes, giving the chicken neck, and the sassy attitude to go with it.

Anyway, when we had our next meeting on the same tenement steps—Lina came along with her best friend, Eva. They had grown up together in the same building. Eva didn't say much. Actually, she just stood there looking for Lina to give her the signal on whether to join or not. Either she was the quiet type or she just followed Lina's lead. She was tall, about five nine, with a cocoa complexion and light brown eyes. She was somewhat shy and very attractive.

After two or three meetings, Lina and Eva decided to join the crew too. The Mercedes Young Ladies were growing at a fast pace. The guest list was so full, we even had to turn some girls down—especially if the vibes weren't felt among the other girls. I wanted to recruit my younger sisters Lizzy and Camela, but Moms wasn't having that. She did not want them to hang out with me, because she now considered me a bad influence—so that was out of the question for now.

Everyone agreed Boston Road would be our meeting place. Then the dues started. We all chipped in to get the sweatshirts with MERCEDES YOUNG LADIES in black letters on the back. I got the money from my brother Cooley, the other girls were getting money from their moms—nevertheless we got it. Now we were officially in effect! We couldn't wait for the next jam to profile as the newest crew.

That night on Boston Road, everyone was curious about us. We walked through the jam with the matching sweatshirts and Lee jeans—yep, our presence was felt.

"Mercedes Young Ladies!" the guys would yell as we passed. But we paid them no mind.

Yeah, baby, eat your hearts out.

None of us were ugly chicks—a little rough maybe, but we looked even better rolling together. We always made sure to meet before a jam and come through together. As an all-female crew—not a branch-off from a male crew—we were mysterious and rough, but in a ladies' style. There were a lot of us, which made us look more powerful. The more we appeared at jams all over town, the more popular we were becoming.

We knew we were on the right track when MCs started incorporating our names into their rhymes. People were all over us, some wanting to be down, some just curious, and other female crews trying to test us to see what we were made of. Whenever they tested us, they saw we were no punk-ass female crew. We represented as hard-core young ladies, who were not taking any bullshit. You messed with one, you messed with us all. In other words, no matter if we were wrong or right, when it came to beef we would kick ass.

Yeah, this was a good feeling for me. Coming up as a child, I never felt like I fit into anything. I didn't know my purpose, why I was born, and could never find the right answer. Now I finally felt I belonged to something in my life that was just for me. This was my newfound family, The Mercedes Young Ladies. Yeah, we were family now, and the focus was to build up a Mercedes Ladies movement. Strong sisters who had each other's backs regardless. Meanwhile we were becoming real ghetto celebrities. Every time we showed up at a jam, whoever was on the mic would start chanting our names. Everybody wanted to know, who were these Mercedes Young Ladies?

Chapter 18

The Rasta Mon

All eyes were on us as we walked through a jam in the school yard at 165th and Boston Road one summer night. Of course we had on our full outfits from the yellow sweatshirts with black velvet lettering to the Lee jeans. We held our heads high and represented The Mercedes Young Ladies to the fullest. Grandmaster Flash was on the turntables while the Furious Five were rockin' the mic. The block was jammed, and it seemed like everybody was out there. Back then Grandmaster Flash and his MCs were the shit. You had Melle Mel, Kid Creole, Rahiem, Scorpio, and Keith Cowboy—they were considered the celebrities of every hood in the five boroughs. Nobody else could do the things Grandmaster Flash did on the wheels of steel. He was the father of the turntables, especially in the Bronx. If you were recognized at one of his events, you were somebody.

The music was pumping. My eyes were on the MCs, and I was just astonished at the way Melle, Scorpio, Cowboy, and Kid Creole were ripping the mic. I was in heaven with the bass from the beats just thumping through my body. The way Flash was scratching and the crowd's ecstatic reaction just made you forget about any worries in the world. Next up was this kid named Grand Wizard Theodore who had some ill turntable tricks of his own. He would pick up the needle and drop it without losing the beat. MCing with Theodore were the L Brothers, Kevie Kev, and Master Rob along with Mean Gene and Cordie O—these brothers were the Furious Five's competition, just waiting on the sidelines for their turn to outdo Grandmaster Flash's crew. When these MCs got going they definitely had the ladies' attention because they were also cute.

While I was standing there, here came a tall man with dreadlocks approaching me. He was somewhat attractive with a slick type of smile on his face. In a heavy Jamaican accent, he introduced himself as Trevor, the L Brother's manager. Before I could even get my name out, he told me he already knew who I was. I was cool with that because I knew we were popular at the time.

"I heard you had an all-female DJ and MC crew," said Trevor. "You're making a lotta noise in the street. And me hear ya know how to emcee on the mic too."

I nodded my head like, *Yeah*, but in reality we were amateurs. Stacey used to play around rhyming, and Nettie knew how to spin on the turntables a little. That was a start but we weren't really serious about it. For some reason I played it off like, Yeah, we do that.

We engaged in a very interesting conversation about different crews, MCs, and the like. I had a feeling he was pitching something, so I cut to the chase.

"What do you really want with me?" I asked him point-blank.

"Hear this, daughter," Trevor told me. "I am looking to start an all-female DJ and MC crew in the business. We got the muscle if you got the hustle. If you're interested, bring the rest of the girls to meet my partners and we'll discuss the matter further."

We agreed to meet on Saturday at around 4:00 p.m., at this spot on Tremont Avenue in the Bronx, which he said was his grocery store. I suppose it could have been a setup, but my crew wasn't scared. Hey, ya never know. If opportunity knocks, why not open the door?

Chapter 19

Meeting the Dreads

Before the meeting with Trevor, the girls and I decided to meet to discuss how we would handle any propositions that might be presented. We always tried to be well prepared for any event; this gave our crew the appearance of being organized. We decided that we would listen to their offer, and show no emotion in front of Trevor and his partners until we were all in full agreement. Some of the girls said they would not be able to attend, but as long as the original members were there—like Nettie, Stacey, Beebe, and myself—that was cool. Lina and Eva said they would show. So did Tina, but I knew she wouldn't make it, not that early in the afternoon. She was more of a night person.

Walking toward the grocery store, we saw Trevor standing out in front. He noticed us too, because you could see that slick grin a mile away.

"Mercedes Young Ladies," he said as we reached him. "Nuff respect!" I didn't always understand that heavy Jamaican accent of his, but it sounded good to me.

Trevor motioned for us to come inside the store and he nodded his head to each girl as I introduced him. Stepping into the store, we noticed some guys inside with dreadlocks like Trevor. They looked like they were on guard for the store.

One sat behind the counter, one by the door, and two stayed standing. They looked each of us up and down, one by one, but we did not sweat it. *What?* We were Mercedes Young Ladies. You know our motto, "We ain't never scared!"

They knew who we were. We could tell by the looks on their faces that Trevor must've told them we were coming. Not a word was said. They just slowly nodded their heads with their ice grill facial expressions as we walked toward the back of the store, as if to say, "Ya'll got the green light to proceed to the back."

Trevor led the way, and it felt like a scene out of a gangster movie, and we were getting ready to make a big drug deal. Although the building looked like a grocery store from the outside, you didn't see a lot of groceries on the shelves once you entered. The store was huge, with three midsize aisles lined with shelves, but it looked like some of the stuff had been sitting there for a while. Behind the counter was some outdated shampoo, Vaseline, and who knew what all else—nothing much in large supply. It looked like a store about to go out of business. There were about two of everything, and four guards—but guarding what?

At the back of the store we pushed through a doorway covered with strings of hanging wooden beads. This led to the room where the meeting would take place. Once we passed the beads, we saw another dread brother who offered us a friendly greeting.

"Nuff respect," he said in Rasta patois. "Me name Ruben, Trevor's partner."

Ruben was kind of short, not as tall as Trevor, with dreadlocks down his back that were all tied together. I mean, the man had so much hair he could sit on his dreads. And even though he had a bushy beard, he was very cute. For a moment my mind started playing tricks on me. The thought flashed through my mind that maybe we were being set up, like as soon as we got comfortable they were going to start spraying us with bullets. *Stop bugging*, I told myself, but when I looked at Nettie's and Stacey's faces, I realized that I wasn't alone on that thought.

The dreads told us to "hold a seat," but there was nothing but some empty milk crates and a beat-down sofa in this dark and dreary room. We chose the milk crates. As we tried to get more familiar with Trevor and Ruben, I was wondering what they could possibly offer our crew, especially based on the conditions we saw in their store. Trevor kept looking at his watch every couple of minutes, probably wondering where the rest of the crew was. And by the way, where the hell *were* Lina and Eva? After about twenty minutes, here they came with curious looks on their faces, never apologizing for their lateness.

"This is it?" Trevor said. "No more crew comin'?" He knew that we usually ran ten to fifteen deep.

"No, this is it for now," I replied. "We can start the meeting."

Trevor started walking back and forth, checking us out with the chew stick hanging from his mouth and his dreads spilling out of a wool hat that was tilted so far to the side it was barely on his head. Of course the girls peeped him and his man out.

"Oh *no*," said Lina with that sassy mouth of hers. "What's this? I know y'all ain't checking us out like we merchandise or something. I mean, like, damn!"

Maybe they were being a little aggressive with the eye-balling, but Nettie and I both looked at Lina at the same time and gave her that *shut the fuck up* expression. She picked up real quick.

Trevor looked at her. I thought he was about to respond to her sarcasm; instead he pulled out this fat-ass joint from his shirt pocket. Then he removed the chew stick from his mouth and replaced it with the joint, struck a match, and set fire to the tip.

Only then did he ask, in an ultracalm voice: "Do ya'll mind if me smoke?"

Before we could answer, an aromatic cloud was filling the room. He took a long toke that was so strong you heard it like a vacuum cleaner with super suction—*suuuuu!* While releasing the smoke from his mouth, he smoothly leaned over and passed the spliff to Ruben.

"Give thanks, bredren," he said, accepting the gift of sacred herbs.

"Yes, I," Trevor replied with a little cough, then returned his attention to The Mercedes Ladies.

"Me like the way y'all gals represent yourselves," he said, still trying to control the cough. "You gwan rough and rugged and right now there's nuff hype around ya crew name. And one ting me love—you got no bad reputation in the streets."

Ruben interrupted him to second that emotion. "No jokey business an' thing," he said while smoking the shit out of the joint. "Me love that. Nuff respect to all the nice and decent gal dem."

As I looked at the other girls, I saw different expressions on their faces. Some were just trying to understand what the hell these guys were saying with their thick accents, some were hoping the joint was passed to them, and the rest looked like they were already catching a contact high from the second-hand smoke.

"Me wan' to start the first all-female DJ and MC crew," Trevor continued. "Live and direct—straight outta the Bronx!" Ruben just sat there nodding his head as his eyes got narrower and narrower. Apparently he agreed wholeheartedly.

"Can your crew handle that?" Trevor asked us, straight up. "If not, no problem. We move on."

Our crew was silent, showing no emotions over his proposal, as we had agreed prior to this meeting. After a few moments, I was the first one to speak.

"Who's going to supply the equipment and a place to rehearse?" I asked him.

"Oh, Action to Action will supply whatever ya need," Trevor replied. "That's not a problem."

"*Wait a minute*," the girls seemed to harmonize. "Who is Action to Action?"

"That's the name of our crew, mon," Ruben answered briefly before returning to his zone.

"Yeah, mon," Trevor continued. "We also got a female DJ who go by the name of Lady D. We want to put her down with ya crew." He paused for a second to take another draw from the spliff. "The original rude boy Grand Wizard Theodore is training her as we speak! *Bloodclaat*, she's wicked 'pon the turntables," he stressed with confidence.

Ruben came in with the background effect: "Yeah, mon," reinforcing Trevor's endorsement of Lady D. We almost started to crack up from their dramatic sales pitch. We'd have to judge Lady D's skills for ourselves. But in the meantime, our next move seemed clear. All we wanted to know was the time and the place to set our plans in action.

Chapter 20

Losing Our Composure

As we walked out of Trevor's grocery store we tried to maintain our composure, like we had just finished a major business deal on Wall Street. But once we cut around the corner, we busted out laughing.

"Did you see that shit?" Lina roared. "What the hell was that we just left?"

"Every time Trevor said something," Beebe said as she gasped for breath, "that little motherfucker Ruben was like, *'Yeah, mon!'* Like he's Trevor's backup singer, looking all dizzy and shit."

"Girl, it was so dark in there," I said as we walked and laughed together, "all I saw was their eyes, bloodshot red and yellow. I was almost scared to enter that shit. I thought it was a demon spot. Jamaican vampires—*bloodclaaat!*"

"That was some crazy shit," said Nettie. "And what the fuck was they selling in there? Whoever heard of a store with practically nothing on the shelves?"

"The only stuff they did have was outdated and shit," Lina chimed in. "What the fuck they think they're gonna use us for? To re-up on product? Could you believe they tried to act like we don't know that was a fuckin' weed spot?"

"Yo," I said with a chuckle, "how the hell are they gonna

supply us with anything when their store needs some damn supplies?"

The girls started laughing even louder.

"They were smoking the hell out of that joint, though," Stacey added in her harsh, squeaky voice. "I was thinking, 'Y'all stingy motherfuckers couldn't even pass the shit to *me*?'"

Nettie started mocking Trevor with her best Jamaican accent: "De original rude boy Theodore training her as we *speak*! Yeah, bullshit." Then she added, in a lazy, sarcastic tone, "He just can't put no bitch in our crew like that."

We laughed so hard we had to stop to get control of ourselves again. I think we all caught a contact high from all the smoke. We couldn't stop laughing. Once we pulled it together I put the question to everybody.

"No, seriously, though, what do y'all think? All jokes aside, does it sound like this could work or not?"

"Well, let's at least find out if they're bullshitting or not," Stacey replied, and we all agreed.

"But wait a minute," Nettie interrupted. "Why the hell were Lina and Eva late and they live around the fuckin' corner?" Shit got serious real quick after that.

Eva was looking at Lina to answer, and Lina started with some lame excuse. Then Stacey started coming at them, and after Beebe jumped in, Lina was getting defensively loud. I stepped in and tried to stop whatever it was that we were getting into.

"Whenever there is a meeting," I let them know, "we all have to be on time, no more excuses."

I was not playing. I wanted this thing to work. But I had to break the tension. "Mercedes Ladies," I said, snapping into my Rasta voice, "nuff respect, nuff respect!"

Everybody started laughing and we left all the quarrelling for another day. Tonight we had something to celebrate.

We kept on trodding up to Boston Road, and you know somebody was out there jammin'. We decided to get a bottle of golden champagne and chill. Back then it really wasn't hard to get something to drink if you were underage. See, they didn't really care in the ghetto if kids got liquor or beer. It only became real strict when suburban kids started getting killed in auto accidents and overdosing.

Drugs, at that time, were not my thing. Nettie and Stacey used to smoke a little weed, but every time I would take a toke, I used to get sick. One time we were at a jam and I decided to smoke some weed. I only took two puffs, and the next thing I knew, the room started spinning and the music was fading in and out of my ears. The sounds of people's voices seemed real heavy, and I imagined they were devil voices just laughing at me. I had to find a corner to sit in until I got my head together. I didn't like that feeling and vowed that I would never touch another joint again in my life. Hey, I tried to hang a couple of times with the weed, but it just did not suit me at all. (So let's kill that bullshit stereotype that all hip-hoppers smoke weed!) It was like kryptonite to Superman, or in this case, Superwoman.

Chapter 21

DJ Lady D

We met for rehearsal as planned in the building on the corner of 165th Street and Freeman Avenue, just off Boston Road. Walking up a slight hill from Webster Avenue, we saw a torn-down tenement building about six stories high. There were dudes hanging out in the front of the building, and more watching us inside as we entered. The hallways were covered in layers of graffiti and the atmosphere was a blend of urine, stale beer, and weed smoke that hit you in the face as soon as you came through the door.

"*This* is where our rehearsals will be held at?" the girls said while checking out the scenery. We found the apartment on the first floor in the back. We knew it was the right door because of the bass vibrating through it. It sounded like a party was in full swing. I knocked hard on the door to penetrate through the loud music.

We heard a voice sounding hard: "Who is it?"

"Mercedes Ladies," I answered with the quickness.

This short, stocky guy opened the door. "What's up?" he said with a smart-ass tone. "Y'all the ladies . . . Mercedes." Then he laughed to himself like he'd been rehearsing that greeting line all day. He acted like he couldn't wait for us to arrive and try it out, but unfortunately we were not amused.

He let us into a dark, crowded apartment. People were packed in there smoking and staring us down as we came in. It felt a little uncomfortable, but we had our poker faces on. They stared at us and we stared back.

Who the hell are all these people? I thought to myself. *Trevor said this would be our first rehearsal.*

Then I looked behind the turntables and saw someone I knew.

"What the hell is this?" I said with a smile spreading across my face. "Oh, shit, it's Theodore!"

When I looked to his left, I saw Kevie Kev staring at us, holding a mic in his hand. The scene paused for a minute before I realized that we were walking in on Theodore and the L Brothers' rehearsal. We searched for seats and waited for our turn to rock. The apartment was full of equipment—turntables, mics, amplifiers, and lots of wire. By the front entrance were a lot of large garbage bags stuffed full of something, and I noticed that more garbage bags were lined up in the bedrooms. I saw Trevor there, conducting business, and of course Ruben wasn't far away.

Once we got settled in, the atmosphere was cool. A lot of smoke circulated the room while the L Brothers were rockin' the mic. It looked like one big hangout spot with Theodore providing entertainment on the turntables. Then from the back came a short, brown-skinned chick with braid extensions in her hair and a white net hanging from the back of the braids. She had a sassy type of attitude, not nasty but confident. You had to respect that.

Trevor stopped what he was doing and introduced her as Lady D, the DJ he was telling us about.

"How y'all doin'?" she said in a friendly but curious fashion. As we introduced ourselves, one by one, she checked us out while we checked her out. The vibes I felt from her were like, "All right, I want to be down, and I am confident about mine, so what's next?"

Just as we were about to get down to business, the doorbell

rang and in came another chick. She was kind of tall with a long, chubby face and sort of a permanent grin on her face.

Okay, who's this? I was thinking, because the way she entered the room felt like she was saying, *Y'all are in my territory.*

She looked us up and down while making her way toward the turntables and gave Lady D a nod and a "What's up?" Then without missing a beat, she grabbed the mic and started rhyming with the L Brothers. It's like she came right in when it was her turn to bust. After she got off the mic, Trevor introduced her as MC Smiley.

As luck would have it, we'd heard of her before. She was the female who would MC with the L Brothers from time to time. Actually I thought she was kind of nice on the mic. She could almost go toe to toe with Sha. She didn't seem too excited about meeting us, but she had no choice, because our presence was felt by everybody in the room. She knew better than to say something slick out of her mouth.

Once the L Brothers were finished rehearsing, they were introduced to us, but we already kind of knew each other from the jams. Kevie Kev was the cutest out of the whole L Brothers crew, and he knew it too. The rest of the crew was more laid-back, but he had a devilish type of demeanor and always felt that chicks were clocking him.

Lady D was obviously very interested in joining our crew. Trevor wanted MC Smiley to join the crew too, but I felt she was hesitant. During rehearsal Lady D jumped on the turntables eagerly, while MC Smiley gripped the mic with a touch of attitude. We sat and observed the presentation. They were both giving their best, whether to show off or just to impress us we didn't know. After a couple of minutes, Trevor stopped the show.

"All right," he said, looking dead at us, "who's going to MC and who's going to spin?"

At the moment it hit us that this thing was about to be on, no more bullshitting. MC Smiley and Lady D watched us to see which one of us was going to step up to the plate.

"I know how to MC," Lina said, "but I have to write some rhymes first." Miss Fearless was not going to let anybody outshine her, even though we never heard her say a rhyme. *Who cares?* I told myself. We told the man we could do this, and our crew would do it!

Stacey then stepped up and said, "I want to be one of the MCs." Nettie walked over to the turntables where Lady D was standing. Lady D gave Nettie this look like, *You better bring it, girl.*

I was still sitting there on an amplifier, and Trevor gave me a devious look.

"So what ya goin' to do?" he said.

"I'm gonna be the leader of the crew," I said, staring him dead in the eye. After all, I was the most serious one and very business-minded. I wanted to stay in control of The Mercedes Ladies—this crew meant too much to me. Plus all the girls agreed. So that was that.

The L Brothers were checking us out as if they did not like the idea of us using their equipment. But since Trevor was clearly in control when it came to the equipment, I guess they could bitch if they wanted to.

Lady D stopped messing on the turntables, took the headphones off, and turned to Nettie.

"Girl," she said, "let me see what ya got."

Nettie stepped up to the turntables like, "No problem." She took the headphones from Lady D, put them on, and began to mix. I had to admit I was impressed with the way my girl stepped up to the plate and brought no shame to the crew.

"Let me hear the scratchin' with that mix," Lady D said, upping the DJ challenge.

"I know how to mix," Nettie said, "but with the fancy scratching shit, I am not there yet."

Just then Lina and Stacey grabbed a couple of mics. They were doing a little somethin', somethin' with the rhyming. My girls were definitely representing—not bad for a first rehearsal.

I looked at Trevor like, *Yeah!* But in my mind I was thanking

God that my girls could do a little something. I think he was impressed too. MC Smiley was still holding on to the same mic. When Stacey threw it to her, she said about four lines and then stopped abruptly with this expression on her face like she was not really interested in being a part of some amateurs fooling around with the mic. I had to give it to her for skills. She was nice on the mic, but she did not have to act like all that.

It was cool, though, because the girls ignored her ass and kept on doing what they were doing. After a while Trevor called our first rehearsal a wrap and scheduled another one for the following week.

"Nuff respect," he told me while we were leaving. "At least me can see y'all know the basics and ting. But they gotta work on some more rhymes and create routines."

I looked over at Ruben, who gave me his famous "Yeah, mon."

"No problem, Trevor," I said. "They will be ready."

Chapter 22

Stepping Up My Game

A week passed, and everyone showed up for our next rehearsal except MC Smiley, who supposedly had something else to do. The L Brothers were finishing up their rehearsal just like last week. As they were leaving, they exchanged a couple of words with us. I still felt that they were not that happy with us using the equipment—not so much Theodore, but the MCs did seem to have a problem. Oh well, they could talk to Trevor about it.

Stacey was late because her mom was giving her trouble about going out. But Lady D was already there, waiting for us. One thing I liked was that Lady D seemed as serious and humble about this as I was. Before we started to rehearse, the question was raised about whether we needed another MC, just in case. Smiley obviously wasn't in it for the long haul. Trevor must have sensed that she really did not want any part of us.

"Why can't we just go with three?" I asked.

"No, that won't work. It look better with four gals," he said, then gave me this sly look. "Why don't you be the fourth, Ms. Lady?" he challenged.

"*Yeah*, Shelly, you can do it," the rest of the girls echoed.

I was very reluctant, because I did not really aspire to be an MC. The crew was so important to me that I was more interested in overseeing all the activities of The Mercedes Ladies. I

saw myself as being about the business more than the show. I
gave in, though. It wasn't like I had a choice with everybody
comin' at me.

"Okay," I said after much cajoling. "I'll try it, but if I don't
like it, y'all can hang it up and we'll find another MC." Not to
stroke my ego, but once I got started we soon realized that I
had that commanding sort of tone that got people's attention.
Now, what would be my MC name? The girls all tried to give
their two cents, but I was like, "No, no. I'll think of my own
name, thank you!" After a while it hit me—Shelly Shel. Yeah, I
felt that name. It had a little ring to it. "I think that's it: Shelly
Shel."

"*Bloodclaat*, me like that!" Trevor said.

Then here came Ruben, "Yeah, mon, yeah, mon, that sounds
sexy and ting."

We all laughed. But the girls were like, "Yeah, that's dope."

"But let's not get it twisted," I said. "Even though I'm an
MC now, I am still in charge of the crew for making sure y'all
show up to practice on time and making sure everybody is
doing what's required of them."

"Me don't have no problem wit' that, mon," Trevor assured
me.

The next thing to do was start writing rhymes and collaborating with the girls on some routines. Back then, routines
were very important when you put on a· show. Even though
you performed in the streets, if you did not have your steps,
choreography, and routines together, you would look wack.
People actually expected to see a free performance as if it was
showtime at the Apollo Theater.

We started collaborating on routines for the groups. For
instance, "We're the M.E.R.C.E.D.E.S. / The girls you know
with the most finesse. / We're calm, cool, and collected too /
So, fly guys, what ya wanna do? / One for the money, two for
the show / Come on, Lady D, just let it go." Lady D scratched
a little *zigga, zigga, zigga* to set it off; then the beat dropped,
and we started rappin' in unison, almost like we were harmo-

nizing. "Let's do it . . . Let's do it . . . Let's do it . . . a-*huh!* / We are the girls that's here to rock your world. / We know we can be the best and put ya in a twirl. / That's why they call us wonder girls. . . ."

Trevor had been right about Lady D. She was like a female Theodore—the girl truly knew her way around those turntables. Nettie, who was now called Nettie D, was our disco DJ, and she was pretty good herself. She would specialize in playing the disco mixes at our shows—disco was still in at this time, so in between the routines, scratching, and rhyming, a rap crew's DJ would play a few disco songs. Like most MCs, we would rhyme over any kind of break beat that sounded fly, sometimes even disco beats. *Good Times* by Chic was considered a disco record, yet it was one of the hottest hip-hop beats for any MC to rock over.

After rehearsal ended, Stacey, Nettie, and I wanted to hang out. We invited Lady D, but she decided to stay behind and practice some more on the turntables. Lina and Eva were going back around their way. And don't let me leave out Beebe, who was in charge of Mercedes Ladies' backup crew. In other words, she watched our backs while we were performing. Whether we had static with anybody or not, Beebe and the girls would be onstage or in the crowd rocking those sweatshirts and representing our name while we did the damn thing. It was just our way of making sure everybody's back was covered.

Even today, when rappers perform in plush air-conditioned arenas, they make sure to have their entourage with them at shows. It's always good to have your peoples around just in case somebody starts some shit. When your entourage is with you, you're supposed to be able to concentrate on performing while they handle all the rest of it. Some members of your entourage were just along for the ride—they hung around hoping to be recognized. Hey, they need their perks too.

Chapter 23

Moms Ain't No Joke

We decided to go to Stacey's house, being there was nothing happening on Boston Road that day. When we entered Stacey's house, I heard a female voice yelling like crazy before we even got through the door.

"Where the hell you was at?" she was yelling. "You know I don't play that shit!" Now here she came heading straight at us. This woman was no joke. I wanted to turn around and run right back out of the house.

Nettie used to warn me about Stacey's mother. She always said she was very strict, but I didn't understand fully until I got to meet her. She was a big lady with a scarf on her head and she just looked mean. She wore these thick glasses that amplified the mean look even more, and she had a mouth to back it all up. As the woman laid into us, I looked at Nettie in disbelief. She just shrugged her shoulders like, *That's Stacey's mom for you.*

Stacey just kept walking, looking sort of embarrassed. It wasn't that Nettie was there—she was used to this sort of thing, I guess—but because I was experiencing her mom's temper for the first time. The tirade did not end until Stacey's mother instructed us to leave. Trust me, I was okay with that.

I walked swiftly to the elevator and punched the button

twice. If the doors did not open fast enough, I was prepared to run down the stairs. Her moms acted like she was ready to come after us with a bat or something. I couldn't believe there was another mother who outdid my moms on the ranting tip. I was outy.

Nettie and I walked a ways down Webster Ave before discussing what had just happened.

"I told you to get ready for her," Nettie said with a smirk on her face. She was a second away from cracking up. "Stacey's moms is like that all the time. She don't want Stacey out in the streets. She's the only girl so she catches the heat, but it's nothing. Stacey and I just be laughing."

In a way, I felt good knowing that I wasn't the only one going through drama at home. Maybe my mom didn't have a real boisterous attitude like hers, but between the beatings and the yelling, it could be a lot sometimes.

Then Nettie and I looked at each other and we couldn't hold it back anymore. We started laughing so hard, we had to hold our stomachs.

A few nights later, we were into the groove of rehearsal when someone started pounding loudly on the door. *Bang, bang, bang!* Before Trevor answered, he told us to stop the music, and then in a whisper he ordered his boys to start moving those big garbage bags toward the kitchen window. Once he saw that everything was in position and two of his boys (including Ruben) were behind him with their hands wrapped around something in their waist, Trevor cautiously walked to the door and looked through the peephole.

"Who is it banging on me fuckin' door like that?" he inquired in a harsh tone. They were so overcautious, it seemed like they were expecting the police. I could tell the way they were getting ready to throw those large garbage bags out of the window. We didn't move. We were just as curious as they were. Our eyes were watching the action as we wondered what the hell was going on.

Then a voice rang out loud and clear. It wasn't the cops. But it was serious.

"This is Stacey's mother," the voice said. "Stacey, *bring* your ass out here *now!*"

Trevor turned around and looked at Ruben and his boys as if to say, *What the fuck?*

Nettie and I couldn't look at each other. We were too scared we'd bust out laughing.

"Oh *no*," said Stacey. "She found our rehearsal site!" From the look on her face, I could see she was devastated.

"Come on, Stacey," the voice said. "I told you I wasn't having this shit!" Trevor gave Stacey a look that said, *Come and handle this shit.* She put down the mic and walked to the door. Once the shock wore off, we all felt bad for her.

As they were leaving, Stacey's mother stuck her head in the door.

"You too, Nettie," she said. "Come on!"

"My mom knows I am here," Nettie replied with a sassy demeanor.

Stacey's mom shook her head and mumbled something, then left with Stacey. We could hear her mouth from the window screamin' on Stacey all the way down the block. Trevor locked the door. From the look on his face, you could see he was heated.

"*Bumbaclaat!*" he said, sucking his teeth. "Me can't have dis shit, knocking upon me door like *bloodclaat* police, mon. That girl's mother could have caught a buckshot, ya know!"

"Yeah, mon," Ruben added as usual. "That woman wicked, mon. We can't deal wit' that. Strictly business, ya know!"

"Now every bloodcot time that wicked woman can't find her daughter," Trevor continued, "she think she gonna knock upon me door! She may even call the police ya know!"

Okay, here we go, I was thinking. *We gonna hear this shit all night.*

The rest of the girls were quiet, except for Lina, who kept

making faces like she was about to say something, but just didn't know what. After a while she just decided to keep quiet because she was scared she'd be the next to get screamed on.

Meanwhile Lady D was tryin' to shut Trevor's mouth. "All right, Trevor, fuck!" she kept saying. "We got the picture." But he still had to get a few more words off his chest.

"Me nah playin'," he said, riffing. "This is some serious shit, mon." Trevor finally ended by saying, "Shelly, we gonna have to talk about this nonsense later, mon. We don't need people's mothers comin' at me door."

"Okay, Trevor," I said. "We'll straighten it out. Can we get back to work now?"

I knew he was worried about his down-low stash house. He didn't need someone's mom blowing up the spot. I was sure that my moms would never come and look for me—she would just wait until my ass got home. I also felt sure that the rest of the girls' moms gave them freedom. In fact, it seemed like they never went home or even checked in—especially D.

Come to think of it, every single one of us was being raised by our moms—no fathers in sight. This fact explained everybody's strong personalities and independence. It also explained why our mothers could sometimes be a little overprotective. All of The Mercedes Ladies faced somewhat similar struggles.

We rehearsed a little bit more, but you could feel that the whole situation with Stacey's mother sorta killed the vibe we had going earlier. That is, until Trevor broke up the monotony with a surprise announcement.

"You better keep working hard, Mercedes Ladies," he said. "Your first show is in two weeks, and we're already giving out flyers."

He handed us a few flyers, and our faces started lighting up as we read them:

Come check out the first all-female and DJ crew ever, featuring DJ Lady D and Nettie with MC Shelly Shel, Eva Def, Lina-Lee, Stacey B, and MC Smiley.

The flyers were phat! And our first gig was right around the corner at the famous '63 Park! You had to be the shit to rock the park or your name was considered mud throughout the boroughs. Everybody from Flash to Bambaataa played there, and the yard was always packed. It was sort of like performing in the Apollo—the audience showed no mercy. But we were not afraid. True to our motto, we were never scared.

Chapter 24

Finally, It's On

Those two weeks passed much faster than we thought. The show was right around the corner. We might not be scared, but we were sure nervous. Still, we'd put in our work. We had been practicing hard, walking four times a week to and from rehearsals, putting in long hours, and hearing all that riffing from both Trevor and my mom. I was more than ready.

On the day of the show, Trevor wanted us to meet him at the rehearsal site early. We thought we were going to have one final run-through, but he really just wanted us to carry the equipment to the park where we were performing. Even though it was just around the corner, we were breaking.

"Damn!" said Lady D. "Where are all those motherfuckers that hung around during our rehearsals, all up in our face? *They* can't carry this shit?"

Trevor just gave us a look that said, *Just pick the shit up and let's go.*

What the hell, it was our first gig, and the show must go on. Trevor told us the park was already crowded. "Everyone and their mother wants to see the first all-female DJ and MC crew," he said with a smile. Of course this made us more hype than ever.

You *know* we had our wardrobe together. We all had our

matching yellow sweatshirts with the black velvet lettering on the back. Our jeans were stitched down the middle in the latest style. (It was better to have them sewed down the middle than ironed—that was the trick to having those permanent creases.) We had the white Pro-Keds sneakers to bring out the flavor even more. Of course the hairdos looked tight. And being that we could not afford the real big shrimp earrings, we settled for putting on the fake ones. You could buy them for a dollar at those little Chinese any-and-everything stores. If you put clear nail polish on them, they wouldn't tarnish that fast.

As we were packing our records and equipment and getting ready to go, Trevor gave us a heads-up. He told us that if anything jumped off in the park and somebody tried to come for the equipment, inside the crates under the extra wires were some loaded guns.

"Go ahead and use them if you have to," said Trevor. "But no worry yourself, ladies, 'cause you know Action to Action have your back."

That was cool, but we knew the Boston Road Crew was out there watching over us too. And we weren't no punk females anyway, so we didn't sweat it.

Approaching the park with the equipment in our hands, we realized that Trevor wasn't kidding about the park being jammed. You couldn't even see the chain-link fences because there were so many people packed in there. Nervous didn't even begin to describe the way we felt. We were over the moon. All of us except for Lady D, who was just as cool as you please. For some reason, it seemed like nothing made Lady D nervous. She was straight-up hard-core and had the mouth to go with it. I thought I was mouthy, but this girl could get downright vulgar with hers. Everything was "Fuck this, fuck that"—"fuck, fuck, fuck," all the time! She would curse someone out at the drop of a dime if she felt like it. Cussing was her way to release her tension.

We started setting up our equipment onstage. Well, it wasn't really a stage, but a space on the concrete playground where we were going to perform. While Trevor and Ruben were hooking up the wires to the mixer, we heard Lady D, still mouthing off.

"I don't believe this fucking shit," she said, setting down a heavy crate full of vinyl. "We got to carry all this fuckin' equipment! That's fuckin' bullshit, Trevor!"

Then Lina joined in like Miss Follower. "Yeah, I am a fuckin' girl," she complained. "I shouldn't have to lift no equipment, and besides, I almost messed up my shit carrying these dusty boxes."

Back and forth, her and Lady D kept going at it without a pause. Trevor was just ignoring them while he helped put the equipment together. Lady D was *his* girl, after all, so he should have known what to expect.

The crowd stood around watching us with puzzled looks all over their faces, like, *What the hell they gonna do?* It was understandable. They'd never seen an all-female DJ and MC crew before. Now the waiting was over.

The equipment was finally hooked up.

"It's showtime, mon," Trevor said with a sly grin.

The crew got in position on and off stage. The crowd fell silent. Lady D put the headphones on, placed her hands on the vinyl on her turntables, and spun a record to warm up the crowd, which seemed more curious than amped. Then the four MCs grabbed the microphones, stepped to the middle of the stage, and we had the park's full attention. Lady D started scratchin'. *Zigga, zigga,* zigga . . . zigga. That was our cue to start our routine. "One for the money, two for the show, come on, Lady D let's rock this motherfuckin' show!"

She let the beat go, and it was on! "We're The M.E.R.C.E.D.E.S. / The girls you know with the most finesse. / We're calm, cool, and collected too / So, fly guys, what ya wanna do?"

The crowd went nuts. Then we broke off individually, each MC taking a verse. The way the audience responded, I knew we had something. When we said, "We are the girls that's here to rock your world," we were not playing. We noticed a few other crews coming up to the front to give us our props. The people loved us so much we kept rocking for more than three hours straight, including Nettie cutting up disco records in between routines. And in this neighborhood, if they weren't feeling your show, they would run your ass out of there quick.

Things were going great when all of a sudden we heard a sharp *Pop! Pop!* Someone was shooting in the crowd. Everybody started running, people were falling, some were getting trampled while others tried to find hiding spots. We stayed cool and stood by our posts, right next to the crates with the guns in them, in case the drama started coming our way. Action to Action stood in front of us, like they were forming a shield. Next thing we heard was the sounds of the sirens. When people knew the cops were coming, then they *really* started running. Any drug dealers or whoever had any dirt on their hands had to get out of the police's way without delay. The show was over.

The cops may have shut it down, but we accomplished what we set out to do: putting our name in the street. While we were packing up the equipment to go back to our rehearsal site, Trevor announced he wanted to have a quick meeting back at the house. Everybody was amped up by the time we got there. We knew we did our thing—all that rehearsing had paid off. It was crucial to be dope on your first time coming out or you'd be dismissed as a joke, especially as the all-female crew. But now the word spreading out in the streets would be that Mercedes Ladies were no joke.

Trevor gave us our props, but then he warned us to not get too happy because there was more work that needed to be done.

"If you want to be the best," Trevor said, "you have to pay the price." He sounded like Debbie Allen on *Fame*, but I wasn't mad at him. We knew it was the truth. And at that moment we were prepared to do whatever it took to succeed.

"Oh no, my mom is going to *kill* me!" Stacey exclaimed as she noticed the time.

Trevor was like, "Yeah, mon, we don't want no problems again wit' ya mother." So we called it a wrap for the night.

Leaving rehearsal, we noticed more people outside the building than usual. Our first fans were waiting for us, mostly boys, but that was okay with us. They kept their distance, but as we were walking away from the building, we heard them chanting over and over, "Mercedes Young Ladies!" I am not gonna front, that shit had our heads blown up.

Chapter 25

We Just Lost One

Trevor began lining up more shows, whether in parks or at school yards—we didn't care; we would have done a hundred a week if we could. Our status and respect were already building up in the streets from the first few gigs. One of the main goals for us was to be able to perform at the P.A.L. That would be huge.

The P.A.L. or Police Athletic League was a big athletic center on East 183rd Street and Webster Avenue that was set up by the Patrolmen's Benevolent Association. During the daytime it was like an after-school center, where a lot of activities (from basketball games to learning centers to karate lessons) took place. If your child was missing, you would find them at the P.A.L. Even if the police might not have appreciated hip-hop, they appreciated keeping kids off the streets at night, so the P.A.L. was where all of the best DJ crews played. You really had to be somebody in order to play there. The rules were very strict there, because it was associated with the police department. At the P.A.L. you could not have an all-nighter jam. They usually had to close by 2:00 a.m. And forget about anybody trying to act up, even though fights would break out occasionally. A gig at the P.A.L. was The Mercedes Ladies' next big ambition, and we were steady working to reach that goal.

During one of our rehearsals, Stacey showed up and said that her moms did not want her to be a part of The Mercedes Ladies anymore.

"Yeah, mon," said Trevor. "We got that impression the other day."

"No, this time she's serious," Stacey said, clearly upset. "She said she doesn't want me out at such late hours of the night." She went on to say that she was still a Mercedes Lady in her heart, but she wouldn't be able to make some of the shows.

The girls had disappointed looks on their faces, but since there was nothing we could say or do, we kept silent. All the routines we had developed were built around four MCs and two DJs. We had to figure out how to break them down for three MCs. We had to get back to rehearsal—there was a lot of work to do!

After practice, Nettie and I decided to hang out with Lady D to see how she was living. She stayed on Intervale Avenue, in a wild area known as the South Bronx, made infamous by Boogie Down Productions' song of the same name. The South Bronx had a lot of abandoned tenement buildings and was known for stickups. A lot of people used to get robbed in that area. It was also known as gang territory. Walking down the block you could not help but notice all the people hanging out in front of broken-down buildings. Lady D knew everybody we passed—this was where she grew up. We went to her house so she could change her clothes. As we entered her house, her moms began yelling at her about something, but D just ignored her. It wasn't hard to tell that they didn't get along. There was no communication between them.

Her mom called her "Diana"—now I knew her real name was Diane—and D started yelling back at her.

"Why don't you just shut the fuck up?" D said while changing her clothes. "All you do is bitch about everything!"

Of course her moms went off. "You stupid little bitch," she yelled back. "I'll fuck your ass up. Who the fuck do you think you're talking to?" Lady D was in her bedroom shouting at her moms while her mother stood in the hallway closer to the living room where Nettie and I were sitting, waiting. They went at it for a while that way, back and forth. They didn't even seem to care that they had company in the house.

"That Borah is something else," her mother said to us, as if she'd suddenly remembered we were there. "That stupid bitch don't respect me at all and has a smart-ass mouth."

Now I saw where Lady D got all the cursing and the hardcore attitude from. They were two of a kind even if they did not realize it. Finally D came out of her room like, *Let's go, y'all*. Still totally ignoring her mother, she headed for the door. As we made our way down the steps of her building, you could hear D's mother shouting, "Don't come back here!"

Stepping into the street, she was like, *Whatever.*

We walked away in silence for a while. Then D spoke up: "My Moms stay drunk," she said. "That's why I don't feed into her bullshit." That was her final word on the subject, and I had nothing to add myself. Sometimes the best thing a friend can do is listen and keep her mouth shut.

Chapter 26

No V.I.P. Status

We heard there was going to be a jam at the P.A.L. that night, and Grandmaster Flash, Kool Herc, and Bambaataa were all playing. We called the rest of the crew and made plans to meet up there. Bambaataa was a former gang member from the Bronx River Houses, but his new crew was called the Universal Zulu Nation, and Bronx River Center was their home base. The Gestapos was the branch that would get down and dirty if need be, and they were known to be notorious. Zulu was the branch that practiced peace—they were all about reconciliation between the different street gangs—but when they rolled they rolled deep.

We'd always heard about the Zulu Nation, but never actually met them. Bambaataa was like the king of Bronx River. He had mad respect, but he was always soft-spoken. Everybody admired the way he carried himself and the way he ran his crew. He always made a point to incorporate peace into all his events, but it could get nasty if you stepped out of line at a Zulu jam.

That night we all met up at the P.A.L. with our sweatshirts and jeans on, ready to represent. Approaching the door of the P.A.L., we noticed the place was extra jam-packed, but we proceeded to the front of the line at the door.

"Hey, we're The Mercedes Ladies," we announced to the doorman.

"Oh yeah?" he said with a dumb-ass expression on his face. "*And . . . ?*"

It was reality-check time. Even though we thought we were popular, apparently our juice wasn't helping us here. Of course D wasn't having it.

"What! You big black motherfucker, you better recognize!" D started babbling on with the mouth at the doorman. "We're The motherfuckin' Mercedes Ladies, fool!"

"Yeah, and I'm Grandmaster Flash and the Furious Five," he said in an overly sarcastic tone. In other words he wasn't trying to hear us. Then he told us to step the fuck off like we were some punk-ass chicks. As soon as he said that slick shit, we all started screaming on his ass.

"Fuck you, you big black-ass nigga," said D.

"Yeah, fuck you, Sasquatch!" Lina and Eva continued.

"Kiss our ass, you big black Bigfoot motherfucker," Tina and Nettie added.

And I finished it off on the serious tip: "Check yourself before you wreck yourself, you Uncle Tom–ass motherfucker. We The fucking Mercedes Ladies. Are you crazy? Don't ever disrespect us."

Needless to say, all this babbling back and forth did not help our situation as far as getting in was concerned. Hearing the music jammin' from the outside made us even more furious that we could not get in. But the crowd standing in line seemed to be enjoying the show we put on. The doorman did seem a little embarrassed. He did not expect us to come at him like that. Our whole crew was pissed. Yo, we had to walk there, everyone's funds were low—as a matter of fact, we had no funds at all. It seemed like we hung outside the place for hours, trying to get in. As the night went on, we would see Cowboy, Melle Mel, even the L Brothers, and try to get them to bring us in. But everybody was on their high horse that night. They would all be like,"Hey, what's up! You wait here and I'll be right back," but you would never see them come back out. At this time hip-hop wasn't making any real money, but the fellas still had this High Post attitude, because of their reputation in the streets. They didn't exactly welcome us into their world with open arms. At this time females were not respected in the game, period. That explained the coldness on the doorman's part. After a while we were like, *fuck it.*

After all the screaming and intimidation, we ended up just going home. All the way home we kept talking that shit.

"That's okay," said Nettie. "We're gonna be hotter than them one day."

"Yeah," I said. "They're just jealous because we can do the same thing they can do—and we're females."

Chapter 27

Bam and the Zulus

The next day Trevor called a meeting. He stood in our rehearsal space with Ruben by his side.

"Me have an announcement to make," he said, "so quiet down, ya hear?"

"Yeah, mon," Ruben repeated. "Quiet down, ya hear?"

"Me set ya up with another gig to do your ting in the 118th School park, along with the original rude boys, Afrika Bambaataa, the L Brothers, and some other crews who going to be playing and ting, ya know. So, ya got to continue to come with the rough and ruggedness."

"Yeah, mon," Ruben echoed. "Rough and ruggedness."

"Set that *bloodclaat* park on fire!" Trevor said.

These niggas must be high, I thought to myself. *Why do they get so dramatic just to tell us that we have another gig?*

Maybe I was a bit less enthusiastic than usual because some of these guys we were performing with had just fronted on us last night at the P.A.L. But hey, it was a Bambaataa event. This was big. Plus it would give us the chance to get to know Bam and his crew. I had to get my mind right.

When we got to the park, it was jammed. Different crews from all over NYC were representing with their crew names on the backs of their shirts. The turntables and audio controls were roped off to keep the crowd back. Cops stood around behind the ropes, waiting for some shit to jump off. You could see this freckle-face red-haired guy rocking the turntables and this little short guy with an Afro standing beside him digging through the crates of records. As soon as we reached the ropes, this big guy with a smile that looked like Mr. Rogers—all big and bubbly—came over to greet us.

"I am Bambaataa," he said warmly. "Y'all must be The Mercedes Young Ladies."

We were like, "Ah, yeah," smiling back at him as we appreciated the hospitality.

Bam started introducing us to the rest of his crew. Most of them said that they had heard of us. Come to find out, Beebe was related to Bambaataa through her father. I was like, *So this is the Zulu and the Gestapo crew!* They were some real wild individuals, acting very devilish toward us in a fun way. It was all good. As we were waiting to go on, they kept playing around, chanting our name. He then introduced us to the red-haired dude and the little guy behind the turntables. They turned out to be Kool DJ Red Alert and Jazzy Jay. Both of them would go on to become legends in their own right, but they started as the main DJs for Bambaataa.

Here came Trevor and Ruben, with the L Brothers alongside them. They nodded at us, glad to see we were on time and ready. Letting bygones be bygones, we didn't mention the drama at the door last night.

"Are y'all ready?" Bam asked us. "Will ya go on after the L Brothers do their thing?" That was cool with us. Most of all, we liked the respect Bambaataa was showing us. Most guys were on that male ego thing, but Bam was confident enough in himself that he didn't have to put his sisters down.

Before we knew it, it was our turn up to bat, and we stepped to the plate for real. By this time, our shit was down tight. We rocked the crowd with no mercy. This was our biggest and toughest crowd yet, but not once did The Mercedes Ladies feel intimidated. There was no doubt that our names were circulating out there in the hood. We were sure we wouldn't get dissed at the door next time.

After the jam was finished, Bam gave us our props and invited us to hang out with him and his crew. They were going to this club called the Black Door, up in the Bronx near Bronx River. This was the club where Zulu and the Gestapos hung out—their home away from home so to speak. Top DJs like Grandmaster Flash would spin there on certain nights. The place was a hole in the wall, but you couldn't help but spot it, because it was the only door on the block that was painted all black. The walls inside were also painted black with graffiti written all over them in glowing paint.

People were standing around holding up the wall, while those in the middle danced to DJ Jazzy Jay spinning records from the turntables in the corner. The music was pumping, and a forty-ounce was being passed around while the aroma of weed filled the air. Nettie and Stacey decided to pull out their stashes while Lina stood there, eyes wide open, waiting for them to light up.

"Damn, Lina," Stacey said. "You always act hungry when somebody pulls out weed, and you never have none."

"Yes, I do," Lina said with the chicken neck going and the eyes rolling. "You just seem to forget when I look out for y'all. But if you don't want to pass it, that's cool with me. I'll get some myself."

"Why don't y'all chill with that shit?" I said. "Damn!" I couldn't believe they were getting ready to argue over a stupid joint.

Now, I ain't gonna front; I did not know my limit when it came to drinking. Sometimes I'd take a sip or two too many until I got sick and threw up. Eva did not smoke or drink. She was the innocent one of the crew, but she would still be hanging tough. Lady D didn't smoke either, but she would take a sip or two from time to time. She was more like the flirt of the crew.

After they lit the joint, the aroma started getting thick. The smell was making me nauseated for some reason. This weed did not smell the way I was used to weed smelling. I turned to Nettie and said, "What the hell is that smell?" She started laughing.

"Oh, girl," she said casually, "that's dust mixed with weed." I had to move away from that smell.

Still laughing, Nettie was like, "Try a puff. It won't kill you."

I was like, "Hell no," backing away from them. "That shit smells horrible." Anyway, I had heard about angel dust, or PCP, making some people act crazy for real. I wanted no parts of that.

On the way home from the party, Nettie and Stacey brought it to my attention that they thought D was a little loose when it came to men. First, she'd start with the body language, and then move to the sassy mouth attitude to get his attention. Then she'd go for the gold without hesitation, and didn't care who was watching. The other girls started noticing this pattern every time we hung out.

"Did you see how she worked it?" they would say. "Damn, she was all up in homeboy's face."

"I don't like that shit," Stacey said. "Every fucking time guys are around, she gotta act like a desperate ho. That shit ain't cool." She was obviously furious. I guess the high was bringing it out more.

"Yeah, girl." Nettie backed her up. "I be wantin' to fuck her ass up sometimes. She's going to give us a bad reputation. You gotta talk to her, Shelly, before I go off on her ass."

I could see what they were saying, but I guess I kind of liked D's style, the confident attitude she had. On top of that, I was feeling nice off the drinks, and I just was not in the mood for hearing any drama. I knew once I got home, I would hear enough of that.

"Yo, as long as it don't interfere with what we're trying to do, don't worry about it," I told them. "Y'all ain't no fucking angels anyway."

Reaching home, I expected Mom to be up waiting for me to come through the door. I didn't know whether I was going to get the fist or the mouth, but whatever it was, I had to prepare myself before entering the house. When I got inside, the light was on—yep, she was up waiting. I saw the look on her face and I knew right then that Moms was ready to bust my ass. She came at me before the door was even closed.

"Where the hell was you at all night?" she demanded. "You left the house at five p.m. and did not do your chores. I am not having this shit. You got to go. I am calling some boarding schools tomorrow. I have too many other problems to deal with without worrying about your ass running the street. You got to go!" She kept coming with all kinds of shit and I couldn't get a word in. I really didn't hear everything she was saying clearly because I was drunk and trying to hide it. All I was thinking was, *Just let me make it to the bed so she doesn't notice the smell of alcohol on my breath.* She was all up in my face, but I kept my mouth closed tight. I was aching to say something back, but I knew the alcohol would reek out of my mouth, so I just kept heading for the room, not knowing if she would creep up behind me and start kicking my ass for walking away. But I took my chances.

When I finally reached the room, I thanked God that she did not smell anything. I could still hear her fussing as I lay down in bed.

"What the hell is a MC? We need money in this house, and you're standing on corners rhyming with some MC shit!"

My sister covered her head with the pillow, but I could hear her next to me, mumbling. "Dag, why you keep doin' that to Mom?"

I took my clothes off and went straight to sleep. I had to suck in the consequences and pay the price for hip-hop. Besides, I knew in my heart that she was just worried about me, and that was the only way she knew how to handle me—intimidation. Sometimes when I came home she would be waiting with a belt or a fist, whatever method she thought would work at the time. What else could she do? Lock me up in the closet? Tie me to the bed? I was going out no matter what.

Chapter 28

The New Chick

By this time it was clear that Stacey could not be a part of our shows or rehearsals, and it was even more clear that MC Smiley wasn't really interested in being a true Mercedes Lady. The rest of us just kept it moving. We were determined to make an impact in this game. Even though D was wild and a bit loose, I felt she was more real toward the goals of the crew than some of the other girls. Plus we were becoming closer as friends. Nettie was still my dog, but D and I clicked more. If something went down, I felt that she would truly have my back.

Occasionally I would go hang out at D's house in the South Bronx. Her mother was getting used to me, even though she would still be breaking on D. And don't let her moms get drunk or she would start cursing D out like a sailor with D arguing back at her. This was happening on the regular. I never saw her mother hit her. D said they almost came to blows a couple of times, but she would just leave the house instead of hitting her mom. She said her mother's drinking was the reason for their constant fighting. One time she was so drunk she accused D right in front of me of sleeping with her boyfriend. D just shrugged it off and said her mother was buggin'. I really didn't know who was telling the truth.

D came to my house to meet my family. It was funny how she clicked with my family, like she was just meant to be there—or crazy like the rest of us. Moms even started breaking on her too sometimes. But when it came to my mom's yelling, she paid it no mind. But as close as D and I were getting, she still had some tricks up her sleeve.

One day we came to rehearsal and were surprised to see this new chick sitting there with thick glasses and red hair. At first sight she had a sort of nerdy Poindexter look about her. When Trevor introduced us, out came this husky-ass voice, like a dude's.

"Yo, what's up?" she said. "My name is Dora."

"She is a DJ," Lady D explained, "and she wants to join our crew."

We looked at D and Trevor as if to say, *How in the hell y'all just bring somebody in our crew like that?*

Even though Dora seemed enthusiastic and had a few ideas to bring to the table, we were still a little hesitant to have some stranger come join our crew out of nowhere. Besides, every new crew member had to go through an initiation. Our initiation wasn't like a gang initiation. It was more like a probationary period. It consisted of a series of tests to see if the new girl could withstand our nastiest attitudes, carrying the equipment, and being at every jam with the appropriate outfit on (whatever we agreed to wear on that particular night). Of course new recruits couldn't talk back. Also they had to have a good knuckle game or at least act like they had one—we did not want no weak-ass girl representing our crew. Only after you passed all the tests were you considered worthy to wear The Mercedes Ladies name on the back of your sweatshirt.

Because Trevor and D brought her to us, we agreed to try her out. We didn't exactly need another DJ, but we decided that Dora could be the disco DJ while Lady D and Nettie mixed the hip-hop. Dora was from Gunhill Projects, located up around Tina's way. She seemed pretty cool, but you could sense that she had a controlling type of personality. She was the type that acted like she knew it all, with a very aggressive manner. From day one she was like, "Oh, let's do it this way," or "I know y'all do it this way, but let's try this." That husky voice of hers made everything she said seem even more commanding. I knew one day she would get into drama with somebody. It was only a matter of time.

Dora started showing up at rehearsals and eventually started doing shows with us. Even though she seemed dedicated, her and Lady D started butting heads as I predicted. Come on, she was a new member trying to be in control of something that was already established. D wasn't having it, especially when it came to the turntables. That was her world. There was a lot of arguing before and even during shows, but we were learning how to cover up our dirty laundry.

Chapter 29

Building a Rep

The Mercedes Ladies were starting to do more and more shows all over town with a host of well-known hood celebrities. I say "hood celebrities" because hip-hop was not internationally known yet, so basically the hood was our whole world. A few Manhattan clubs were booking rap acts, but for the most part hip-hop was still very much a ghetto thing. Even though we didn't make much money, it was like we lived or died by our reputation.

But money pressure was real, and it was causing problems in the camp. First of all, we had to walk to a lot of our shows; then once there, we had to wait for Trevor to bring the equipment in his van, unload our own equipment and help set up, and play all night. For all this work we never saw a dime. We really didn't care about the free shows in the parks or out on the corner somewhere, because we knew the value of promoting ourselves in the street. This was the real grind, getting street buzz. But we did not understand why we were not getting paid for shows we did at certain rec centers and dance clubs.

Trevor would always have an explanation.

"*Rasclaat*—this one is gonna get y'all known all over the

boroughs," he'd tell us. "It will lead to even bigger shows, mon. Y'all goin' to get paid, just be patient, me daughter." With high hopes, we just went along with the program. But as the leader of the crew when it came to business, I was feeling more and more pressure every day.

Finally, we got the chance to play at the P.A.L. It was our turn and we were excited about it, because we knew that once you played at the P.A.L., you were definitely "in there"— wherever that was.

It was a Friday night in the summer, and we were packing up the equipment getting ready for the big event. All of a sudden MC Smiley fell through saying she was going to rhyme with us onstage tonight. *How convenient*, I said to myself. Smiley rarely showed up at street gigs, but now she wanted to tag along when we were playing the P.A.L. But I kept my mouth shut. We had a show to do.

D wasn't really with it, though, and she let Smiley know.

"Oh, you wanna be down *now*, huh?" D taunted her. "Just the other day you didn't want no part of Mercedes Ladies!"

I'm sure Smiley had a few things to say but I cut them both off. This was not the time to be debating. Trevor's van was loaded up and we had to get to the club. When we rolled up to the spot, the sidewalk outside was jammed and there was a line running from the front door all the way around the corner. A huge crowd was patiently waiting for the club to open up.

The streets were buzzing about this new female group that was performing tonight. Some had heard them on the streets; others just overheard the hype around The Mercedes Ladies. Everybody wanted to see how they performed alongside the other heavyweights in the business on a big stage like the P.A.L. Then you had a few other girl crews in line, with the jealous mean mug faces on. Yes, they were hating, because they were just regular hangout crews. We could DJ and rap, we looked good, we could fight, and there was nothing they could do about it. So all they could do was stand around and sip their "Haterade." Whenever we noticed any vibes like that, we always told Beebe to let our floor crew know to be on the lookout while we were performing.

Trevor's dudes started unloading the van and helping us carry the equipment inside. It felt pretty good to walk through that front door because this was the same place we had such a hard time getting into. Now we were performing there, with full V.I.P. status. As we took the stuff off the van, we saw our old friend "Sasquatch" the doorman. He couldn't say shit to us. We all just kept staring at him, rubbing it in his face. He looked like he would love to fuck us up but he wouldn't dare.

"Yeah, asshole," D said as we headed upstairs. "Tell us you don't give a shit who we are now, motherfucker."

Once we got established inside, we realized that we were the only ones scheduled to perform that night with the L Brothers maybe doing a routine or two. But you know us—we were not one bit fazed. The show must go on. After all, our reputation was on the line.

Grand Wizard Theodore came on before us to warm up the house before our segment of the show. He was the perfect DJ to start your jam. He was every bit as nice as Flash skills-wise and he got mad respect from everyone in the streets. The difference between Flash and Theodore was this: Flash was a genius when it came to cutting records, but Theodore was a wizard at scratching records. He was a very quiet dude who rarely held conversations, but when he hit the turntables, forget it! The crowd would go nuts. See, it was one thing to be just a good DJ who knew how to spin, but when you were a DJ with special skills—like turning around in the middle of a scratch without losing the beat or cutting records together so well that the crowd thought it was a whole new tune—that's what separated the good ones from the greats. And Theodore was a true turntable wizard. By the time we were ready to perform, the crowd was fully amped.

We rocked the P.A.L. within an inch of its life, and kept them chanting "Mer-ce-des Young La-dies," until the place closed. If we were looking for street respect, then our mission was accomplished. I always knew when we had a successful show because afterward people would stand around just to get close to us. After that P.A.L. show we were getting approached with offers of more gigs and requests to take pictures with them. I am not going to front. We were on ghetto star mode for sure.

But after the show our bubble soon burst when we asked Trevor about the money. As usual, he started blabbing on and on about how there was no money involved. He said it was a charity event for the community and we had previously discussed this. Strangely, none of us could recall that conversation. But what could we do? We may not have made a dime, but at least our name and respect in the game were growing. Being that it was still early, we decided to go hang out—of course, after helping Trevor put away the equipment first.

Every time we went out, guys always tried kicking it to us. They would step to whoever they could get through to, which usually meant D. Most times guys thought Nettie was evil looking, so she was not easily approached. I do think that was her way to keep them off of her, and it worked. Some guys said The Mercedes Ladies were stuck-up. That comment never bothered us as long as they weren't saying we were hoes. We had rules, and one of them was to keep a clean reputation out there in the streets. The other rules were simply showing up on time for rehearsals and shows; not getting high before a show; and if you had a problem with someone, to discuss it at meetings—no talking behind anyone's back about matters concerning our crew.

I was starting to see another side of D. Don't get me wrong, that was my girl and stuff, but I started noticing that every time we had a gig or just went to hang out, she would leave with a different guy. Some of the other girls were taking notice of it too, so I decided to bring it up at the next meeting before things got out of hand.

Trevor called us to tell us that we were going to have to rehearse even harder because he was getting demands for more gigs. Stacey was trying to come to some of our shows, but the pressure she was getting from her moms didn't allow her to commit herself to The Mercedes Ladies. Beebe would support us at a lot of our shows. Even Tina would come to some of the shows with a little liquor stash—always late of course, but she would show up. She was still the same old Tina. Nothing came easy with her. We used to have to stress to Tina which colors we were wearing for the night. Like if we said, "Yellow sweatshirts," she would try to debate why she could not wear a red one.

We were doing a lot of shows now, playing out at least twice a week—and sometimes twice in a day. But our patience was wearing thin with Trevor. We heard the same old story after every show about why we did not get paid. We talked about leaving him, but did not know what we were going to do for equipment. It was like a bad relationship. You are not feeling the dude any longer, but you can't leave. He pays the bills, and you never have money for yourself, so you feel locked in. But we were itching to break free.

Chapter 30

Beef With Another Crew

One hot summer night we decided to go to another Bambaataa jam at the schoolyard across town. We were just going to hang out and show support since Bam and the Zulus had showed us mad respect at their last event. As we passed through the metal gates and made our way through the crowded yard, we saw this guy named Smalls bum-rushing his way toward us. Even though he was a little guy, you could not help but notice his crooked-ass teeth and that dingy hat he always wore. From the sides of the hat, it looked like he had never combed that nappy hair of his. We knew him from hanging around the jams. He was the kind of guy who was not part of any crew, but would front for whatever crew was playing on any given night. He couldn't exactly front like he was one of The Mercedes Ladies, so instead he decided to just be cool with us.

"Oh, shit!" he cried out, all dramatic and shit, putting his hands on his head. "My girls!" Then he started the chant: "Mer-ce-des Young Ladies, Mer-ce-des Young Ladies," while doing some stupid dance to impress us and get all the attention he could from anyone in the jam—basically trying to let people know who he knew.

"Okay, Smalls, we see you," I said, while trying to back him off of us. But he just kept coming closer.

Smalls was a real slick talker who gossiped more than any woman I knew. He was always up on whatever was going on in every neighborhood, and he could be really irritating. All of a sudden, a serious expression came over his face. He looked around all paranoid, like he was telling us some real top-secret shit.

"Yo," he said, in a conspiratorial tone. "I got to tell y'all something. Yo, check this shit out. I overheard some niggas talking about y'all." Our ears perked up at any hint of treachery.

"What could you have heard about us?" we responded with curiosity in our voices, ready to hear the street gossip.

"Nah, for real," Smalls continued. "Some dudes were spreading some bullshit about your crew. Y'all know me. I was about to step to their ass 'cause y'all my motherfucking girls. See what I'm saying?"

"All right, Smalls," I interrupted. "Enough beating around the bush. Get to the point—What did your irritating ass hear?"

"You always got some fucking dumb shit to say, Smalls," Lina added in an agitated way. "Hurry up and tell us—*shit!*"

"Well, the word on the street is that your whole crew are freaky deakies," he said. "Yep . . . straight freaks of the week!"

We looked at him, trying to figure out whether to fuck him up or what.

"Who the fuck said that shit, Smalls?" Lady D asked, getting up in his face. "You better fucking tell us now."

"Hey . . . hey," he said defensively. "Hold up. I didn't start this shit, so why y'all down *my* throat?"

Once you have a snitch in the corner, he starts singing—especially when he knows these chicks will bust his ass. Smalls started looking around like he was a secret agent, then spoke to us in a scratchy whisper.

"Yo, y'all didn't hear this from me," he said, still looking around all paranoid, "'Cause I don't wanna have to hurt somebody. Ah, but it was them Zulu cats."

"What!" we said, furious.

First of all, we were mad because we didn't want to believe him. The Zulus always showed us much respect. Second, we were working very hard at not being labeled as hoes or anything of that nature. We wanted to be respected for our talents on the turntables and on the mic, not for anything else. We finally let his ass go and headed over to the ropes around the DJ stand to approach some Zulu brothers we saw over there.

Those poor dudes caught a bad one. We did not give them a chance to say shit. Our mouths were ready for action, with the eyes rolling and the necks steady snapping. When we were done venting on them, the Zulu brothers had to aggressively defend themselves.

"What the fuck y'all talking 'bout?" they said. "We ain't said shit. Matter of fact, we want a meeting with your crew to take care of this shit, because we ain't going out like that." Yeah, we were street, but we had a little business savvy about us too. We agreed to the meeting before it turned into a fight, then walked away slowly to avoid creating a bigger scene.

We heard them in the background as we were walking away: "Yeah, meet us on our turf in Bronx River around six o'clock tomorrow evening if y'all want beef with us."

We were, like, "Yeah, whatever, nigga. We'll be there—*what!*"

We didn't flinch or get nervous once. "Fuck that" and "fuck them" pretty much summed up how we felt at that moment. Nobody was going to spread any type of bullshit rumors about The Mercedes Ladies. Not *our* crew.

The night of the meeting, we were ready for war with scarves on our heads, sweatshirts, Lee jeans, sneakers, and a jar of Vaseline to rub on our faces so we could avoid scratches. In the hood, that was the dress code for fights among girls. You could be in the middle of an argument with another chick; then before y'all fought you'd say, "Hold up!" while your girls supplied you with the scarf and the Vaseline. After that it was on, and may the best girl win. If you did not have time to get prepared, you just had a straight throw-down and said your prayers that your hair didn't get pulled out and your face didn't get filled with scratches.

Anyway, as soon as we made it to Bronx River, we saw them walking toward us while we walked toward them. It was sort of like a scene out of *West Side Story*, except the guys and girls were not in love, they were ready to rumble. Both crews came to a halt right in the middle the projects. They looked us dead in the eye as we stood our ground with our arms folded like, *Yeah, what?* Everyone had the mean mug expressions on. It was silent for a while before the Zulus spoke. This time they caught us off guard, because instead of saying something slick out of their mouths to set it off, we got an apology. They swore that they did not start the rumor, and expressed their sincere regret for any wrong interpretation anybody might have had about us. I don't know if Bam told them to squash it or they decided to do it on their own, but the important thing was that the beef was squashed. We ended up hanging in Bronx River with them for most of the night, and they showed us love with maximum respect. That's how The Mercedes Ladies became official Zulu Queens. It was all good, and we remained cool from that day on. I think they liked the way we came to represent ourselves with no fear. Yes, we were ladies, but rough and rugged.

Chapter 31

Pressure Finally Broke the Pipe

Even though it was summer, our next show was inside a gym. Trevor arranged for us to perform at this junior high school. The best part was that he assured us we were going to get paid this time. The school had approved the budget ahead of time, so it wasn't like were we depending on some shady promoter. The jam was kind of packed. We ran through the usual drill, setting up the equipment while the crowd looked on with anticipation. Although there were a few older kids in there, this was a younger crowd than we were used to. Sometimes kids are the best critics. They don't listen to hype, they just judge for themselves.

It was fun playing for a crowd of kids. They enjoyed the show fully and you didn't have to worry about somebody shooting the place up. When the show was finished, here came a lot of teenyboppers bum-rushing us for autographs. We were amused, and it made us feel really good. Some of the girls even asked how they could be down. We thought that was cute. We put some of them down with our junior league by placing a hand over their foreheads and saying, "You are now officially a Mercedes Lady." A few boys asked to get down with us and we advised them to start a fan club.

After all the excitement of the show, we were tired. We saw

Trevor waiting over by the van, and just as we were about to pick up the equipment and start loading the van, I was like, "Hold up, let's get our money first."

For some reason, I felt Trevor was up to something. I don't know if it was our past experiences with him, the look on his face, or just a gut feeling. Whatever the reason, we started walking toward him empty-handed. He had a smirk on his face as if to say, *What y'all doing? Where's the equipment?* But we just kept walking toward him.

We came to a halt and stood there with no expressions, our hands folded in front of us. There was an awkward silence while Trevor tried to figure out what to say.

"Ah, what's up?" he said, finally. "We gotta get movin', ya know?"

"No, we don't," I said. "Where is our cut, Trevor?"

Ruben wasn't there this time to supply background vocals, so Trevor seemed somewhat tongue-tied. We stood there looking him dead in the eye, and the atmosphere was getting downright uncomfortable. I knew Trevor could feel the vibes. Seeing we were not playing this time, he removed the smirk from his face. His boys that were with him backed away. They felt the vibes. We were waiting for a reasonable response. Something like, "Okay, girls, here is your cut." Instead, he cleared his throat and tried to prepare a speech on the spot.

"Ah yes," he said, "me get paid, but hear wha gwan yah . . ." He could see the intense look on the girls' faces. "Me only have seven dollars left. The other night during the gig, this speaker blow out, and me did haffi fix it. And gas nuh cheap neither."

We knew something crazy was coming, but we truly couldn't believe he had the nerve to offer us seven measly dollars to split among all six of us. Pissed didn't even begin to describe how we felt. Looking at the other girls, I thought it seemed like they could not decide whether to cry, curse, or simply kill his ass. The pressure finally broke the pipe, and we started breaking on him.

"What the fuck, Trevor?" said D. "Why we never fucking get paid?"

"Yeah, Trevor, this shit ain't right," said Nettie. "Fuck this." Salty remarks came from all the girls left to right.

You could see Trevor was starting to get heated too. His defense game came on strong.

"What kinda joke you making? Me did haffi pay a lotta money for dat speaker, mon! Anyway, I supply all the equipment. And what ya tink me van run on? Free gas?"

The argument was growing louder but getting us nowhere. After all the talking, that same seven dollars was all that remained to compensate us for our night's work. We were so disgusted that we just left his ass there to put the equipment back by himself.

Then we walked away into the night. By this time the backup crew had left, so it was just the DJs and the MCs. We didn't know where we were walking to, we just kept walking, crying, and laughing at the same time.

"I can't *believe* this shit!" D yelled out. "That motherfucker thinks he's our pimp or something. Man, fuck this, we should fuck his ass up. What the fuck Action to Action gonna do?"

"No, no, better yet, let's go take them garbage bags," Nettie suggested. "I'll bet we'll get all of our money then."

"I still can't believe he had the guts to hand us seven dollars," I said. "That was almost worse than no money at all."

We were still walking and breaking when inspiration struck. We would punish Trevor with the most powerful weapon at our disposal.

"Let's come up with a rhyme to put his ass on blast for the next show," I said.

"Bet, bet," everybody said.

Eva set it off. "We got seven and a quarter and a penny to our names," she rapped with passion behind every word. "Trying to put Mercedes Ladies in the hall of fame."

"But that's okay 'cause we just begun," I said, jumping in. "And in no time we'll be number one."

Lina kept on rhyming in a jovial manner. "We had this manager, his name was Trevor / He thought he was clever . . . until we *left his ass*." Everyone busted out laughing.

"That shit don't rhyme," said Eva. "Come on, let's make a fly-ass one."

We took that seven dollars and decided to get a bottle of liquor and get drunk. We stopped walking and sat on a car that was parked on the corner of Webster and Tremont avenues in the Bronx. As we passed around our bottle of golden Champale—you know the rules, two sips and pass—the effects of the alcohol just intensified the vibes of the situation at hand.

We got so heated, we started devising all types of wild plans.

"We got to put an end to this shit from Trevor," I said. "Any future business dealings will be handled correctly."

"*Yeahhh*, girrll!" Lina responded, her voice slightly slurred.

"Fuck him and all his *bumbaclaat* fake-ass Rasta posse," Eva added.

"They're a bunch of fucking wannabe original rude boys tryin' ta be managers," said Lady D with a look of pure disgust.

We decided to take a vote to open a can of whup-ass on Trevor. I started the voting process with the bottle in my left hand, my other hand raised in the air.

"If we're not gonna murder this punk-ass Jamaican nigga, I vote to catch him when he least expects it and whip his motherfucking ass!" I said, eyes burning. "Who seconds that vote?"

Lady D immediately raised her hand. "You know I second that vote," she said with alarming intensity. "Not Trevor or nobody else is gonna fucking disrespect our crew from this day on."

"We should just murder his ass!" Eva and Dora said at the same time.

"Throw his punk ass off the fucking roof or something!" Dora continued in her husky voice.

"No, we should push him off the damn train platform right

before the train comes," Eva interrupted. "It will look like an accident!"

Money was so tight, we were even talking becoming down-low stickup chicks, buying black pullover hoodies and going downtown to get paid. We weren't going to rob anybody in the hood. They were as broke as us. No, we wanted rich people. We were setting up the whole blueprint. With enough Champale in us, we might have been crazy enough to try and pull it off, but the bottle was empty and we were broke.

Even though we were drunk, deep in my heart I knew that we were going to have to get ruthless in order for our crew to be taken seriously in all aspects of this game dominated by males. That was one of the first lessons we learned: business is never personal.

By the end of the night, one thing was sure: we were not going to fuck with Trevor as a manager. We vowed to start doing shows on our own until the right manager came along. Trevor and his posse were history.

Chapter 32

Eat or Die

Trevor kept calling us, leaving messages with my moms, trying anything to find out why we weren't showing up for practice. Of course he knew damn well what the problem was, but we eventually agreed to a meeting so we could tell our ex-manager that he was fired.

"All right," he said when we told him it was over between us. "That's what y'all want, so be it." He knew we didn't have any equipment and couldn't afford any. But we could still perform at places that had their own equipment. Trevor probably figured that we would eventually fold, but he didn't know us well enough. Some of the girls, like Lina and Eva, might have had mixed feelings about leaving him, but the rest of us would not budge. We were sticking to our guns.

A few days later D and I were chilling at my house, deciding what to do that night. Neither of us had any money, but we heard there was an MC contest going on at this club in Harlem and the first prize was a hundred dollars.

"Come on," D said. "Let's go down there and enter." Even though she was a DJ, D also had mad skills on the mic.

It was pouring down rain that night, but we were so hungry we set off on foot. We walked from 180th and Tiebout Avenue three long-ass Bronx blocks up a hill by the police precinct toward the Grand Concourse. Then we walked down the Concourse all the way to 138th Street until we hit the bridge that took you into Harlem. All this to enter a contest without any idea whether we had the slightest chance of winning. We were soaked by the time we reached there, even though we had an umbrella to share. During our journey there, we tried to hitch a ride a couple of times. We knew it was dangerous, but we took our chances. If Moms found out, she would have killed me.

Upon arrival we ran into this older guy at the door. When he stopped us to pay, we told him we were there to enter the MC contest. He instructed us to sign our names on the list he kept on a clipboard. As we signed our names, we noticed that there were ten other contestants who had signed up before us. We were the only females in the competition.

The place wasn't that big, but it looked full, with an older club type of vibe. People sat or hung around the bar. Most of the guys were looking around to see who they were going to pick up that night. Others figured we were there to represent for our peeps in the contest. While we were signing our names to the list, this dark-skinned big guy, about six two, came over with a curious look on his face, as if to say, *Who are these females signing the list?*

He was in his thirties and he looked sort of mean—not real scary, but just enough to intimidate others enough to stay in control. It turned out he was in charge of the contest. We explained that The Mercedes Ladies were in the house.

"I heard of y'all," he said in a booming voice. "Where is the rest of the girls?"

"It's just us two tonight," we replied.

"Okay," he said. "These are the rules. You get, like, two minutes to rhyme, and the judges—along with the response from the crowd—will determine the winner. Good luck," he said and then faded into the crowd.

While we were looking around trying to figure out who the judges might be, we noticed a makeshift stage across the room by the bar. Then the music stopped and the DJ announced the host with great fanfare. We had never heard of either the host or the DJ before. I guess the club was their home base. The host did his best to get the audience amped before announcing the acts. You know, he was kicking the usual phony shit: "How ya doin' tonight? Oh, I can see everybody looking fine. Boy! Have we got a show tonight!"

Then he would tell a few jokes, but they weren't that funny. Instead of making me laugh, his comedy routine made me think, *Wow! It must be tough to stand up telling those lame jokes with that hot velvet suit on, trying to look cute while wiping the jheri-curl juice sweat dripping from his forehead.* But I didn't have time to let my mind wander. We had a contest to win.

D and I stood there absorbing the atmosphere, running through our lyrics, and checking out whom we were up against. As each contestant came up and did their thing, we gained confidence.

"Yo, this competition is weak!" I whispered to D.

"No sweat, girl," she replied with a grin. "We got this."

With all our experience doing shows, winning that hundred dollars was going to be a breeze. We could tell that a lot of these acts were MC wannabes who were up there fronting. Sometimes the crowd could turn out to be difficult, but we had learned to blot out the assholes in the audience. There's always one in every crowd, so we were prepared for them too. Our feet were tired, our clothes were damp, but we felt invincible.

When our turn at bat came up, we stepped to the plate and knocked that shit right out of the park. From the moment we started rhyming, everybody at the bar put down their drinks and turned their bar stools around. The bartender even paused while pouring the drinks, and people started moving away from their corners and walls to take in the action. We didn't even have a routine planned, so we just hit them with the hungry flow—eat or die.

D rhymed like she was a seasoned MC. I guess she had been paying attention during all the gigs watching us rip the mic.

But she had plenty of natural talent. Skills like that couldn't just be learned. They were a gift. And of course I held up my end of the bargain. By the time we were done, the club went bananas. Even the ones who came representing for their peeps couldn't front on the skills.

Now came the moment we'd been waiting for all night. It was time for the host to announce the winners.

"And the winner is . . . Mer—"

Before he could finish the word, we started screaming. Of course we deserved to win first place, but it had been a while since we got what we deserved. The promoter winked his eye at us while handling his business, giving us the thumbs-up for a job well done.

We snatched that hundred dollars and ran out of there like the devil was chasing us. We made sure the stickup kids didn't get to us. Hell, that was the first real money we had ever seen from a gig in our lives. We split the pot fifty-fifty. It felt good to be compensated for our hard work—even if the actual performance took only ten minutes. On the way home, we started talking about doing this contest thing to raise money for equipment. It would take a long time, but at that moment, anything seemed possible.

On the way home we took a cab, more than happy to spend eight of our hundred dollars. D decided to spend the night at my house because it was kind of late. On the way home we joked about whether my mother would be waiting for us at the door with a bat. Of course she was up, but instead of a bat, she used the deadliest weapon of them all: her mouth.

As soon as we opened the front door, she started yelling at both of us.

"This shit ain't right!" she railed. "Where the hell y'all was at?"

I went in the back to use the bathroom, and by the time I came back, my mother was even angrier.

"Y'all gone," she said. "You too, D. I'll beat both of your asses! This is gonna stop. . . ."

It was almost funny this time. D was trying to get a word in, but I warned her, nobody could outtalk my mother. She was in the habit of yelling back at her mother—but not my moms. Even though we were victorious in the club, when we got home D had to take it on the chin like a defeated champ. It felt kind of good to have someone to share the heat with. Moms refused to let us eat anything and said we better not think about sleeping late, because she'd make sure that the both of us got up extra early for staying out so late. This was our so-called punishment. That was Mom for you. The next morning we were starving and sleepy. Moms woke us up early to clean the house. But it was all good. At least we made some money for the cause.

Chapter 33

New Management

That same week I received a phone call from this guy named Gary. He claimed to have gotten my number from this promoter we once played for. He wouldn't mention the name of the promoter, but he said he was interested in managing us. He said he was from the Red Hook section of Brooklyn, and claimed to be well known.

"I can get you a lot of shows throughout the boroughs," he said. Sure, it sounded good, but I really wasn't one to talk business over the phone. So I cut the conversation short and told him I'd rather meet in person, along with the rest of the crew, to discuss his proposal.

I called a meeting with the rest of the crew to figure out our next step. When I told the girls about this cat Gary, they all wanted to hear what he was offering. So we called him and set up the meeting. He suggested that we get together at some after-hours spot that his brother ran in the Bronx.

Gary was a tall Spanish-looking guy with short curly hair. He was dressed very conservatively with an ironed button-up shirt, sharp slacks, and dressy shoes—not the normal dress code during this time in the hip-hop era. He was a real smooth guy with his Kangol slightly tilted and shades covering his eyes. I had seen him around at various jams. I didn't know what he did, but he was always on scene, checking out the scenery and chatting with whoever was promoting the jam in question.

He met us outside this dingy-looking down-low spot located in the middle of the block. It was sort of like a basement apartment in a tenement building. Inside was a pool table, some chairs, and a makeshift bar. There were a couple of older cats playing pool and drinking beers. He introduced one of them as his brother, invited us to have a seat, and got right to the point.

"Yo, I can get y'all gigs all through the boroughs—what? Y'all stick by me and we gonna fuck everybody's heads up in the street—what? Ya know what? Motherfuckers don't play with me when it comes to money. I got a reputation in the streets—what! I'm a straight go-getter. I'm gonna make sure y'all crew gets paid. You can motherfuckin' bet your bottom dollar on that shit—what?" I appreciated the fact that he didn't waste time discussing business, but every sentence out of his mouth ended with that "What?" I couldn't tell if he was waiting for us to respond or just questioning what the hell he was saying.

Homeboy was talking fast, making a strong attempt to sell himself. We just sat there listening to what he had to say. Okay, so he was a slick talker, but what did it all add up to? Between all that street lingo and the hand and head movements, he was hard to read. If we learned one thing with Trevor, it was that actions speak louder than words.

After he finished his presentation, we told him we'd get back to him regarding our decision. He seemed okay with that.

After much debating, we let a week go by before we gave him our decision. We did not want to appear desperate. When we finally called him, we invited him to our meeting instead of breaking it to him right away. But we had pretty much agreed to give him some play on the manager tip. "What do we have to lose?" was the general consensus. Besides, he acted like he had street smarts along with his gift of gab. We all heard him promise we'd get paid for the shows, so if he failed to hold up his end, we were out of there.

Our crew was known in most of the boroughs by now, but people in Long Island, Queens, and Brooklyn had never seen us perform. The girls were ready for our new adventure with a new manager. We didn't have equipment, but we could still practice our routines, and he said most of the venues already had equipment set up. I was glad to see that the girls weren't losing enthusiasm in the crew. They were still doing their thing and keeping the faith in The Mercedes Ladies.

Our first show with Gary took place at a big club called Harlem World. Located on 116th Street and Lenox Ave, Harlem World was the site of numerous legendary battles, from Cold Crush Brothers vs. Fantastic Five to Busy Bee vs. Kool Moe Dee. A DJ by the name of Donald Dee happened to be playing there that night. Donald Dee was one of the hottest DJs in Harlem. Along with his brother B. Fats, you could say Donald had some spots in Harlem locked.

By the time we arrived, the club was already popping. We looked over by the DJ booth and noticed this stout, neatly dressed brown-skinned guy with a short shaped-up Afro. He was spinning the hottest joints around at that time, and he even had skills on the mic. This brother had the crowd seriously amped. I was impressed. Gary walked us over to the booth to meet him, and he picked his head up from the turntable, looked at us, smiled, then kept on doing his shit. He had one of those Colgate smiles that lit up his entire face. He wasn't a bad-looking guy, with his round 'fro and belly. We stood there for a moment more watching him catch wreck when he surprised us by grabbing the mic to announce that we were in the house.

"Mercedes Young Ladies," he said, taking his headphones off his ear. "How ya doin'?" He talked with a lisp but it was kinda cute with that Harlem swagger type of attitude. "So, y'all ready to rock the spot or what? Let's get it rockin'," he added bluntly. "Who's the DJ and who's the MCs?"

By the time he finished his sentence, D was taking her position on the turntable. Donald looked at her in a skeptical way, as if to say, *You better not fuck up.*

"You sure you know what you're doing?" he said, like he was concerned, or trying to be helpful to D. But by this time she already had the headphones on her ears. She was so focused on what she was about to do on the wheels of steel, D didn't even notice that Donald was talking to her until she looked up and saw him moving his lips.

"*What?*" said D in an irritated tone, taking off one ear of the headphones. Even though he tried to play it off, I could see Donald was embarrassed that D had clearly ignored him. He was used to being the center of attention, and Lady D made him feel like she was the headliner up in this spot.

"What you mean *What?*" he shot back, all defensive and shit. "You better stop playing, girl. I know you heard about me, and if you don't know, you better ask somebody!"

D just looked at him with that "eat shit" smile, and Donald looked back at her with the same. The chemistry between them was not starting off well. Meanwhile, the other young ladies were giving him that *Who the fuck he think he is?* look. But Donald paid them no mind. At the end of the day, he was about his business.

While D was picking out the records she wanted to start off with, and the other girls were trying to figure out where the other mics were, Gary took the opportunity to go mingle in the crowd. I began kicking it with Donald, really trying to see where his head was at.

"Yeah, I heard about y'all," said Donald. "Y'all be out there doin' the damn thing."

"Yeah, we be holdin' it down," I responded, feeling confident about my crew. "Good looking out on the guest spot," I added.

Something about the look on his face told me that he was not overly impressed.

"Yeah, I did this for Gary," he told me nonchalantly. "We go way back, so I let him give y'all some shine up in Harlem."

I could have taken that comment offensively, but I realized that was just the way Donald came off. No harm intended, he was just a blunt person. You either accepted it or not. But I could see right through that attitude of his. He was actually a cool-ass dude. For some reason, we hit it off like we had known each other for years.

I always respected people who were straight up with theirs. I never felt for phony-ass people who camouflage their true selves. I'm not saying you're supposed to reveal everything about yourself, but it's better to be up front with people than to be shady.

After the show, we exchanged numbers, because Donald said he could arrange for us to play at other spots in Harlem.

"Good show," he said in an unemotional tone. "Y'all all right," he added, "but I see where y'all could use some help on the routines." There he was with that blunt attitude again—Donald was a real critic.

"Yeah, okay," I replied. "Thanks for the constructive criticism."

But Donald could see I wasn't trying to hear him. I guess my head was somewhat swollen being a Mercedes Lady. The rest of the crew wasn't trying to hear that shit either.

"Shelly, let's get the hell out of here," they said.

"Go ahead," I told them. "I'm right behind y'all."

Being that Donald was so blunt, I decided to return the favor and be blunt with him.

"Uh, Donald," I told him as he was about to go back to the DJ booth. "That's cool and shit, but we make our own routines—and they got us a name so far."

He gave me this look like, *Yeah . . . so?*

"Well, call me," I told him in a blasé voice. "And I'll see what you got."

Chapter 34

Big Willy

About a week later Donald was on the phone asking if I wanted to hang out. I was cool with that, because he never gave me the notion that he wanted something more than friendship: a sister and brother vibe I got from him. One night of hanging with him developed into every weekend; whenever there was something popping, Donald would call me to hang. He was like a brother to me. I enjoyed hanging with him, because he was popular, and it was a breather from hanging with the girls all the time—plus it came with perks. He would pick me up, always in a phat-ass ride, and pay for everything whenever we would go out. I would get dropped off at the end of the night.

Donald was very generous. After whatever event we went to, we'd go out to eat, and he would always pay for everybody's meal. Sometimes Donald would roll with a crew of about ten, and was never shy about footing the bill. At one point I thought Donald must be selling drugs, because in all the spots we used to go to, guys would be handing him money all the time. He was kind of a show-off who had no problem pulling knots of cash from his pocket. I knew he had a lot of DJ gigs, but I didn't know what else he was into and never questioned it. When I think about it, Donald had the mentality of a Big

Willy, the type everybody wanted to be around. He always kept plenty of cash around, drove phat rides, and never got stressed about anything. Hanging with him, you could get fat and spoiled.

You could tell he loved the ladies. Everywhere we went, chicks were up in his face. But Donald had a serious girlfriend, whom he called "wifey." They were childhood sweethearts, and they had a beautiful little girl. I was the only female she would trust Donald around. I guess because I presented myself as genuine to her. When I met her, she appeared to be somewhat hard. Not that she looked rough—she was very attractive—but she obviously didn't take any shit.

Sometimes Donald would bring me up to the apartment, and she would be in the kitchen cooking. I'd go in the kitchen and say, "What's up, girl?" showing respect, and she would turn around and give me this blank look. "Yeah—how ya doin'?" she'd say, and then turn back around to continue whatever she was doing. I guess she felt like, *Who the fuck are you always hanging with my man?*

I don't blame her. I probably wouldn't have liked having another chick hanging around my man. Hell no. But the more I came around, she eventually started speaking with me and saw it was truly just business between Donald and me. I could tell Donald must have put her through some shit. Like any big DJ he spent a lot of time hanging out in the streets and having chicks around him. No matter what, I respected the fact that he took care of his home. The refrigerator was always filled, "wifey" always had some fly shit on, and the baby was well kept. Even if she did go through shit occasionally, his responsibility outweighed the drawbacks.

Sometimes I would go hang out with Donald's family on 143rd Street and Seventh Avenue in Harlem. Going there was like walking into the house of music. They had a piano in the house, and his mother used to give singing lessons. The entire household was talented. Everybody that hung out there was into music. I used to be up there chilling and taking in all musical vibes. His moms reminded me of Barry White's wife, but without the long nails. She walked with a graceful, diva-type attitude and talked in a high-pitched voice. She was also a foster mother, and no matter how long it took, she'd always get those kids into music too.

I wanted D to hang out with us sometimes, but Donald always said that she had a name for herself out there in the streets that wasn't good. They used to argue all the time, so I tried to keep their friendships separate. Whenever they were together he would sometimes make salty comments that got her heated. I didn't really listen to that shit, because that was my girl, and she had my back, just like I had hers.

Chapter 35

Beef in the Schoolyard

By now The Mercedes Young Ladies had a lot of static in the camp. From the outside looking in, it looked like we were all tight with one another, but there were issues simmering beneath the surface. For starters, D and Lina kept clashing because one claimed the other was a ho. Nettie and D didn't always see eye to eye either, and Nettie was fed up with D's reputation as well as her habit of picking up guys after shows. Dora was having run-ins with everyone over that controlling shit. All of a sudden, it seemed like she wanted to run all the routines. I was always having to break up a D and Lina fight or a D and Nettie fight or a Dora and everyone fight. Trust, the picture was getting ugly. Eva was a quiet girl who did not start arguments with anybody, but she followed behind Lina in any situation—whether Lina was right or wrong. Remember, they were girls, who grew up together outside of the crew, so their loyalty ran deep. It was obvious that Lina was a bad influence on Eva. Lina would start shit with her big mouth, but deep down she was really a punk.

Although it seemed like everybody was ready to kill one another, when it came down to showtime, we were usually ready. And when it came to throwing down, we would throw down as one—if we had to.

One day we heard that Stacey had beef with this chick from her school. Even though Stacey didn't MC anymore, she was still a Mercedes Lady. This girl was supposed to be some tough chick in school and she kept talking shit to Stacey during their classes, testing her like she was trying to start a fight. One day me, Beebe, Nettie, Lady D, and Cowboy from the Furious Five went up there. Cowboy was down with Stacey's brother's peoples, the Boston Road Crew, the same crew that served as our male backup whenever necessary. Cowboy always showed us respect and would casually hang out with us when he wasn't busy performing. Maybe he was amused with us, 'cause we used to make him laugh. Also, I thought he had a thing for Lady D, but he never acted on it.

As one of the original MCs from the Grandmaster Flash crew, Cowboy had a style of rhyming all his own. Out of all Flash's MCs, he would always be the one to get the crowd going. Remember that famous line that goes, "Throw your hands in the air / And wave 'em like you just don't care! / Say, 'Oh, oh, oh' "? That was Cowboy all day. It was like he had the crowd under his spell. They would do or say whatever he told them to do on the mic. Cowboy was a naturally sexy guy. He was a tall, brown-skinned brother with bowlegs, and back then men with bowlegs were considered fly. So that gave him a big girl fan base.

This particular day we skipped school to roll up to Walton High School, a school for troubled girls, to see what the deal was with this girl who was messing with Stacey. Our timing was perfect. As we approached the school, we saw Stacey by the gates waiting for us. She was ready for this chick—she had her scarf on, her sneakers were tied down tight, and her face was all Vaselined down. Once she saw us there, she had the eye of the tiger. We stood there waiting with her for this chick to come out of school. A few minutes passed and here came this big burly-looking chick, about six feet tall with her hair all braided up. We could see the Vaseline shining on her face, so we knew she was ready to throw down.

As soon as they spotted each other, they just started swinging. They didn't care who was there for whom; it was on. We kept it fair, forming a circle around the fight to make sure nobody else jumped in. I heard Nettie yelling at the crowd that was starting to form.

"Back the fuck up," she warned. "Ain't nobody jumpin' in."

"Yep," Beebe backed her up. "Nobody better even *think* of jumping in."

The rest of us stood there watching the blows fall. Stacey had the girl on the ground, just hitting away. The girl grabbed Stacey's hair, holding on for dear life.

"Let go, bitch," Stacey yelled. "Let go of my fuckin' hair!"

Then all of a sudden, this grown man came out of nowhere and started pulling on Stacey. We didn't know if he was somebody's father, uncle, or what, but he was trying to pull Stacey off the girl. He had placed something that looked like a briefcase on the floor, and just as he went to grab for it, Nettie kicked it away. It seemed like he was trying to reach for something inside the case. That's when Cowboy pushed him back. "What the fuck you think you doin'?" he said. "Let the girls fight."

From the look on the man's face, you could see Cowboy intimidated him, because he slowly backed away with his hands held up.

Then out of nowhere, here came some other chicks from the school who came to the other girl's defense. We didn't know where the hell all these people came from, but now it was time for us to jump in too. Boy, did we go for the kill—it was one big brawl outside the school. It must have looked like we were fighting the whole school, but that's how we rolled. You messed with one, you had to mess with us all. We kicked ass, and then we went home with our heads held high and our skin a little bruised up—just a little.

Chapter 36

Sabotage

The next time we got a call from Gary he sounded excited.

"I got a show lined up for y'all," he said. "It's at the Hotel Diplomat—what!"

This was going to be a big show; everybody was supposed to play there: Grandmaster Flash and the Furious Five, Grand Wizard Theodore and the L Brothers, Kool Herc, Dr. Jekyll and Mr. Hyde, Love Bug Starski, Busy Bee, Cold Crush Brothers, Donald Dee . . . You name it, the list just went on and on. The show was being promoted by this big-time promoter named Redd. It was even being advertised on the radio. We were very excited about being a part of a jam like this, especially thinking that we were going to get paid. After this show our name was going to be well, well known throughout every borough.

This time my mother could tell how seriously I was taking this MC thing. She backed off of me and let me prepare for this event. Though she didn't understand the first thing about hip-hop, I think she respected the fact that I was so determined and she could tell that this was a really big deal to me. The eagerness and excitement shown by all Mercedes Ladies helped too. Moms even agreed to let my sisters Lizzy and

Camela come watch the show—this would be their first time
seeing me perform.

We knew our show would be tight. Now we just had to figure out what to wear. We knew we had to look correct. The
usual sweatshirts and jeans were not going to make it for this
show. We wanted a classier look. Plus, being the only female
crew featured on the show, we wanted to make a hell of an impression. After some discussion, we voted to wear cowgirl outfits, with the cute hats, skirts, and boots. In those days that was
considered a fly look. All of us saved our little money up, and
with some help from our mothers we got it done. We all went
together to pick out the outfits on Simpson Avenue in the
Bronx, a shopping district where you could talk down the prices
for almost anything—and they were already cheap to begin with.
After a long day of arguing and haggling, we had everybody's
outfits—different-colored brims with the feathers hanging on
the side, cowgirl shirts that buttoned up to the neck with matching black ties, miniskirts, and cowgirl boots with the fake white
cowhide-looking material.

On the day of the show we had serious butterflies in our
stomachs. Gary had assured us that we didn't have to bring any
equipment, because we could use the equipment onstage, which
I believe belonged to Flash. That was cool. All we had to do
was bring ourselves and put on a hell of a performance.

It was like one of us was getting married. Everybody was all
nervous and shit as we pulled on our brand-new boots. Our
hair was all curled up under the hats with the fake baby hair
gelled and a little lipstick to match our skin tone. You couldn't
tell us nothing—we looked *good*.

The Hotel Diplomat was located in Midtown Manhattan,
on the east side. That in itself was big. Gary rented a black
limo—really, a friend of his who worked for a limo company
did us a favor and drove us there. We were still impressed. As
the limo pulled up in front of the hotel, we couldn't help but
notice the long line of people waiting outside to get in. This

was no surprise. The show had been promoted for weeks, so we knew it would be packed.

The driver got out first to open the limo door for us, and the crowd was fighting to see who was getting out of it. One by one, the driver helped us out, and we strutted slowly to the entrance with our high-heel cowboy boots on—a far cry from our usual footwear—carefully making sure we did not fall on our fly asses. We felt like stars, and tonight that's exactly what we were. The only things missing were the red carpet and the paparazzi.

Inside two big guys greeted us, instructing us where to go and where the other entertainers were. As we entered the huge backstage area, it seemed like everybody turned around to look at us with shocked expressions on their faces. Nobody had ever seen us dressed up before especially looking girlish—ya know, miniskirts, lipstick, stuff like that. We acted like it was nothing, slowly strutting our asses across the room, with the *yeah, what?* expression. The tables were filled with trays of finger food, soda and bottled water were neatly lined up—tonight was strictly V.I.P. status. Every hood celebrity from Flash to Theodore to Love Bug Starski was in the house, and nobody made a bigger entrance than we did.

"Shelly Shel," a voiced called out. "Over here!"

I walked through a sea of V.I.P.'s and spotted Donald Dee, my man. Seeing him relaxed me a little more.

"Where the hell is y'all equipment?" he said with this stern look.

"They told us we didn't have to bring any equipment," I replied.

"What?" he said, in a tone that said *I can't believe y'all fell for that shit*. Then he added, "Yo, I don't think that was a good idea."

"We're just here to turn this place out," I told him in my best nonpanicky voice. "I know there better be some equipment for us to use onstage."

"Okay, Shelly," he said, shrugging his shoulders and shaking his head. "Good luck. I'll talk to you later." And then he was gone to handle his own business.

We stood behind the curtain near the V.I.P. section to watch the acts as they did their thing onstage. And then we heard the announcement.

"Ladies and gentlemen, next up we have the first all-female DJ and MC crew. Are y'all ready!"

The crowd got so hyped, it made us even more nervous. My stomach was doing flips.

"Here they are, ladies and gentleman, *The Mercedes Ladies!*"

I never once heard anybody tell us "you're next," so it was a good thing we were all standing there watching.

As we took our places onstage, I heard Lady D's voice screaming on someone.

I turned around to see what was happening and one look at D's face told me that we had a problem.

"Yo, they don't want us to use their equipment," she said.

"Says who?" I replied.

"The DJ who the equipment belongs to," D answered in a rage.

I was puzzled as to who really owned that equipment on the stage.

This whole scenario played out while we were onstage with a huge crowd checking us out from head to toe. I tried very hard not to stare back at the crowd. Since we had the fly cowgirl outfits on, we were trying to maintain our composure. Outfits can do really amazing things to your mental state. If we were up there wearing the usual sweatshirt and jeans, we probably would have just started cussing or fighting. But here we were onstage, looking cute in our cowgirl outfits—and somebody told us they didn't want us to use their equipment! We were outraged! How were we not breaking?

The truth was that we were slowly starting to break, especially Lady D. At this point the crowd was still seeing a group of classy ladies onstage, but they were about to see another side of us in a minute. Luckily, the promoter decided he didn't want to create a chaotic situation and set off the crowd. He gave the order to tell us to go ahead and use the equipment.

At last, we were ready to perform—or so we thought. But as soon as we tried to say "One for the money," the top part of the mic fell off. Then when D went to scratch, the turntables went dead. Yep, somebody sabotaged our asses at one of the biggest hip-hop events ever.

All of a sudden the crowd began to get restless and started to boo. We felt like putting bags over our heads, but we knew our reputation was on the line. There were so many faces in that room, and all we could hear was the sounds of booing. It was like that scene from the movie *Carrie* when the girl stood there with the crazy look of embarrassment on her face and pig blood running all over her face. This was truly a nightmare, and it wasn't a movie. It was real.

Keeping her cool under pressure, D started messing with the cords and reattached the system. Having to quick-fix problems at many shows, DJs basically become part-time electricians. Suddenly the music came on, and the crowd stopped booing. Meanwhile we found one microphone that worked. No, they could not stop our shit. The crowd was starting to feel us a little something, between our cowgirl outfits and the way we battled back to overcome the "technical difficulties." We shared that one mic, rocked the house, and that was all she wrote.

But when we got offstage, we were ready to fight. Of course everybody (all the men, that is) started blaming each other. Basically, we weren't trying to hear *nobody*. We did not care who you were that night. We knew it was a setup. Somebody— we had no idea who—wanted to see us fail. But we didn't.

We started looking for our so-called manager, and he popped up from somewhere like, "Oh, that shit was messed up." We didn't really want to hear that either.

"Where is our money?" we asked, and Gary started that bullshit babbling.

"Ahh, well . . . the promoter told me that the door did not

make much money," he stammered. "And after he got through paying the high-profile names, he had nothing left."

"I don't really care what the door made," I shot back. "What do we make?"

We were so pissed after the humiliation of being booed that we simply couldn't believe there was no cash left for us. But Gary had nothing more to offer us. All we knew was that our new manager was on his way out.

After that fiasco, we were reluctant to do any more shows with Gary. What was it with these punk-ass managers? Instead of bringing us excuses, he should have been breaking for his girls to be paid—especially with all that "go-getter" street shit he was always poppin'. We did do a couple more shows with him—never receiving a dime—but we told ourselves we were just using him to put our name out there. That was better than going home broke and feeling foolish.

Chapter 37

Another Manager

Next up on the manager merry-go-round was Curt from Brooklyn. I met him backstage on the night of the Hotel Diplomat disaster. He asked for my number to discuss business, and I gave it to him. He must've sensed that we were going to get rid of Gary after everything that went down that night. He called us that same week while we were still at a vulnerable stage—our brains were pretty much toasted, so you could have said anything to us and it would've sounded good. He wanted a shot at managing us, and our crazy asses gave him that shot. We really just wanted to keep doing shows, so our name could stay out there. But at this point it was hard as hell getting Lina and Eva to keep up with rehearsals. Curt did start getting us booked for shows and paid us from a hundred to a hundred fifty dollars to split. It wasn't as much as we felt we deserved, but it was a definite improvement over nothing at all.

He booked us on a show at this Holiday Inn in Queens, right by JFK Airport. Upon our arrival we met with Curt and he told us we were going on after Grandmaster Flash and the Furious Five. It was cool. The place was somewhat crowded, and a lot of Queens people were there—a new market for us. Grandmaster Flash played for about twenty minutes and then they were out. As we got onstage, we were wondering who else was going to play after us. To our surprise, there was no one else scheduled to play, so we ended up performing all night. The crowd loved the show and everything was cool until afterwards when we tried to get paid. Curt kept stalling and had us waiting in a room. Finally he came in with this stupid look on face. He didn't even need to say anything.

"Yo, I got some bad news," he began. "*Ahh* . . . the promoter said he had to pay Flash. The money off the door paid for that, and he paid for the club, and has no money left." It was really starting to trip me out how these managers would come tell us all about the promoter's finances instead of taking care of our finances.

We looked at Curt quietly for a minute, but we couldn't stand the sorry-ass look on his face—so we headed for the promoter ourselves. Yes, we were ready to fight him. Our so-called manager looked scared, like he didn't have the heart to step to the promoter, but we did. In fact we were about to bust his ass and cause a scene. We must have made quite an impression because the promoter threatened to call the police.

While hiding behind his security guards, he promised us that the next jam he gave, we would be the first paid. We weren't concerned about the next jam—we wanted our money now. But no matter what we did, we still couldn't get any money from this guy. We broke on Curt, and he said he was going to pay us out of his own pocket when he got some money. We were about to jump him and kick his little punk ass. Lady D swung on his ass, almost hitting him in the face. I was going to let her go, but with the threats from the promoter to call the police, I had to keep the situation under control. We told him he better get us some money, and he could tell we were not playing. . . .

At this point I was starting to feel like there must be a rumor out there, and managers were waiting for their turn to pimp us. I could just imagine them talking shit: "Yo, they might break on your ass or throw some punches, but they'll do a show." This was getting crazy.

The next show was scheduled in Long Island at a skating rink. We played and got paid, but Curt never paid us for the Queens jam like he promised. In fact this time he cut out before we could get to his ass. That was probably the best thing he could have done. But unfortunately this led to the crew arguing with each other that night. We started coming at each other about who was serious and who was not. Some of the girls were getting on D about her flirtatious ways. The DJs were arguing with each other about whose scratch was off. Man, the scene started getting ugly. It was time to call it a night before a fistfight broke out. We were really angry at Curt, but since we couldn't get to him, the only way we knew to express it was by lashing out at each other.

Chapter 38

The Turning Point

When I walked through the door my mom gave me a look. But this time it was not an angry look, but an "I can see you're fed up" expression. I looked back at her with tears in my eyes. I couldn't hold back. I started telling her about all the problems me and the girls were going through. As bad as I felt right then, this moment was a special one. For the first time this overwhelming feeling came over me because my mom was listening to me. She was starting to understand my drive for this hip-hop stuff, and she wasn't yelling or hitting me.

This felt so good; it was a turning point in our relationship. As we sat there talking, she started opening up to me. She told me how she never got to fulfill her dreams of being a singer. She always wanted to be a singer. While she was talking to me, I started remembering how as a little girl she used to sing this one song that always stayed in my head. The way she sang it sounded so beautiful.

"Summertime and the living is easy, fish are jumping, cotton is high / Your daddy's rich and your mama's good looking, so hush, little baby, don't you cry. . . ."

I used to love when she sang that song; her voice was so smooth and sweet. She sounded like Lena Horne or somebody in that era, but she said everybody said her voice was more like Sarah Vaughn's. Mom went on and told me the whole story about how she had her first child at the age of fifteen. This was the only way she could get out of her grandmother's house. Even though her husband was abusive and she had two other children, she still wanted to be a singer. My moms wouldn't let her dreams die so easily.

"I went to New York to fulfill my singing career," she told me.

While her husband was out working, she would go sneak into certain clubs and sing. She was getting gigs at several nightclubs, and she even sang with Billie Holiday once.

"So what happened, Mom?"

"Life happened," she said with a sigh. "As I started having more kids, reality started intruding on my dreams. My children always came first."

I was glad she had decided to open up to me. Our conversation made me understand and have a certain respect for my moms. I started to see her as a young lady instead of just my mother. In fact, while she was talking I noticed that she did have a sort of star quality. Here standing in front of me was this strong, gorgeous woman, who could've given Lena Horne a run for her money in her prime. And to think that she was my mother . . . I was deep into the moment, until she made a surprising suggestion. Then my ass snapped back into reality when I heard her say . . .

"Shelly, have you girls ever considered singing?"

That broke it up. I looked at her like *what?*

"*Sing?* Mom—MCs and DJs don't sing!"

All right now, that was the end of that conversation. Back to reality. Mercedes Ladies singing? *Picture that!* I thought to myself. *That would ruin our reputation.* Before she could elaborate any more on that subject, I was outy.

Chapter 39

Girls Fight

After going through all these knucklehead-ass managers, we decided to go on our own. Besides, we were getting demands from promoters all over to do certain shows. I was sure we could do better without anybody managing us. But then the problems started brewing up. First of all, when there was a show, Lina and Eva started coming late. Then when they would show up there would be serious arguments going on amongst Lina and D. I mean they had it in for each other with a passion. The tension between them was getting serious until one day it finally broke. We had this one show set up for us at the Brooklyn Armory. This promoter had called me to see if we wanted to play there. It was a few bucks involved, like a hundred dollars plus carfare, what the hell? It was like a spur-of-the-moment gig.

It was a Saturday. We were scheduled to be there at 6:00 p.m. Lady D said she arranged for a friend of hers to drive us. I'd met him before through D. His name was Alonzo, this cat that liked her who lived around her block. She did not feel the same way about him, but would use him for rides and shit like that. I got the call from D, saying that her and Alonzo were going to pick us up at my house. Eva and Lina showed at the house, Nettie, Dora, and the rest of the crew were going to

meet us at the Armory. We stood outside in front of my building waiting for D and her friend. The ride finally arrived
around 5:00 p.m. They pulled up in this old black two-door
that looked like a 1970 Chevy. It was a good thing the other
girls took alternative means to get there, because the car was
small. We got in, and then D introduced Alonzo to Lina and
Eva. So far the ride was going smooth, until about halfway
there Lina decided to say some slick shit out of her mouth to
D, something like "Oh! By the way, D, how many guys you
taking home tonight?"

What the fuck was wrong with her? Out of nowhere she
said this stupid shit, like she wanted to start some shit with D.
I looked at her, but she tried not to look back at me. She was
stuck in the "I feel like starting some shit" mode.

I was like, "Shut the fuck up, Lina. What the fuck is wrong
with you?"

She just ignored me and kept going with a silly-ass look on
her face.

"Well, it's true. When do D not leave with a guy?" She
knew damn well D wasn't gonna let that remark fly like that.
Eva had this expression like, *Oh, shit, it's about to get ugly*—
knowing her girl was dead wrong. I looked in the rearview
mirror at Alonzo, and I could see he did not like what was
being said. I noticed his eyes started squinting, the face was
getting tight. I didn't know if this cat was going to throw us
out of his car on the highway or not. First of all, he had a thing
for D, so you know he did not want to hear that shit. On top of
that, his car was not a big car, it was hot, and he was not in the
mood for no big-mouth hussies.

Before we hit the Triborough Bridge it was on and poppin'.
Lina and D were arguing back and forth, then the name-calling
began.

Lina was the first to go there: "You ain't nothing but a
whore, D."

Soon D was getting heated too: "You just mad, bitch, 'cause
nobody want your stinking ass."

Oh no. Once you heard "Bitch," you knew they were getting ready to fight. Those are some fighting words.

Lina shot back: "Who the fuck you calling a bitch . . . ho!"

Without waiting for D's response, Lina reached into the front of the passenger side to swing on D. D turned around in her seat, resting on her knees, and started swinging back. Alonzo had to stop the car—yep, right in the middle of Bruckner Boulevard. They got out of the car to fight, and he didn't know what to do, especially with mad traffic behind us.

I just said, "Hell, let 'em fight. Please let them get it over with." Eva was trying to stop them, but I was pushing Eva out of the way. "Let them fight, girl." After a couple rounds of punches and pulling hair, I figured they would eventually get tired. Besides, this had been brewing a long time between them two. It was going to eventually happen anyway. As this went on, a long line of weekend traffic was backing up behind our car. People were blowing their horns and yelling at us, but the fight did not stop. Then me, Eva, and Alonzo finally broke it up and pushed their asses back in the car. Alonzo threatened that if they said another word, he was letting their asses walk. The threat worked somewhat, but you could feel the vibe between them two. They wanted each other's blood. Believe it or not, once we arrived it was showtime and the show went on. They did not go back home the same way, though. Hell naw!

Chapter 40

The Battle

A couple of months passed by, and we did not hear or see Dora until this one night. We heard that the T Connection was going to have some type of MC and DJ battle going on. T Connection was the home spot for all the hottest DJs from uptown and crosstown—anyone from Herc to Flash, Breakout, DJ Baron, Red Alert, and the list goes on and on. When you heard the T Connection mentioned you know the place was gonna be packed. So ya know we was up in there. Plus, we had built-up emotions dying to come out—what perfect timing. This was a huge club on White Plains Road under the train station. It was this big building in the middle of the block. Once inside, you went up a steep flight of stairs into a big ol' room with a stage. When we arrived, we saw the place had a nice crowd and the stage was all set up with equipment. The DJ was rockin', and everybody stood around like they were waiting for something to happen. Electricity was in the air. Then out of nowhere we heard this familiar voice coming from behind us, "Hey, hey, Mercedes Ladies . . . What's up!"

We turned around and saw a familiar face. "Oh, shit, our homegirl! Sha Rock!"

We were like, "What's up, girl?" with excitement in our

voices. Sha was our girl, one of the few other females in hip-hop who was really doing it like us.

She was like, "I know y'all gonna enter the battle tonight."

"Hell yeah!" we replied. "Who else did you see signing up?"

The T Connection was one of Sha's home bases, being that she was from uptown, where the place was located. We figured we were probably gonna go against some wack-ass male crew that was trying to get a rep. Besides, there were no other all-female DJ and MC crews that we knew or heard of.

"Come on to the back of the stage to sign up," Sha said. She was really there to chill.

While we were walking with her, I noticed that her crew was nowhere to be seen.

"Where are the rest of The Funky Four?" I asked, curious.

She answered, "Girl, I am here solo. I don't know where the hell they at." The way she answered me, I felt she was mad at them or something close to it. When they performed as The Funky Four Plus One More, Sha was always the "one more" because she was the only female in the crew. I could only imagine what might be bothering her tonight. Nevertheless, I left the topic alone. While we were standing behind the stage mingling and bobbing our bodies to the music, wondering who the hell was gonna battle us, I looked in the crowd and noticed a bunch of girls coming toward the stage.

"Oh, shit!" Lina said. "That's Dora with those girls."

We all stopped to look, overcome with curiosity.

"What the fuck is she up to?" D said.

Nettie backed that comment up right away. "I know she ain't bringing some chicks to fight us," she said while removing her earrings. "'Cause if that's the case, it's on."

We did not really end up having beef with Dora, so why would she do some shit like that? I had no idea. Still, we stayed defensive from that moment on. I could hear the rest of The Mercedes Ladies talking their shit in the background, getting ready for shit to go down. "I *know* that bitch don't want none of this," they said while taking their positions, just in case she did. With Dora you never knew.

It seemed like a long time before Dora and the chicks finally reached the stage.

"Mercedes Ladies!" she shouted out with a grin all over her face. "What's up? I want y'all to meet my crew."

They just stood there looking us up and down. We stared back with the *What y'all gonna do?* grill faces. Dora was the first one to break the tension.

"Yo, these are my girls!" she told her new crew, pointing to us and sounding all excited. We weren't impressed. We did not care if we were still her girls or not.

"Well, Mercedes Ladies," she said, still babbling excitedly. "I want y'all to meet the Inner City Crew from Queens."

Yeah, okay, I said to myself, waiting for the other shoe to drop. She couldn't hang with The Mercedes Ladies so Dora had gone and recruited her own all-female crew. Then, with a smirk, she added, "Ahh, by the way, we are entering the contest. Are y'all going to enter?"

Yeah, that's Dora all right. She could never rule us, so she had to get a crew she could rule.

"Yeah," I said calmly.

"Then I guess we'll be battling y'all," she said in an innocent voice, still smirking and looking around for our responses. But we decided to save it for the stage.

Then out of nowhere, Sha said, "Fuck that—ain't no chicks from another borough gonna come to battle my girls. I am a Mercedes Lady tonight."

Oh, it was on.

The crowd started pushing up toward the stage; you could feel them getting amped. They just felt a monumental moment was about to take place and we were the main event. Things got so heated between the crowd, the new group, and us that the house DJ couldn't even properly announce the event. He just said, "Let the battle begin." Even though the contest was supposed to be a DJ and MC battle, our DJs could not get on the turntables. It was some political bullshit about them not bringing their needles or something. We did not have time to argue the point, so we were like, "Fuck it, it's a crew MC battle."

Of course we blew their wack asses out of there. First of all, nobody from the Bronx had ever heard of them before, so if they were coming to battle us on our turf, they had better come with a tight routine. Instead they had some lame-ass rhymes—then they ran out of rhymes, like they did not write enough. They were not as aggressive as we were when it came to ripping the mic and doing routines. But when they started MC'ing off beat, it was over for them. They started to get booed.

But once we got on, *What! Come on, you wanna battle Mercedes Ladies* and *Sha Rock?* The crowd let them know whose house they were in. All Dora said before taking her makeshift crew out of there was, "Ah . . . y'all got that."

Damn right, we got that . . . how *dare* you?

That night was almost like a setup. Nobody else even signed up to battle, which I found highly suspect. But anyway, it was truly a historic hip-hop moment. We never heard from Dora or her crew after that.

Chapter 41

The Hustle Takes Its Toll

Despite our triumph at T Connection, it seemed as if no one was getting along at this point. Of course I knew it was stress taking a toll on us. It was starting to be a big mess: some of us were getting high, some of us were drinking, and some of us were hoing. It seemed like we were falling apart. The time of the signs was definitely coming. At this one show we had, when it was time to get onstage, Lina snatched the mic—not routine format, mind you—and she started saying the same thing over and over. For example, she was like "Yes, yes, y'all" like eight times in a row and then follow that up with "let's get high, y'all," which she repeated another eight times. Anybody listening to her must have realized that she was real high. We later on found out that she had smoked some dust and was completely out of it. On top of that, she did not want to give up the mic. We practically had to fight her to get the microphone out of her hands right in front of the little crowd that was there. The whole shit was crazy. Needless to say, the show was a disaster, but we still had to finish it out.

At that point I knew we were really falling apart. It looked like the interest in the crew was starting to fade. We were mostly making appearances and doing certain shows, trying to keep our name out there. I found myself drinking a lot every time we went out; I would get stoned. On top of that, D and I decided to try this little paper you lick with a cartoon character on it. You know it was more to it than just licking the cartoon character. We did not really know what the hell we were taking, but it made us laugh a lot. We got introduced to it from going to a party one night that we were invited to by this guy named Dwight from around D's way. It was a house party up on University Ave in the Bronx; it was actually his cousin's place. We went because we had been promising Dwight that we were going to hang with him one night. He was a hype type of dude, who loved to party and was always excited about anything. "Hey, what's up? Y'all know I am your number-one fan, but y'all got to hang with a brother sometimes . . . come on, D," he'd say with this devilish look on his face, eyes always red. "We grew up together! You know how I do!" Each and every time we saw him, damn, he started making us feel guilty for not hanging with him. This one night we decided to hang with the devil—I mean, Dwight. He claimed his cousin was giving a party that was going to be off the hook, not to mention that he promised his cousin that he was going to bring The Mercedes Ladies. It was a night where nothing else was planned for the crew. The party was in this small-ass apartment. Inside shit was cramped, I mean, literally standing room only.

Dwight acted all happy and shit, because D and I were rolling with him in to the joint. While we're walking in with him, he stopped to talk to everybody. "Yo, yo, what's up! Yo, I am chillin' with my girls, Mercedes Ladies, and shit. You know me!" Smiling from ear to ear, he was showing off to his boys, like, "Hands off—they're with me!" So that night we found out why Dwight was always so hyped and happy with that evil grin on his face. We were at the party, and the first thing he did was make us a drink of some spiced-up punch; you know, the kind that tastes good but eventually sneaks up on you. We sipped away, listening to the music, checking out the scenery, hearing hyped Dwight running his mouth. As the drinks hit us, our vulnerable stage kicked in. We were officially nice and

Dwight said, "Yo, yo, check this out." He pulled out this little paper with a cartoon character on it. We never saw nothing like that before. D said, "What the fuck is that?" It looked like one of those lick-on tattoos. "Oh, shit, it's Snoopy!" Dwight started laughing. "You lick it all right, but it ain't for your skin." Still laughing, he added, "Snoopy is going to seal the drinks y'all just had."

D and I were still curious about this little cartoon paper he put in his mouth, sucking it like it was some candy and shit. He pulled out another, tore it in half, and said, "Yo, just try this shit. It ain't gonna do nothing but make you laugh a lot. Trust a brother. Try it." Our silly asses popped it in our mouths and started sucking away. At first I was like, "This shit is wack. I don't feel no different . . . Dwight, you play . . . ing . . . *gaaaa*. . . ."

Before I could finish my sentence, I just started laughing. D started laughing too, and suddenly everything was looking funny as hell. We laughed so hard we had to leave. By the time we got outside, the laughing was so intense our faces hurt and tears were rolling down our faces. The crazy part was we did not know what the hell was so funny. Then we learned where to cop it at, in the park on Fordham Road in the Bronx. We started getting hooked off the laughter. I guess after all the stress Mercedes Ladies were going through, it felt good to let go and just laugh. I would come home and ma could be yelling and coming at me hard, but Snoopy made that shit *sooo* funny. She did not realize that I was high on something. For the most part, I knew how to contain it in front of her, and by the time I got home, the high was worn out a little. I did not like the way it made you feel the next morning, though. Yo—my stomach would be cramped up. After about a couple of highs, we then found out that Snoopy was some form of acid called "mesca-line." Bottom line, we were dropping acid. Once that idea sank into my head, it kind of scared me, so we both stopped before it got out of hand.

D was slowly but surely certifying the bad reputation out there in the streets about herself. Most of the arguments were mainly about her rep—a lot of things were getting back to us. Lots of times guys thought we were all easy because of the rep she was developing around the way. The girls started coming down on D hard, but all she would do was get defensive and attack back with the mouth, "Mind y'all fuckin' business!"

I got tired of defending her ass. In fact, I was getting tired of it all.

Chapter 42

White Lines

One hot summer night, we had just finished making an appearance at this block party we were invited to. Afterward I decided to call it a night early; I was not feeling very well. As I arrived home, I noticed the house was in a sad mood. My sisters were sitting around with tears in their eyes. I went to look at my mom, and she just held her head down.

"What happened?" I asked, thinking somebody had died or something. I got a little panicked. Then mom raised her head slowly.

"We have a seventy-two-hour eviction notice," she said in a monotone voice.

I didn't know what to say.

"I tried everything and could not get any help," she added.

While I stood there looking at my mother, my sisters started crying again. I felt like crying too, but I knew we had to make moves. What was crying gonna solve? We'd been evicted so many times I was almost getting used to this shit.

"We have three days to find somewhere to stay until I find us another place," said Mom, regaining her composure. "Just pray."

Damn, I said to myself. *If only I could contribute something. I do all these shows and ain't making shit.* That thought made me feel even worse.

Moms called my older sister Tori to see if we could stay there, but her husband wasn't having it. His mean ass wouldn't even let us have a sleeping spot on the floor. At least he could have let my mom stay there with my little sisters. But no. I couldn't stand his ass anyway.

My brother Ronnie let Mom and my sisters stay with him in his apartment; it was a small one-bedroom. I went to stay with my Uncle Pleas and cousin Essie, who lived in Harlem on Convent Avenue. I felt bad about being split up from my mother and sisters, but I liked the fact that my uncle wasn't strict. He would let Essie come and go as she pleased, without any hassle. The first week staying there was kind of hard, but after I got used to my new lifestyle, I started hanging with Essie. She was a nice-looking girl with a great shape, age twenty-one. She had a spoiled demeanor, but it wasn't irritating to be around her. You almost wanted to be like her. She was actually cool to hang with because everyone in Harlem knew her, especially in the after-hours spots. Essie used to bounce from club to club until daybreak. She made life seem so easy.

I was still in touch with the rest of The Mercedes Ladies, but business was slowing down because everyone was getting really frustrated. Meanwhile I was temporarily homeless. It was a vulnerable time for me, and hanging out with my cousin wasn't such a good idea—as I soon found out.

This was the time I was introduced to the white devil known as cocaine. It just happened one night. Hanging with Essie at one of her favorite after-hours clubs up in Harlem. When we entered the club, she saw some guys she knew. They spotted her and invited us to their table. On the table was a lot of Moët and dollar bills—yes, money—full of this strange white substance. This was the first time I actually came into contact with cocaine. I had always heard of it, but no one I knew was doing it—at least to my knowledge. Where I grew up, there were mainly heroin, dust, and weed heads. I couldn't stand the smell of dust, marijuana made me too paranoid, and I wasn't about to put no needle in my arm.

"Come on, Shelly," my cousin said. "Sit down." She was all hyped and shit even more than her usual free-spirited demeanor. They were some older-looking cats sitting there looking me up and down.

"Oh, this is my cousin Shelly from the Bronx," said Essie. "She's kinda homeless right now, so she is going to be living with me."

No, she didn't *just say that shit,* I thought to myself. My cousin had put my situation on blast for real. But I played it off and smiled, shaking their hands and saying, "Nice meeting y'all."

She went on to explain that I was one of The Mercedes Girls.

"No," I interrupted her, "it's The Mercedes Ladies."

At this she picked up a bill off the table and pulled out this straw. I was thinking, *What the fuck is she doing with that?* It was cut in half, and the top was cut at the sides to create an oval shape for scooping. She dug the straw into the bill and carefully brought it up to her nose, making sure not to drop it. I heard the snorting sound and her eyes popped wide open. That shit must have gone straight to her head. Essie was open. It was like her whole face lit up. She quickly went into her purse and pulled out a little bottle filled with some more—I guess it was her own stash. She started passing the powder around to whoever was sitting there.

When the hell did she cop that? I was thinking. *We came straight to the club.* Maybe that was when she supposedly had to go to the store before we left. My cousin had a nose like a fucking Hoover—no fronting, she was sniffing them lines like a vacuum cleaner. After a few minutes she got out of her zone and looked at me, realizing, *Oh, my cousin is with me!*

"Come on, Shelly," she said. "Try a line. It won't hurt you.

This is nothing you're gonna get hooked on. Besides, if you don't like it, then I won't bother you any more about it, okay?"

I hesitated. It seemed like everybody at the table paused to see my response.

"It's nothing, girl," Essie said, egging me on. "You acting all shy and shit."

After a bit more pressure from my cousin and her friends staring me down, I finally gave in. I examined the straw for a minute, making sure no leftover boogers were on it, then I picked up the bill and studied that for a second. My cousin was signaling me to hurry up.

"Girl, just snort it up," she said, "what the fuck?"

I dug the straw in the bill as I lifted the filled straw up to my nose. My hand slightly started shaking, and they all looked at me like, *She better not spill that shit.* Finally it reached the tip of my nose. I tilted my head back slightly and sniffed. Oh, here it came—my first sneeze. My cousin quickly snatched the bill out of my hand, so the tremble from the sneeze wouldn't blow the rest of the blow. Damn—they really were protective of this powder.

I felt a strange sensation once the powder passed through my nose tunnel. Damn! I felt good. All of a sudden I was hyped. I felt like I was on cloud ten, twelve, twenty—I couldn't count no more, so I just let it flow. I don't know if I was buggin' or what, but it seemed like everybody was all happy and shit, like they were proud that they broke me in. I almost expected them to get up and give me a standing ovation.

The Moët was just flowing. Every time I downed one glass of champagne, somebody would fill up my glass again. I noticed that the music was really jamming. With a few more sniffs and another sip of Moët, I was ready to hit the dance floor. This combo of Moët and cocaine made me forget about any stresses in my life. Hell, what stress? This was my *life*. We hit one club after another that night. I did not care. Yo, I was feeling good. I could see why my cousin had such a carefree spirit.

My cousin wasn't into the hip-hop jams; her thing was the older sophisticated atmosphere, the after-hours spots, and clubs where the music was mainly R&B and disco. In the places where she would go, DJs like Hollywood, Eddie Cheba, and Love Bug Starski would be playing—those were some of the hottest DJs on the club scene. I guess she figured that's where people with money were. Even though she was from the hood, she had this ghetto-princess attitude. Coke to her was a symbol of high class. If you were into cocaine and champagne, you had to be about money.

The next morning I wanted to kill her ass. I felt horrible. My nose looked swollen and my allergies started kicking in. I didn't want to leave the bed. My cousin was up like it was nothing. She sprang out of the bed like a champ.

"Girl, get up," she said. "You act like you ain't used to hanging. Don't you Mercedes Girls go out a lot?"

I lifted my head off the pillow to respond to her sarcastic ass.

"Yeah," I said, "but we don't be putting shit up our nose."

"Yeah, girl," she laughed, "but it felt good, didn't it? Besides, I have another club for us to hit tonight, so get it together. . . . And don't worry—the swelling goes away. Just stand under a cold shower for a minute." Of course she knew all the remedies.

Then I heard Uncle Pleas, "Y'all come get some breakfast now! I cooked."

I liked my Uncle Pleas so much. He was real cool. A very handsome man with a dark complexion, he never seemed to let anything or anyone bother him. He really was my mother's cousin, but since he was an older man, we called him "Uncle." Essie's mother never said much. She was a very fragile woman who would just sit in a chair with a cup in her hand. I think it was full of booze, because she always acted so out of it. All I ever heard her say was, "Essie, where you think you goin'?" Always in a slurred tone. "Damn, don't your ass know how to stay home?"

Then Uncle Pleas would say, "Woman, leave her alone,"

with that southern twang that he never lost, even after several years of living in New York.

"She's a young girl who don't need to be stuck in no house." Then he'd look over toward us, digging in his pocket with a smile on his face. "Y'all girls got enough money?" he'd ask, and Essie would hold out her hand while he just peeled the bills off. Yep, that was Uncle Pleas—he was always so nice to me and my siblings. Meanwhile Aunt Emma was trying to lift her head up. "Okay . . . *ba*–by", she said, then took another sip out of that cup she so tightly held in her hand, put her head down, and then go back into her zone, mumbling shit to herself without the cup even tilting.

As fragile as Aunt Emma was, I was surprised to see how well the house was always kept. I mean Ester ran the streets at night and slept all day while Uncle Pleas worked, but somehow the apartment stayed neat. Maybe after cleaning all day, taking sips out of her cup and zoning out was how Aunt Emma liked to wind down. Hell, I didn't know.

By nighttime Cuz was ready to hit the streets again, and I was all set to go tagging along with her. This time her plan was to hit the Cosmo, this popular club on 167th Street in the Bronx. I had heard of the Cosmo before. Mercedes Ladies had tried to get up in there a couple of times, hoping to land a gig or just make some connections. But unfortunately we never made it past the front door. For one you had to pay at the door, and then you had to have money for drinks. Bottom line— Cosmo was financially out of our league.

In order to get booked to perform there you most definitely had to have a name buzzing out there in the streets. Cosmo was one spot where only the best disco and street MCs and DJs played—not that we weren't considered one of the best, but because we were females it seemed like our street buzz didn't count.

The spot was jam-packed that night, with a line stretching all the way around the corner. Rolling with Cuz, we had no problem getting inside. She soon spotted some peeps she knew.

"Oh shit, there go KC," she said, looking towards the bar.

"Not the KC who has a record out?" I replied.

She was like, "Yeah girl—he grew up with me on Convent Ave."

I looked over there and recognized KC right away. I also noticed this light-skinned guy sitting next to him, along with this short white guy who was standing behind the bar talking. Essie started pulling me to get through the crowd over to them.

"Come on girl," she said with a gleam in her eye. "We got to push our way through. I want you to meet KC. Maybe he can help y'all Mercedes Girls. Oh, and the white guy behind the bar is Joe—he's the owner."

We finally reached the bar, but by this time Joe and the light-skinned dude had both disappeared. KC was sitting there alone now.

"What's up, KC!" my cousin said. "You performing tonight?"

"Naw, I'm just chillin' tonight," he replied, all nonchalant. While sitting on the stool he twisted his body in my direction. As I stood there checking him out, his eyes slowly moved to meet mine.

"Hello," he said with a big ol' smile that complemented those light brown eyes of his. With his redbone complexion, he was a real pretty boy. He reached out to shake my hand, so I extended my arm just as Cuz started with the introductions.

"Oh this is my cous . . ." she began, but I interrupted her because I did not want her to say that homeless shit again as she introduced me.

"Hi, I'm Shelly from the Mercedes Young Ladies," I said.

KC shook my hand with a smile, then started chanting— "Mercedes Young Ladies," almost like he was going to break into an MC routine. "Yeah, I heard of y'all," he said.

From the corner of my eye I could see the short white guy with curly black hair approaching us.

"Hi, I'm Joe," he said in a friendly Italian accent, while shaking my hand. "Welcome to Cosmo, I know your cousin is gonna make sure you have a good time." Then he turned to the barmaid. "Yo Karla—give them a drink on me, whatever they want." He whispered something to KC and walked away.

Just as we were about to order our drinks, the light-skinned guy I saw earlier came back. He seemed more business like, with a laid back type of demeanor.

"I'm KC's manager," he said. "You can call me Ron."

"Yo Ron," KC said with excitement in his voice, "she's one of the Mercedes Ladies."

Ron was like, "*Yeah*? Your crew name gets around. I need to check y'all out one of these days."

I was like, "Cool, I'll let you know when we have another show coming up."

By this time they were ready to leave. "Nice meeting you," I said as they headed for the door.

As soon as we grabbed our drinks, Cuz was like, "Girl, let's move the party to the back." Then she added, with that up-town Harlem fly girl attitude of hers, "ya know, the V.I.P. section." Don't get me wrong—I was adapting very quickly to her carefree fly girl world.

Outside the V.I.P. section stood this big bald-headed dark-skinned brother who was one of the bouncers for the club. He had to be 6'4" and 300 pounds with one purpose in life—to make sure nobody got in without either the owners' or the DJ's approval. But of course you know Cuz had the platinum status.

"What's up Boe?" she said, smiling as she approached him. He just nodded his head and the next thing I knew we were in. Well the "V.I.P. Section" was a big room full of red velvet benches and small round tables. The lighting was dim enough to make everybody in the room look good. All I could see was dollar bills folded in half being passed from hand to hand. Then the straws were carefully guided to various nostrils, never worrying about a spill. There were bottles and bottles of Moet champagne and a silver ice bucket at every table. I just paused for a moment to take it all in. *Wow*, I said to myself. *So this is the Cosmo*? It was most definitely the place to be. The atmosphere looked so glamorous, ya just felt important even if you were a "nobody."

After we made a couple of rounds to different peeps Cuz knew, it was time to hit the after-hours spots. This was my cousin's hangout routine on a regular. Yo, no frontin'—the cocaine made you feel so uplifted, you'd be down for whatever.

After-hours spots were down-low establishments where people went after the clubs and bars were closed. They could be in a basement or in a brownstone—anywhere that was not considered a legal club. You could do whatever you wanted there—gamble, smoke weed or whatever your chosen activity—until the middle of the following afternoon. When you finally did come out, eyes all red and shit, you felt like a vampire once the sun hit you in the face. And don't let it be a Sunday morning—you'd be coming home to your building looking and feeling like hell while your neighbors were all dressed up and on their way to church, looking at you all shameful and shit.

This time Cuz wanted to hit this after-hours spot on 149th Street off of Alexander Ave, in this building that looked like an old warehouse. You had to go up some narrow stairs and at the top was this big loft with a makeshift bar and tables and chairs all around. There were a couple of people in there, and of course my cousin knew everyone. We spotted an empty table so we sat there while Cuz got up to order us some drinks. My cousin never had a job but she always had money. I figured my uncle and aunt kept her pockets full of cash. She was their only child and they spoiled her.

While sitting there waiting for the drinks, I felt somebody staring at me. I slowly turned and saw this well-dressed dude at the table across from ours surrounded by a bunch of guys. He smiled as I looked, and I smiled back at him. The next thing I knew, he stood up and started coming in my direction. I couldn't help but notice the bling-bling shining from his neck and wrist. He was dressed in all black with a short mink jacket on.

I didn't even focus on his headpiece yet—whether he was cute or not—I had to get past the fly shit this man was wearing. Besides, it was kind of dim in there anyway. When he finally reached my table, he introduced himself.

"Hello, my name is Gee," he said, and I told him mine.

"What's a girl like you doing here?" he asked, and I said I was hanging with my cousin, pointing Essie out to him.

"Oh, *she* is your cousin?" he said boldly, like she was bad news or something.

I was like, "*Yeah*, that's my cousin, why do you say it like that?"

"Oh everybody knows her," he replied. "She has quite a nose."

"Maybe she do," I said, "but that's my cousin and I am staying with her until my moms finds an apartment, so I don't care what people think about her."

He laughed and asked what time I was leaving.

"In a couple of minutes," I replied in a snappy voice. "Why do you ask?"

"When you're ready to leave I'll drive you home," he said with a smirk on his face.

I hesitated at first. "I don't know about that," I said. "I just met you." But he was not trying to hear that. He had this princely type of charm about him. Finally I said, "Okay, but just me, you, and my cousin!"

"Seriously, I'm gonna drive y'all home," he said as he turned and went back to his table. "Plus a girl like you shouldn't be out this late."

By that time my cousin had returned. "*Girl*," she said, "do you know who that is?"

"Noooo," I said.

"He got Harlem locked. The man got money for days and he don't usually kick it with just anybody." She seemed more flattered than I was. When I told her he wanted to drive us home afterwards, she smiled like she just won the lotto.

When it was time to leave, I looked over to his table but didn't see him or the guys he was with. We get downstairs and I saw this brand new black Mercedes Benz parked in front. The window rolled down and there he was waiting to drive us home like he promised. I got in the front seat while Cuz got in the back.

When I finally got to get a good look at his face, all I could say to myself was, *Wow*. This man was gorgeous. I got all butter-flied up inside. I had never come across someone like him be-fore—a true hood prince.

He looked over to me with this smile. I guess he could feel that I was somewhat nervous. Whenever I got nervous, I would start talking—especially if a good looking dude was staring at me.

"This car is nice," I said, stating the obvious. "By the way it's the name of my group—Mercedes Ladies?"

"Yeah?" he said. "You're in a group?" To my surprise he'd never heard of us. *Damn, he's a real classy man*, I thought to my-self. *Not into that MC stuff*.

"What does your group do?" he asked. I gave him a brief description and he seemed amazed that there was an all-girl MC and DJ crew out there.

After this brief conversation he pulled off the highway. I gave him the address. Cuz was quiet I guess she was back there just chillin'—this was right up her alley. On the way he did not have a lot to say, maybe because of my cousin's presence.

He pulled in front of the building and as I was leaving the car he said, "wait a minute." He gave me his number and said he was giving a dance and wanted me to come. Before I could say anything else, he put a knot of money in my hand. "Buy yourself a dress and come," he said, then he drove off. I stood there like, *what the hell?* Before I could tell him to take his money back, he was gone . . . just like that.

My cousin was like, "Girl, I think he likes you," sounding all excited and shit. "How much money is that?"

I had never accepted money from a man before, because I always wanted to have my own by earning it. But I'm not going to front—it made me feel special. And that was something I never felt before. Somehow I just felt that he knew I was different from the other girls out there in the streets. Why else would he go out of his way for me like that?

After hanging out with my cousin for a while I was starting to feel burnt out. When Mercedes Ladies did shows all night, it was cool because I was doing what I loved doing—performing. Plus I wasn't getting high, so I didn't feel burnt out. But now I felt that the "fly girl" lifestyle was taking its toll. Besides, I had goals that I was determined to reach.

But Cuz had other plans. One night she was going out with this guy and she set me up with his cousin.

"Yo Essie," I protested. "I don't like blind dates."

She assured me that it was cool because she knew his cousin. She went on to say that he was cute and just wanted to take somebody out to show them a good time. I was still somewhat hesitant, but then I thought, *Why not? It's got to be better than the usual night of club hopping.*

So we went to go meet up with them. As we approached, there were two cars—Essie's friend was in one, and his cousin had his own car. She walked me over to meet Jerry, a light-skinned freckle-faced dude with a dumb-ass grin on his face.

"How you doing," he said. "Come on, get in."

"Hi," I said, keeping it real simple. I really wasn't feeling him. But as we pulled off, I notice the other car going in the opposite direction.

"Aren't we going to hang out with them?" I asked.

"Nah," he said. "I have other plans for us."

"Like what?"

"Go out to eat and then catch a movie," he replied.

I was like, "Okay that's cool." I was down to just enjoy the evening for a change. I hadn't been out on a date in a long time—really, not at all. I was always caught up with Mercedes

Ladies business. Hey, I told myself, I could do this for my cousin.

We rode downtown and got something to eat, and after that he headed for the Bronx.

"Aren't we going to the movies?" I said.

"Ah . . . first I have to make a stop," he replied.

For some strange reason I started getting butterflies in my stomach. That wasn't a good sign. I asked where we were headed and he said Dykeman Ave, up past Fordham Road in the Bronx.

I was like, "Yo, it's nothing up there but an old power plant." But he just kept going. Then before I knew we were pulled up next to the train station and he just parked.

"Yo, I am ready to go home," I said, but he was not trying to hear me. Then all of a sudden he was in a rage, trying to have sex with me. He actually pulled his little thing-thing out! His face turned red and he started foaming at the mouth like a wild animal.

I was like, "I'm getting the fuck out of here." This man had rape written all over his face. I had seen shit like this in the movies. I knew it was do or die—fight my way out of his car or be killed.

You know me—I bit him, and it was on. We were throwing down right there in his car. He was trying to overpower me, but something was with me that night because I was fighting my ass off. Finally I got free from his car and ran. I could see his headlights on my trail, but I kept running. I saw a store under the train station with some Spanish men outside. They could see I was out of breath and they asked what happened. I told them this man in a car was chasing me. As soon as he saw me talking to them he drove off quickly.

I was so out of it, I tried calling my cousin but she wasn't home yet. I couldn't call my mother because she would only ask what the hell was I doing out with a man by myself? The Spanish men were kind enough to put me in a cab home.

When I finally met up with my cousin, I went off.

"I can't believe it Shelly," she said. "I thought he was nice. I'm sorry."

I was just thankful that I had escaped with my life and just a few fighting scars. Those would heal, but this episode was the straw that broke the camel's back. I was tired of life with Cuz. I just wanted to get back to our Mercedes Ladies ventures.

Chapter 43

Time For a Change

I was starting to feel the wear and tear of running around with Cuz. I kept calling moms to see what was going on and finally—after a couple of months that seemed like years—there was good news for a change. Moms had found an apartment.

It was called "River Park Towers," located on the West side of Tremont Ave on 179th Street. It was a fairly new complex of four buildings right by the Hudson River. I really didn't care where the place was or how it looked, I was just happy to call somewhere home again. Moving in made me realize how much I had missed everybody.

After settling in the new place, it was time to get back to Mercedes Ladies business. The first thing was to call the girls to see where their heads were at. The phone calls put my mind at ease. It seemed like our little separation had made everybody that much more eager to get started again, so I arranged for a meeting.

When the girls arrived at my house they were ready to roll, and they all seemed happy to see me back in the game. This meeting turned out to be a little different than the ones we'd had before. The twist was that moms asked to join in. I didn't have a clue what for, and neither did the other girls. She just sat there listening as we went back and forth about past issues of not getting paid and all the dirty-ass managers we'd been through. After listening to us go on like this for a while, she stood up in the middle of the living room and blurted out the crazy idea that had just come to her.

"Why don't y'all let me manage the group?"

She waited for a second for a response, but nobody said anything—that's how shocked we all were—so she kept going.

"You girls work hard," she said, "and I am tired of seeing you doing shows with no money involved." We were all as silent as lambs while respectfully hearing her out. "First thing y'all have to do is incorporate singing into the routines."

Ooooh no, I thought. *Here she goes again with this singing shit—* but I held my tongue. Still the room remained silent. The girls all had puzzled expressions on their faces, just staring at one another to see who would give the first reaction.

"Rehearsal could be here at the house," she said—that sounded like a plus to me. "Don't worry," she added. "I'll have y'all hitting notes in no time."

I wouldn't dare be the first one to speak because it was a no-win either way. If I went moms' way, the girls would all be like, *That's because it's her mother.* If I went against moms, that wouldn't be a good look for me either.

The silence was finally broken by none other than mouth almighty, Dee.

"Yo," she said, "I think that's a good idea. Hell, what do we have to lose?"

That was all I needed to hear. I backed Dee's vote and then the rest of the crew agreed. We were still a little hesitant about singing and stuff, but we decided to give it a shot. Plus she wasn't going to manage us if we didn't.

"Then it's settled," mom said triumphantly. "The Mercedes Ladies are going to incorporate singing into the act."

It was a done deal. Moms was our manager. It felt good to finally see her participate in something I was doing. It had to be better than battling with her all the time.

As usual, Moms was not playing. She made sure we had rehearsal three to four times a week, and she was especially strict when it came to being on time. We spent hour after hour trying to get this singing thing down. It was not quite as easy breezy as we thought it would be. Believe it or not, it didn't take long for us to get the harmonies. I guess those MC routines had trained our voices to just naturally come together. But the solo parts were another thing. That's where the difficulties came in. Of course everybody wanted to be the lead singer. Rehearsals were always being interrupted by arguments about whose voice was the strongest. Mom the manager always had the last call.

We didn't have original songs yet, because we were used to writing MC routines. We usually rehearsed songs that were out already, like "Encore" by Cheryl Lynn and of course "Mercedes Boy" by Pebbles—that was a no-brainer. It must have been funny to watch us trying to learn our dance routines and concentrate on singing at the same time. It remained a mystery to us exactly how this singing and dancing was going to fit in with our MCing and DJing, but we were willing to try and work it out.

There were other little tussles here and there, like the day she suggested that we get rid of the sweatshirts and jeans. *Come on now*, we protested. *What the hell was she trying to turn us into?* She said she thought our image should come across classier, but our crowd was from the streets. *Who cares about wearing classy clothes?* we demanded. We put up a big fuss, but eventually we gave in.

One of our first ventures with manager moms was a meeting that she set up with these producers from Long Island. She had first met them at one of my brother's band events. They wanted to produce a song for his group before they broke up. Moms kept their card and decided to give them a call to see if they were still producing. They were hesitant because of their experience with my brother's band, but she convinced them to listen to the Mercedes Ladies. They even said that they were interested in working with a female group, so our timing was on point.

One Saturday afternoon, this black limo pulled up outside our home. A handsome young black driver, dressed in a black suit with a shirt and tie, got out to open the back door for us. As we were piling in the back, Dee waited to be the last one in line. She paused before she entered, then looked at the driver.

"Oh, the back looks cramped," she said in an unnaturally light voice. "Do you mind if I sit up front with you?" Of course he was not going to object to that.

Yeah right, we mumbled. *Dee's in her flirt mode.*

All the way to our destination we could hear Dee yapping away to the driver. We just kept looking at each other laughing—that was our girl Dee. We were too excited to be mad. This was our first big-time meeting, and it was happening a short time after hiring our first female manager. Now that's what I'm talking about!

Finally the limo pulled up in front of this big white house. We saw two older white guys waiting out front. "That's the producers," Mom said.

"*They're* the producers?" we all said at once, doing a double-take to make sure our eyes were not deceiving us.

We had never met or even imagined white producers who were involved in the music we did. And older white guys at that . . . It just struck us as odd.

The driver let us out and they greeted us, shaking our hands one by one while introducing themselves as Bob and Eric. We entered the house, there was a big room furnished with a grand piano in the middle and a couple of plush chairs.

They told us to make ourselves comfortable, checking us out one by one as we sat down. Then they opened the meeting with a very proper demeanor that reminded me of Mr. Rogers.

"Hi girls," said Bob. "Glad to see you made it. Ahh, like we told your manager, we're looking to produce a song for the right female group. Ahh, Eric join in if you will."

"Well like Bob said," Eric continued, "we're looking for a female group that's serious about making it big."

"They've got to be dedicated," Bob added. "With a lot of passion. If we find the right act we are prepared to produce, record, release, and promote a single on our label."

Then they began peppering us with questions: "Are y'all fast girls?" "Do you do drugs?" and on and on. It felt like we were being screened for a job with law enforcement or something. After the interrogation was finished, they said they wanted to hear what we sounded like. At the drop of a hat, we started singing for them on the spot; then we busted into a rap. We never planned it out that way but it just worked. You could see on their faces that they were feeling us, but afterward they kept steadily picking us apart one by one. I guess they wanted to see who was the weakest link among us. Before they went ahead and invested in the project, they wanted to make sure we were worth the investment. When the meeting was finally finished, they told us that they liked what they heard and looked forward to doing business with us. You could see in my mom's eyes that she was pleased with the whole outcome of the meeting.

That same night we had a show to do, so we all agreed to meet up at the spot. It was just a bullshit sideshow that we'd agreed to do at the last minute, but everybody showed up on time—except for D. We stood in the front of the club waiting for her for over an hour. Then all of a sudden, here came D, pulling up in the front seat of the limo that took us to the meeting. We were mad at her, and praying that she did not do anything stupid with this guy.

"It's probably a trap," I told her. "Bob and Eric probably told the driver to see which one of us he could get. If we turn out to be a bunch of loose chicks, then they won't invest their money in us."

"Why y'all trying to hate on me?" D retorted, but we didn't wanna hear it. We were so upset that we all started arguing with her. D vowed that she did not do anything with the driver, but that was not the point. She should never have mixed business with pleasure. That had always been one of our strongest rules— especially at this point in our career, when we'd finally found somebody who wanted to invest in the group. How could she do that to us?

In spite of us being upset, the show had to go on. But as soon as we were finished, the fighting flared up again. I mean, we were really coming down on her ass. All of us were nervous because we knew what was at stake. My mom found out, and she was furious. She also agreed that it had been a setup to see if we were fast girls, and D had taken the bait. Sure enough, we never heard from those men again, and that was that. We all felt that it was because of D's little escapade with their driver, even though we were not sure what went down. I was so angry at her. Even if they did not set us up, the situation just did not look right.

Chapter 44

Showtime

I could hardly believe my eyes, but Moms was really doing her thing arranging shows for us. I was surprised how many people she knew. She was always on the grind, doing some major promotion to any- and everybody she met shopping for groceries, in the number spots, on the elevators, you name it. Her mouth was better than any advertisement money could buy.

"You know I manage my daughter's group," she'd brag. "They are real popular. I know you heard of them—The Mercedes Ladies."

Once she got them open to realizing who we were, she would go in for the kill: "And by the way, they do shows, so if you or anybody you know needs some singers, here's my number." That's all it took, the power of the word of mouth. Like Marvin Gaye, everybody heard it through the grapevine.

You'd be surprised about all of the gigs that were coming through for mom's "singing group." Once in a while she would say, "And they also rap," but she focused more on promoting the singing. One of the gigs came through this old-school lady she met in the supermarket who was known for putting on shows. She told us that this was a more adult crowd we would be playing for.

"Girls," she said, "you've got to come with some *style*."

Now, this was too much.

"So our usual hood style isn't good enough?" I replied. I understood she wanted our image to be classier, but, damn.

Here she goes: "Why don't you try something a little more, uh . . . *sophisticated*," said Mom.

Trying to be sophisticated was fine, but we didn't have the funds to buy new outfits. Mom suggested getting material and having someone in the family sew our outfits. It would certainly be cheaper than a shopping spree. My sister Tori was the first seamstress we tried to recruit, but she said her time was too tight between her husband and kids. Then Nettie mentioned her brother Terrence.

"He knows how to sew and he'd love the opportunity to show off some of his designs!" Nettie called Terrence right then and there.

"But of course," he replied. "Just supply the material, because ya know I am on fixed income, girl."

Mom, D, and I came up with the money for the material. Mom went to the fabric store and came back with something gold and shiny that she called metallic. At first the girls were not receptive to the idea of wearing these shiny suits, especially Nettie.

"I don't know about y'all," she said with that bully look of hers, "but I ain't wearing no shiny shit. I don't want people to think I am some type of punk chick."

But Moms was like: "Hey, money is scarce, so y'all are going to work with this. Besides, the material looks classy."

All I could do was hope that Mom knew what she was talking about. I didn't want us looking stupid up onstage with shiny shit on.

We could only afford enough material to have the tops made, and we decided to wear black pants. Nettie's brother told us we had to come to his apartment while he made our tops. Her brother was the hood Versace, a true drama queen with attitude for days. He had a big mouth but you couldn't help but enjoy him—he was real funny.

"Now, girls, what y'all wanna do?" Terrence would say with his legs crossed, puffing on a cigarette with a drink in his hand. "Ya know I ain't gonna put y'all in no bullshit. First, we got to get the measurements, 'cause ya know some of y'all—not calling no names—got boobs all over the damn place and ass for days! But don't fear, when I get through with y'all, ya gonna look fabulous!"

He would walk around that apartment with a switch in his walk and one hand on his hip like he was walking on a runway. "I see I have to teach y'all how to walk like ladies," he'd say, "especially if you're representing my designs. I can't have y'all looking sloppy onstage and shit. With *my* name on the line?" he'd add in a high-pitched voice. "*Hell* no!"

Being there with him, watching him make the tops with the true diva attitude, was an unforgettable experience, and we loved every moment of it. No high-paid superstar stylist in the world could have worked harder to make sure we looked right. Attitude aside, Terrence really knew what he was doing. The finished product was worth all the drama—the Ghetto Versace did his thing. The blouses hugged our body in gleaming gold. They had a V-neck wraparound design that tied in the back. The sleeves were wide so that when we did our routines, they would spread out as we lifted our arms. We still were not cool with wearing shiny shirts, but I'm not gonna lie—they came out phat.

At the show the next night, we got to strut the "Terrence design," and ya know his ass was there, right in the front row. When it was our turn to perform, we entered onstage, and we must have looked like true stars, because the audience started screaming before we even started our routines. Then we saw Terrence standing up in the front row screaming. "Go, girls," he cried. "Those are my girls! Get it, girls! You look like stars!" Terrence went on like that all night, just a-clapping and screaming away. This singing thing wasn't turning out to be as bad as we thought. Maybe Mom knew what she was talking about after all.

Chapter 45

Hanging With the Big Dogs

Doing shows and rehearsing all the time, especially with the singing, was making our work with the group more intense. When D and I decided to take a break one night and hang out, we ended up back in the Cosmo. The place was jammed, as we knew it would be. This night was open mic, so you had all kinds of MCs coming through, blazing the place. We wanted to touch the mic so bad, but in the Cosmo the politics was thick—especially when it came to females who wanted to hit the mic. You had to be known in the street and even then you had to be a male. We just knew it wasn't going to happen, so we decided to chill and hang out rather than play ourselves.

While I was at the bar, I noticed Ronald and KC on the other side of the bar. It had been a few months since the last time I saw them with my cousin. I walked right over and said, "Hey, how are y'all doing?" They acted very pleased to see me again.

As I went to introduce D to them, I noticed her eyes became glued to KC, and he put a big smile on his face. I was like, *Oh no, here we go again.*

My girl was steady, smiling and giggling, and he was grinning from ear to ear too. It was like nobody else was in the room. We moved from the bar to the back of the club's so-called V.I.P. section, to hang with them. Once you were back there, all you saw were bills of cocaine and champagne being passed around. D was so wrapped up in KC, I couldn't even tell if she really noticed what was actually happening back there. Maybe she didn't care. I thought this was her first time experiencing a scene like this—but maybe not. She didn't seem too surprised at all.

While KC and D gazed into each other's eyes, Ronald ordered drinks and I sat there kicking it with him about the group. I liked talking with him, because he was very informative about shows and other aspects of the business. After a while Ron and KC said they were headed to another club and invited us to come, but we decided to call it a night. It seemed like D had tamed her wild ways somewhat after blowing our last opportunity for a record deal.

But on the way home, D kept talking about KC. "Oh, he is so fine. We hit it right off. Me and him would make some beautiful kids."

I was like: "Be easy, D. Slow down. Don't go so fast with this one, please. They may help us get some shows or even perform at the Cosmo, and we don't need you fucking this one up!"

"What do you mean by that?" she replied, suddenly turning into Miss Defensive. "I ain't fuck up the other ones. You need to look at Lina and the rest of the fucking crew."

"All right, D, whatever. But I am serious. I will personally fuck you up," I said, letting her know I meant business.

"Okay, Shelly," said D; then she soon returned to her KC spell. "But isn't he fine? *Mmmph!*"

Suddenly she snapped out of it and cast a glance in my direction. "By the way, what was you and Ronald talking about?" she said with a curious look on her face. "It looked like y'all was in a zone of your own. And you talking about *me!*"

"Don't even try it," I said. "We were strictly talking about music stuff. That's all, D."

D decided not to push the issue. She had moved in with us

after her moms threw her out of the house. D blamed it on her constant drinking and D's mom blamed it on D's disrespectful ways toward her. Whatever the cause, the bottom line was that they were just not getting along. Even as things were getting worse, D showed no emotions at all.

D always had a hustler's mentality. She didn't care what happened, she was gonna survive regardless of what it took. Having her in the house with the rest of my sisters, there was never a dull moment. Moms treated her like she was one of her own children. Meaning that when D got out of line, Moms would step to that ass. One time D decided to go downstairs to the lobby in a see-through pajama dress. When she got back upstairs, Mom saw her coming through the door and greeted her with a look of horror.

"I know you did not wear that outside," she said, her voice rising. "Tell me you didn't."

"Yeah," said D. "What's wrong with this outfit? I was just in the lobby."

Uh-oh. I could see this one coming.

Moms went off on her. "You're not going to be disrespecting this household like that. You can see right through that PJ dress. I don't play that shit!"

D went on to say some slick shit, like, "I wear what I want," and before you knew it, Moms socked her, and then dared her to move a muscle, face, or body part.

D just stood there and took it like a champ. She went in the next room and did not say a word. The whole apartment was silent for a second and then everybody just resumed whatever they were doing—washing dishes, reading, whatever. Nobody dared to say a word, and the whole household remained quiet for the rest of the night.

By this time, D and I were hanging at the Cosmo every Friday, which brought our relationships with Ron and KC that much tighter. D was now officially dating KC, and I was hanging out with Ron. He would invite us to the different shows he would give. We would be at the recording studio with them while KC was cutting his single, "Drop the Beat." When KC's single dropped, it blew up. You could not tell D and me that we weren't on our way. Whenever we went out, they would pick us up from my mom's place in a limo. The limo was fully stocked with champagne and the finest cocaine. The cocaine was sort of a beige color, which I found out was considered raw. I knew my mother would not approve, but fuck it—it felt good hanging around and basking in their celebrity status.

I just knew that Ron would look out for Mercedes Ladies eventually. And why not? D was going out with KC. Plus Ron seemed to like me too, but I always kept it on the friendly tip. *Let's just go along with the flow*, I said to myself. When Ron invited me to go with him on a trip out of state, I refused and blamed it on my mother. I really wasn't feeling him like that but couldn't tell him. I guess I felt if he knew, he would not look out for us, so I played it off.

With KC's success, big things started happening for Ron. Whatever group he was managing, he would always invite us to hang out backstage after the shows. I knew we were on our way. When I spoke to Ron about putting Mercedes Ladies on, he said he would speak with the owner of the Cosmo, since he was a silent partner in the club. I told them my mother was managing us and they agreed to meet with us at the house. When they arrived, Mom did not let them get a word in. She just took over the conversation, stressing that she was the manager, she used to sing, she knew the business, and so on and so forth. From the looks on their faces, I could tell they were not loving the whole stage mom thing, but Ron agreed to start working with us regardless.

Chapter 46

The Betrayal

Ron arranged for us to start doing rehearsals at the house of this guy named Barry. He lived out in a comfortable suburb of Long Island and knew music very well. Barry was a talented man who played instruments and did vocal training, which Ron said would be necessary to get our vocals tight.

On our first visit to Barry's house, we could tell he ate, drank, and slept music twenty-four-seven. He had this big piano in the middle of the floor, sheet music everywhere, and an electric guitar placed in the corner. We would be out there for hours, almost seven days a week but Moms never went with us. Barry wanted us to hit those notes, and he was not playing. We never complained about the endless rehearsals. We were drained but willing to give it our all. After a few weeks, Barry and Ron announced that he was preparing us for the studio.

"What do you mean, the studio?" I asked excitedly.

"You're gonna record a single," he told me matter-of-factly. "But before that can happen, you have to be vocally ready for the studio."

"Record a single—*what!*" We were ecstatic, and that only made us work harder. This would be our first time recording in a real studio. Ron told us that when Barry felt we were ready, then he would book the studio time.

After another week of relentless drilling at the piano, Barry finally felt we were ready for prime time. Excited couldn't describe how we felt; we just knew this would be our big break, the one we'd been dreaming about and working toward from the very beginning. The one that could change our lives forever. At first I really had no clue as to where the whole Mercedes Ladies thing was going to lead us. But now the picture was starting to become a bit more clear, especially with hip-hop getting a little more notice.

Ron told us that we were expected to be in the studio on time, and he told us the time and place. We showed up wide-eyed and ready. The studio was located in Midtown Manhattan, and when we stepped inside—*Wow*, we were blown. There was a huge control room with all kinds of high-tech equipment. A man in a chair sat in front of a huge board with all kinds of lights and buttons that looked like something out of *Star Trek*. Then behind a see-through glass window was the vocal booth where a mic was already set to go with earphones hanging at the ready. The producer could talk to you through the earphones and watch you while you recorded.

We were speechless. Here it was at last, Mercedes Ladies' first studio session! Our time had finally come.

"Okay, let's get to work," said Ron, snapping us out of our daze. "I know this is your first time in the studio, but don't be frightened by all the equipment. Just do your thing. First, I'm going to play the track, so y'all can get the feel of it." The beat he wanted us to use was taken from the classic Aretha Franklin jam, "Rock Steady." He said the record would have singing and a rap on it. The beat was hot, but studio time wasn't as easy as we expected. Ron would make us sing our parts over and over until we nailed it.

"Naw, do it again," he'd say, stopping us in the middle of a take. "Sing that verse *this* way. And put more emphasis on the rap part." Ron was real serious when it came to studio work— no bullshit. So we stayed there for hour after hour, with him yelling "Come on now, time is money!" He didn't have to tell us. Sometimes we'd only have two or three hours of sleep because some of us had jobs to help make ends meet at home.

We still considered Moms our manager, but she had to maintain on the home front. You know, she was trying to keep up with the bills and put food on the table too. With no money coming in, there was no way she could be in the studio with us. We just reported to her about whatever was taking place.

I didn't want Mom to feel that she was being pushed out of being our manager. Even I had to take odd jobs at temp agencies, number spots, and whatever else in between, to at least help financially at home. Somehow I worked it and never missed a beat in the studio. It was rough, but I saw the bigger picture. Finally, the project was completed, and it sounded phat. Even Ron had to admit it.

"You nailed it," he said as we listened to the playback. "Just wait till the final mix is done." We had no idea about the intricacies of the music business, about rough takes, and final mixing and mastering—so we just let that comment ride. If he was happy we were too.

Ron seemed just as excited about the single as we were. We sat there with him in the studio and listened to it play over and over, nodding our heads to the finished project. We were proud of ourselves. Ron told us the single would be released within a month, after the paperwork was finished. You couldn't tell us anything once we left the studio to celebrate. The thought of all our hard work paying off had us sky-high—especially after all the negativity we had been through. The fact that the single had both rapping and singing made us feel even better.

All that month we were nervous wrecks, just hoping for a call or any news about the record. Finally, on the day before the single was to be released, all The Mercedes Ladies came to my apartment. There we were sitting around all afternoon, nervous but excited. It seemed like my whole family was there just waiting to celebrate.

Finally, the phone rang, and everyone gathered around

with their eyes lit up. You would have thought it was a holiday or something. Moms said nothing but you could see what she was thinking. Her girls were finally getting a break. She was so happy and nervous it was written all over her face. I answered, and heard a calm voice on the other end. It was Ron.

"What's up, Ron?" I said, barely able to contain my excitement.

"Ah, there has been a change of plans," he said. I noticed that he did not sound excited at all. As a matter of fact, he seemed a bit too laid-back for such an important occasion.

"Okay, Ron," I shot back, "what's the change of plans? Do we have to redo the song? Is the release date pushed back—what?" My voice sounded serious at this point. From the look on my face, everybody started getting worried.

"She's not smiling," said D.

"What the hell is he saying?" said Nettie.

"Ah, I decided to let a known singer do the song," he said in that same old guilty tone we'd heard from so many men in the business before.

I fell silent, and just looked at the girls and Moms, trying to hold back the tears while I was on the phone listening to this shit. Finally I found the words again.

"What? A known singer? Who?"

"You remember Nona?"

My mind shot back to the days in the studio. One evening when we were recording, we met this chick named Nona Williams. She'd had a record out before that flopped, but she did have a little name in the business. She was supposedly hanging around to help us out with the recording—you know, like give some expert singing pointers. I admit that she had a hell of a singing voice, but this was a rap record with some singing on the chorus. She couldn't rap. Ron began to explain that because she was well known in the business, it was going to be a better business deal if it was released by her. In the final mix, he took the rap part out and turned the record into an R&B single.

I just said, "Okay, Ron," and hung the phone up. Then all you heard was crying and cursing. After a while things quieted down enough for me to break the bad news to everybody as their expressions ranged from disappointment to despair. We cried for days. We did not even want to leave the house. Depressed? *What?!* You had no idea how we felt. It was a devastating feeling to be so close and yet so far away.

Chapter 47

My Spanish Fling

They say that when it rains it pours and that's no lie. I couldn't believe someone could be so heartless. But Ron's betrayal was just the first downpour. Then came the flood.

Mom was behind with her bills. She needed extra money for rent or we might lose the apartment. It always felt like we were a heartbeat away from being homeless again. D had to go move back in with her mother and I was struggling from within, even feeling suicidal at times. I found the streets calling me so I could escape the trials of life. I would hang out all night and day, getting high mainly by drinking. I knew it was no solution, but I just did not want to deal with all the crap in my life.

That's when I met this Spanish guy named Danny through a girl in my building. She kept bugging me to meet her cousin, who had seen me one day coming out of the building. I never used to hang out with anyone from my neighborhood; I used to come and go. But she said he had this crush on me, and she promised him she'd introduce him to me. So, what the hell—I agreed to meet him.

He wasn't a bad-looking guy, with fair skin, a nice build, and curly hair—kind of a sexy Spanish dude. At first I was like, *How is this guy her cousin and she's black?* But I came to find out that he was half black, half Spanish. I started kicking it with Danny to see where he was coming from, not just because he was nice looking—looks weren't all that serious to me. You had to have something special about yourself to gain my attention. Danny had somewhat of a shy demeanor. He tried to appear like he was street, but I saw right through that act.

The day we met he was like, "Yo, yo, what's up with you?" I thought it sounded so corny coming from him, but I played along.

"Nothing, just chilling," I said bluntly.

He had a nice car, and I was kind of impressed. He asked me to go out with him, and I was like, "*Um*—why not?" I could see he was the type of guy who was being taken care of by his parents, but he wanted to act like he was a street dude. Our first date ended up turning into a short relationship. He kept buying things and kept my pockets loaded with cash. See, his father ran mostly every number spot in Harlem and the Bronx. He and his brother would have to collect the money from the spots, and not only did they get paid from that, but they added their own little twist to the game. They would set up stickups to rob their father's number spots. Then they would take the money they made and buy cocaine to sell. So Danny had crazy dough and was very generous too—especially to me.

He would come over practically every day and give me a bag full of cocaine to make my own money. I would hit the Cosmo and sell it. Sure, it was wrong, but fuck it—I was making money. I hit Moms off to help her pay bills, bought her perfume, and gave her pocket money to play her numbers or do whatever she wanted to do. Being broke was the last thing on the menu dealing with this dude. When I went shopping, I would bring whomever with me and let them buy whatever they wanted. I even had a little gold Mercedes emblem made for each of the girls. I invited them down to the Cosmo one night to present them with their medallions.

"I know y'all are wondering why I called you down here

tonight," I said to them as the DJ cut up Cheryl Lynn's "To Be Real." I could see by the expression on their faces that they had no clue.

"Well, The Mercedes Ladies have been through a lot of disappointments this year," I began, and D interrupted me.

"Shelly, please don't tell us you're quitting."

"Far from it," I said. "But I am tired of waiting for men to do right by us. I thought it was time we started to do for ourselves." Then I raised my hand to reveal five gold necklaces with shining Mercedes emblems dangling on the end.

"Whooo, girl, you went and did it now," said Nettie as they all excitedly reached for their Mercedes Ladies chains.

"This is our bond for life," said D her voice suddenly serious. "Whatever they do to us, we'll always be Mercedes Young Ladies for life."

Everybody raised a glass and drank a toast.

"To The Mercedes Ladies!" we all said, and drained our glasses before a night of partying Big Willy style. I made sure my girls enjoyed themselves. The bill was on me.

Night after night, life with Danny went on first-class as usual. I had so much cocaine, I would be in the Cosmo with D giving the shit away. I would bless friends, family, whoever I felt like. I ran into my cousin Essie and hit her Hoover ass off. You know she was loving that. As for me—*what?* I *stayed* loaded off the shit. It was nothing, and I had so much of it.

But after a while, even though the money was crazy, I was not feeling the homie. Believe me, Danny did nothing wrong to me, but I started feeling smothered. I guess I was not used to being in a relationship. I decided to break it off and it was not easy. I had to do what I had to do. The girls didn't understand. "What? Girl, you crazy!" I would hear constantly. "With all that dough he gives you? Yo, you buggin'."

Danny took it pretty hard but I was not scared of him. He would call me on the phone threatening to kill me, but I thought he was all talk. Then one day he came over, supposedly wanting to talk, and my dumb ass let him in. He got in the living room, walked over to the window, and the next thing I knew, this motherfucker pulled a gun out and pointed it to my head.

"You wanna leave me, huh?" he said with tears in his eyes. "You think it's some motherfucking joke, huh? I'll kill you, and I don't give a fuck. Then I'll kill myself before anyone comes." I looked at him showing no fear. I was a little surprised that he had enough heart to put a gun to my head, but I knew he wasn't as street as he acted.

"Do what ya got to do," I told him coolly.

He just looked at me with the Cowardly Lion expression. *Ooo—if I only had the nerve!* Then he put the gun back in his pants and left. Once the door shut, I was like, Oh, shit, this cat could have killed my ass and nobody would know. After his stupid ass left, that's when the fear finally hit me. Later I heard he was trying to start silly rumors about me sleeping around, but I knew it was out of anger. I did not sleep on him, though; I always walked the streets with the third eye open.

Chapter 48

Prince of the Hood

Even after breaking up with Danny I stayed in the mix. One night D and I were hanging out, and guess who I ran into? The one and only gentleman, Gee himself. I was as surprised to see him as he was to see me, and I thought he looked as charming as ever. In fact, he looked even better than when I first met him while hanging out with my cousin. He wore a brown mink jacket with some custom-made pants. His skin was glowing and the haircut was tight. He was looking like street royalty and his attitude went along with the gear. Gee was with his brother and some other guys, and he introduced them to me and D. He inquired what I was up to, and without giving any details I simply replied, "Just enjoying the night," trying to sound all grown-up and shit.

"Why didn't you show up to the dance that I gave you a special invite to?" he asked in a gentlemanly way. I put that innocent young girl smile on my face. He did give me money to buy an outfit for that occasion, but I did not feel I owed him any explanation.

"Oh, I am sorry," I said, "but my family was in the middle of moving and getting settled in the new place. I still have the money if you want."

Before I could finish, he stopped me. It was clear that I

shouldn't insult him by talking about money. I felt he was acting more like a protector than someone just trying to get in my pants. It was like he knew I wasn't really about streets, but the streets were trying to snatch me up. He started scolding me for being out late, and I became defensive.

"Who are you to tell her what to do?" said D, taking the words out of my mouth. But she was no challenge for him. Shit, Gee was the man. You could tell the streets respected him. But we had no idea just how gangster he truly was. We would find out soon enough though.

When it was time to go home, Gee ordered one of his boys to take us home immediately. I could have been offended, because I was not used to any man or woman—except for my mother—telling me what to do. But I was tired of hanging out that night, anyway; plus we couldn't be mad at a free ride home. I promised to meet him the following day at one of his many clubs.

I got home and hit the bed. I lay there for a minute, thinking about Gee. I wasn't on some love shit or anything like that, but I wondered why he was so interested in my well-being every time he saw me. He never came off like he was flirting or being disrespectful, but rather as if he cared about my well-being in the streets. Unable to figure out where he was really coming from, I started dozing off to sleep.

The next evening I met Gee at his club right off of Alexander Avenue as promised. I brought my girl D along, just in case. I felt better having some backup with me. We reached the address expecting to see a clublike atmosphere, but instead we found a long deserted block with a building that looked like a warehouse in the middle. We were about to turn around and leave when we saw some people come out of the door. We went up to them and asked if they knew who Gee was. They looked us up and down like, *What the hell y'all want Gee for?*

"May I ask who are y'all young ladies?" one older guy of the bunch said, in a stern but respectful way. We did not hesitate to answer.

"He is expecting us," we responded. "He asked us to meet him here."

The man with salt-and-pepper hair seemed to accept this answer. He knocked on the door, told the doorman to let us in, then told us to have a seat at the bar. This was one of those instances when being female definitely helped us. If we were some cats looking for Gee, I don't think it would have gone down this smoothly.

As we entered the club, we felt like we were walking into a scene from a gangster movie. Guys, old and young, sat around makeshift gambling tables counting money with cigars in their mouths, drinks at their sides, and jewelry dripping from the neck and wrist. Whether the dice was being thrown or the cards were being dealt, all you saw was money being tossed around on the tables. The chicks in there were sitting around like some sort of decorations. They had the tight-fitting dresses on, and their hair looked like they were in the beauty parlor all day, with dainty jewelry dripping from their ears and adorning their chests.

They all paused for a moment to check us out as we walked in. You could see they were wondering who these new faces were. The guys probably thought, *Oh, just some more gold-diggin' chicks*, while the girls looked at us like, *Who are these hood rats coming up in here?* D and I had our usual jeans, T-shirts, and sneakers on. D had her hair net hanging from her braids, and I had my hair all slicked back in a ponytail with the regular hood jewelry on. Ya know, the big old shrimp earrings and our Mercedes emblems dangling around our necks.

As we were sitting down, the door buzzer rang, and the old guy, who acted as the bouncer of the joint, the one who let us in, looked through the peephole and unlocked the door. In came Gee, surrounded by an entourage befitting street royalty. The whole room literally paused as he walked in. He looked like the black Godfather of the hood. Everyone tried to gain his attention; you could clearly see he was the captain running this ship and everybody else was merely a faithful soldier. One of his soldiers gave him a signal that he had company and when he looked over toward the bar, he noticed us. Gee started walking toward us with a megawatt smile.

"Hey, Gee," the chicks called, trying to get his attention.

"How you doing?" he said smoothly as he looked at them. "I'll catch up with you later, all right?" Ever the gentleman, he returned his gaze to us, still smiling.

I was caught in a daze for a moment. This was the kind of man that commanded my full attention—strong, bad-boyish attitude, classy, mysterious, and well dressed. Whatever he said, people would jump up with no hesitation. He was very secure and in control. I had to struggle to keep everything very businesslike.

I snapped out of it as he sat down next to us. I felt so nervous, and he could tell, because he smoothed it out with his soft-spoken tone and smile.

"Y'all all right?" he asked. "Need anything?"

"No, we're all right, Gee, thanks," I responded.

"You're sure? Did my people treat y'all good?"

"Yeah," I said with a smile. "They was polite."

He kept talking to me, making sure I was comfortable with the atmosphere in the club. D was her usual self, running her mouth, trying hard to be noticed with her ghetto mannerisms.

"Oh, is that a mink?" she asked. "What kind is it? Do you get facials? 'Cause your skin is *so* smooth!" I was trying to catch eye contact with her, like, *Damn, D, chill. You're acting like you ain't got no kind of class about yourself. Shut the fuck up, already!* But she ignored my facial hints and kept right on talking. I could tell that he saw right through her. Come on, I know he had all kinds of Ds throwing themselves at him. She kept trying to throw the bait, but he wasn't biting. I liked this man's style. He was a real class act.

Once I became comfortable with Gee and the setting, I knew I had to get down to business before everyone else came bum-rushing him. You could see that everybody in there was anxiously awaiting his undivided attention, whether for business purposes or just to be noticed by him. I had not really planned on presenting this business proposition to him, but then I was like, Why not? He looked like he knew a lot of people, and Mercedes Ladies needed all the help we could get. I decided to run with the opportunity, even though it just hit me.

"Why did you want us to meet with you tonight?" I said, getting straight to the point. He liked my boldness.

"Why don't you tell me?" he replied.

I started pitching The Mercedes Ladies, how we started and who we were. He seemed very interested in what I was saying, and I appreciated that. It was almost like he had sensed something about me from the start. Like he knew what I was pitching better than I could even express to him. Before I knew it, I was asking him to manage us.

"How much do y'all need to set it off?" he replied without hesitation.

Wow! I thought to myself. *What now?* I really did not know how to answer that question, because I never expected to be having this conversation. Then an alarm just went off in my head, and in all one breath I said, "We need outfits for our shows, a rehearsal hall to practice at, a vocal coach, promotional pictures, a recording contract, and movie deals. Hey, if you can make it happen, we're ready."

I felt like somebody who just was granted three wishes, and I went for more, wanting to get them all out in one shot. Call me crazy, but I was not playing. From the look on his face, I could see that he saw me in a whole different light. No, I was not the normal round-the-way girl.

"I can see that you have goals and you're going after them," he said. "I respect that." After the meeting with our hood prince, he ordered one of his soldiers to drive us home. While being escorted out by the guy who was gonna drive, we could feel Gee's eyes on us until the door closed behind us. By the time we reached home he had called my house to make sure I went straight home. Yo, Gee was no joke.

Chapter 49

A Bed Full of Money

The following week I met with Gee to tell him we had a show coming up and needed outfits. "No problem," he said, but this time he wanted to come to my house. Moms had no problem with that. She had been hearing so much about this hood prince, she could not wait to meet him.

To my surprise, he showed up just as he said he would. This time he was dressed down with jeans, a sweatshirt, and sneakers. He was very casual, but he still had that finesse about him. It was obvious that clothes did not make this man. He was still fine in whatever he wore. I guess he wanted to see how we were living before he invested in the group, but he didn't want to look too flashy in front of my mother.

As he entered the apartment, Moms was grinning from ear to ear. I could just read her mind as she greeted him—*Mmm, good looking with money*. The rest of the girls in the apartment were staring him down too. He seemed very much at home in a houseful of bright-eyed women. He soon made himself comfortable and acted as if he'd known everybody for years, especially my moms. When she liked you, she would talk you to death. I mean, literally talk, talk, talk—but he knew how to handle her with ease.

Still Mom had her way of letting you know who was really in charge.

"Mercedes Ladies need someone to sponsor them," she said, getting right to the point. "I have been managing them without finances, you see. I've been in music before, so I know what I am doing—all we need is a sponsor." She went on and on, but believe it or not, it worked.

"Yeah, tell me what they need," he said. "Like I told Shelly, I need to know how much it's going to cost, outfits and all. I'll make sure they have it." He also mentioned that he wanted us to meet some people he knew in the music business. I thought Mom's approach would drive him away, but he was actually receptive to her demands. When he was ready to leave, D and I walked him downstairs where his dedicated soldiers awaited. The whole block's eyes were on us. You could see the curious minds at work as we walked toward the different-colored Benz sedans that were lined up waiting for him.

We had another show booked for us through the David Winfield Foundation. Before the show Gee called to tell us that he bought us some outfits for our pictures. We met with him to pick up the outfits, expecting some bargain shit. But when he opened up the trunk of his car, we were stunned to see these fancy boxes.

"Go ahead, open them," he said.

We ripped open the packages and inside were these beautiful print dresses, brown with pink leaves on them. The material felt smooth, like you could throw them and bend them and a wrinkle wouldn't even think of popping up. We looked inside the outfits and the labels read, *100 percent silk*. We looked at one another silently like, *Wow!*

The outfits felt fabulous. D and I tried holding our composure, but we had to say something.

"Damn," said D and then we both burst out laughing. Gee told us to take the outfits to the rest of the girls, and then handed us some money to pay for the pictures.

"Make sure y'all go straight home," he said as usual. "There's cab fare in there too."

Here he goes with the authoritative shit, I thought to myself. It was okay, though, I decided as he rode off into the sunset. I was kind of getting used to it.

Everything moved at a fast pace with Gee. Anything we needed, all we had to do was ask and it was given. He even helped Moms out when we got in trouble with the rent. It was all too good to be true, like a Cinderella hood story. I never really took the time to think or even guess what Gee actually did to make all that cash. All I knew was he had loyal soldiers, hot rides, and lots of women and men wanting to be around him. Most of all, he was truly looking out for us. I didn't care about anything else.

One nice spring afternoon, Gee told me to meet him at his spot. He was supposed to give me money for the outfits for our next show. D and my sisters Camela and Lizzy came along with me. Gee was late showing up, but we just waited patiently outside the spot. Finally we saw the Benz rolling up, and to my surprise, he was rolling alone.

"No bodyguards today, eh?" I said jokingly.

He smiled but said nothing.

"What's up, girls?" he said after parking the car and stepping out of the gleaming whip. "Were y'all waiting long?"

"No," we said, lying our butts off—it had been about an hour. But we would never have acted upset—not with Gee. We all had the Colgate smiles on our faces as he approached us. I kind of think he liked that almost "Polly Purebred" look about us. You know—the innocent look. That illusion came crashing down when D began running her mouth like always, but by now he knew her whole profile.

Gee was like, "Do you ever shut up?"

Of course she tried to outtalk him, but he just kept putting the focus back on the group as a whole. By now it had started getting dark.

"I'll drive y'all home," he offered, and we were fine with that. We all piled up in the Benz, talking loud and just enjoying the ride, when we noticed that he'd passed the turn for our block.

"Where are you taking us?" I asked.

"Change of plans, girls. I am taking y'all for a ride. I have to take care of something." He got on the phone and jokingly told my mother, "I am kidnapping your daughters, but they will be returned."

"Okay, Gee," she said in an almost girlish manner. "That's no problem. I know they'll be all right with you."

Yo, Mom, I thought to myself, *how do you know he's joking?* It's amazing what having money can do—sometimes it even buys a mother's trust too. After about an hour on the road to who knows where, we pulled up into the driveway of this huge, beautiful house.

"Who lives here?" I blurted out, already knowing the answer.

"This is my house," he responded proudly.

"Damn!" D said with amazement.

Look how my hood prince is living, I thought.

We strolled through the heavily secured front door and discovered that the inside of Gee's house was just as beautiful as the outside. It was a big, luxurious home, like the ones you see on *Dynasty* or *Lifestyles of the Rich and Famous.* As Mercedes Ladies we tried our best to act cool, but come on—we grew up in projects and tenement buildings. We'd never been up close to anything like this. He saw the expression on our faces and he began to give us a tour of the premises. As he took us from room to room, I was lost for words. We finally arrived in this big-ass bedroom that was bigger than our whole apartment. It was richly decorated with silk sheets on the bed and the windows all perfectly laced with curtains.

As I examined every detail of the décor, Gee said nice and calmly: "This is me and my wife's bedroom."

Hold up! I thought, *Rewind.* Did he just say "me and my *wife's*"? The shit played over in my head again, and this time it hit me hard. It's not like I wanted this man as a boyfriend or anything. It was more, like . . . well—I guess I did have a crush on him. Even though he was an older man, I realized I had feelings for him. But he'd never know from me. I showed no expression, even though my heart felt crushed. We approached another room, down the hall from the master bedroom. This room was like an office/guest room.

He said, "I need you girls to help me," as he opened up the door.

I was thinking, *Okay, now what the hell are you up to? I am not down for no freaky shit. Oh, I get it now. This is payback time for all the money he gave us.* All types of shit was running through my mind. I looked at my sisters, and they just stood there with the innocent little girl smiles on their faces. I looked at D. She was all happy and shit, you know, she was down for whatever.

He opened the door, and on the bed were three brown shopping bags. He walked over to the bed and turned the bags over. Out comes all this money, stacks and stacks. Yes, dough, mulla, dollar-dollar bills, y'all. We were all just lost for words, except, of course, D. She said, "Oh, shit, what the fuck? Look at all this fucking money." Then she said something silly, like, "Oh, this is for us?"

My sister just looked shocked, like, *Oh my God.* He smiled with that bad-boyish look and said, "No . . . but I need y'all to help me count it."

It seemed like we were counting for hours. He even left us there a few times. I was like, Damn, he really trusts us. We could have been counting/stashing it in our bras, pockets, wherever we could stash it, but he must have known we weren't like that. He trusted us, but I didn't get it. He knew we had never seen shit like this before.

We were finally finished, and he said, "I got some food. Let's eat." We were ready for that.

While eating I asked out of curiosity, "Where is your wife?"

He replied, "Her and my daughter is on vacation." He then stated, "Y'all can crash in the guest room, and I will take y'all home in the morning."

Morning came and we were ready to go, but first he

brought us breakfast. I trusted him more than anything now. He did not once try or give any type of gesture to hit on any one of us. Even though D kept swinging her ass at him all night, ya know, throwing the body language, he paid it no attention.

Chapter 50

Stranger and Stranger

Dealing with Gee, shit, all sorts of strange shit started happening around us. I mean, for instance, there was this man that came out of nowhere. He came up to us at one of our shows and introduced himself as Lionel. He was an older man, who looked and sounded West Indian or from one of the Caribbean countries. He started hanging around us; I assume he was searching for the weakest link, whoever he could get to or whatever it was that he was looking for. He got to get closer to us through, who else, D. She felt he was an older man that liked her, so she was going to use him for rides, money, whatever she could get from him. He started coming to the house. He claimed he was some type of spiritual healer from Jamaica. Moms believed him; she thought he was so nice. He was giving her all kinds of herbal remedies, and that caught her attention. She thought he was some man trying to get next to D or really was a God-sent spiritual healer. I don't know, but he just kept hanging around the house. Whenever we had a show, he would pop up, but I could see he was trying hard to win our trust, to be all up in the house.

Another incident happened about three o'clock one morning. The detectives knocked on the door looking for me. My mom woke me up, and they said they wanted to take me downtown to identify a body of a man. They claimed they found this man shot in the head in his car and my name, phone number, and address were in his pocket. My moms said hell no. She refused to let them take me anywhere. Then they tried describing him. I knew who he was. His name was Tee; I met him through Gee, who used to have him drive us home sometimes, or he would volunteer. He had a phat ride, with a sunroof. He was a chubby guy and was always dressed and smelled good. He asked me for my number one time, and I gave it to him simply because he was a chill brother, that's it. He used to call me to go out with him, but I kept pushing it off and usually blamed it on group business. Gee knew he liked me, because he used to tease me about him. He then would say, "You don't need no headaches [referring to men in general]. Concentrate on your career." Hanging around Gee, I used to learn a lot about the streets just by watching, and he used to tell me a lot to school me.

Anyway, I did not give in to any of Tee's offers. He was a quiet type of dude, cool and shit, but no, I wasn't interested. It wasn't any of the detectives' business whether I knew him or not. I told them I didn't know the guy and I didn't know why my address or number was found on him. Besides, I wasn't really sure if it was Tee or not: I used to meet a lot of guys that were chubby and had rides. They finally left after my mom got firm about leaving her daughter alone. According to my brother Cooley our phone was tapped. He claimed he could hear a tapping sound on the phone, which usually meant somebody was listening to our calls. Of course his ass would know. A lot of times it seemed like we were being followed. There was just a lot of bizarre shit happening around us.

Early one morning Mom woke us up in a frenzied state. We thought someone died or something. She was like, "Oh my God, no, not Gee." We were like, "What happened?" She said, "Gee is in the newspaper." We were puzzled as we started reading the article. They claimed to have found all of this money on him and got him for some tax thing. Then they alleged that he was one of the biggest drug kingpins in New York. They had him labeled as a kingpin they had been investigating for years.

Yo, it was like they drove a Mack truck right through me. Not Gee, they made him out to be some crazy killer gangster, who did not give a shit. That was not the Gee we knew at all. They were lying. Someone was framing him, because they were jealous of him. We all started crying, "That's not fair, not our Gee. . . ."

We tried reaching him, but no one was talking. It was all over the media, "The Big-Time Kingpin Caught." Someone snitched, and they had enough evidence to put him away for life. We couldn't write or see him; he was locked away in an undisclosed prison. Away and gone, that was all she wrote for The Mercedes Ladies/Gee phase. I still think about him until this day. By the way, the older Jamaican man, who was hanging around us so much, vanished with no trace. Moms said that he was probably an undercover for the FBI and wanted to know our connection with Gee.

Chapter 51

A Side I Never Saw

The clock was still ticking, and time was slowly but surely eating at The Mercedes Ladies, but we were still determined.

Trying to find which way is up in this game, I decided to give my man Donald Dee a call; besides, it had been a while since we hung out. He was in the studio, by this time, and was producing tracks and shit. I started chilling with him at the studio, and I went to some of his shows. He was happy to have me around again, at least that's the way he acted. He was introducing me to a lot of people, singers, producers, and rappers that he was producing. I was not dating anyone, nor thinking about it. My mind was in sort of a lost state, searching for a piece of this well-deserved pie. I would go and hang out with Donald at one of the clubs that he DJ'd at.

This is when I met this MC duo by the name of Dr. Jekyll and Mr. Hyde. I saw them around before, and they were on the same bill as us when we played at the Hotel Diplomat, but we never really kicked it with them. They were different from other MCs. Their style was more sophisticated, with the way they dressed and carried themselves. Hyde was the tall one with an Afro. He had lips for days and a big bright smile. The other one, Jekyll, was shorter, wore glasses, and had that intelligent look about himself. You could see he was going to be into some type of business when he got older. I used to think of them as the gentlemen MC duo; they were never rude, always polite, with a smile on their faces.

Well, hanging out one night at the club, Hyde and I started kicking it. He was mad cool, and we'd talk on the phone and meet each other at the club, stuff like that. I think we had an attraction for each other; it became a weird relationship. We got along well. It was sort of like a girlfriend/boyfriend type of thing, but we never made out or anything. We did slow-dance one time at the club and almost kissed, but it didn't happen— because of me. It wasn't like I didn't like him or anything, but for some reason, I would run away from relationships if I felt they were going to get serious. I think he became mad at me, because I would not let the relationship go any further. It sort of faded away. I did like him, and I liked being around him, but I didn't know why I ran away from the relationship.

During this one show Donald had, he introduced me to this girl name Sonia. She was working for this New York radio station, 92FM WKTU. She was mixed with Italian and Arab. According to Donald, her parents were rich, but she always ran away from home just to hang out in the hood. She hung around Donald; that's how her and me became close. First, I did not know what the connection was between Donald and her. Every time I came to the studio or one of his shows, she was always there. He used to say, "Yo, Shelly, she wants me bad. When I go to her house, she treats me like a king. I be asleep all up in her bedroom and shit," trying to insinuate that they had something going on.

But after a while, hanging with her, and seeing the way she acted around him, I saw Donald was frontin'. Sonia didn't like him like that. She was the type that liked to hang out with people from the streets to act cool while doing her interviews for the radio station she worked at. She was a very vain person. Being around her, I would say she liked to tease guys; you know, smile all up in their faces, acting like she felt them, but never doing anything with them. This girl loved to stay in the mirror. I mean, she would literally look at herself and put makeup on every two minutes. Then she would carry a blow-dryer in her bag and always found a bathroom to go blow-dry her hair. She would wear purple everything, outfits, shoes, and makeup, because she was in love with Prince. She thought she was Apollonia (Prince's girl)—Prince was popular at this time. She would wear glitter and diamonds—all of this in the middle of the day—and was always dressed like she was going to a big ball. She was a unique girl; one that I had never come across in my life, and for some reason, we clicked, even though we came from different walks of life. She was very good at running her mouth on an intellectual level, and on occasions, she would mix it with the hood lingo that she picked up hanging around. Since she was very knowledgeable about things, Donald was amused by her. I think this was because she was different from what he grew up around.

One time she asked me to ride with her to her house to get some clothes, after we had just came from one of Donald's shows. That was convenient, because I wanted to see for myself this big mansion Donald said she lived in. She lived way out in Long Island in a gated community. She called for a driver to pick us up at the train station; this was at, like, six o'clock in the morning. The driver met us at the train station and drove us to this big-ass mansion, which turned out to be her house.

We got out, and I was just looking around, and then this tall white lady, with long brownish hair and a snobbish attitude, came to the door as Sonia went into the house. She started questioning Sonia with this heavy Italian accent, "Where the hell you been? Who's this girl you're bringing to my house? You know, Sonia, I don't like that." I guess she meant bringing strangers to the house. She was talking and checking me out from head to toe. I just stood there, amazed by this big-ass house.

Then all of a sudden, Sonia started cursing her mother out, I mean, like, "Don't fucking start questioning me. You get on my fucking nerves, that's why I don't stay home," and then proceeded to walk up the stairs. "Come on, Shelly."

Her mother looked at me and said, "I'm sorry about this. Your name is Shelly? Yes, well, Shelly, we worry about my daughter being out there night after night."

I did not know what to say. I just said, "It's all right," and then Sonia started yelling again, "Leave me the fuck alone, bitch, damn it."

Then Sonia said to me as we were approaching her room, "Don't pay my mother no mind. All she do is run her mouth." Then Sonia slammed her door. I could hear her mother still fussing, but Sonia didn't care. I never dreamed of cursing at my moms. It was so bad that I started feeling uncomfortable. I mean, Moms would have beat the living shit out of me before I could get it out, *slap*, knock my ass out. I couldn't even act like I had an attitude with my moms. She did not play that. You know the old saying "I brought your ass in this world, I'll take you out"—the black mothers' anthem.

From the arguing between them, I gathered that all they wanted her to do was go to school, and that's it. I was kind of mad at Sonia. I was like, *Damn! How could you disrespect your moms like that? All of this shit you got going on and you don't appreciate it.* She didn't have to worry about bills, a roof over her head, food for the house, nothing. Just go to school. She was running away from all of this, and I was trying to find this. She put on her clothes and argued some more with her mother, and then we finally left.

Chapter 52

Who Would Believe Me?

That night she had to go to some club for the radio station to interview KC. By now KC was huge, doing well with his single. Rap was starting to hit the mainstream. Grandmaster Flash and the Furious Five had cut a few singles, and there was a big record out called "Rapper's Delight" by these cats called The Sugar Hill Gang. My girl Sha Rock and The Funky Four Plus One More had a hit with "That's the Joint" and there was even an all-girl trio called Sequence with a record called *Funk You Up*. The singles were hitting all over.

Sonia wanted me to go out with her and I had nothing planned anyway, so I went. We got to the club, and it was packed. She started asking for KC and his manager, Ron. The club bouncers directed us over to this bar area, and lo and behold, who do I see sitting there but Ron? He knew Sonia from the radio station she worked for. He saw us coming his way.

"Hi, Ron," Sonia said. "Where is KC? I am here to interview him. And by the way, this is my friend Shelly."

He smiled like nothing had ever happened. "Oh, Mercedes Ladies, I know her. What's up, Shelly?"

Sonia was surprised to see we knew each other, because I never told her I knew KC and Ron. I played it off; it was all business. Besides, who knows, maybe he'd make it up to us and put us on for real this time.

"What's up, Ron? How have you been?" I asked. We acted like two old friends that hadn't seen each other in a long time.

Then KC came from behind and greeted us. He was happy to see me, and he gave me a big hug. Sonia was like, "You're ready for this interview, KC? Where can we go without the noise?" He had a place in the back of the club that was set up already for the interview.

"Come on, Shelly," Sonia said. "You can watch the interview."

Then Ron interrupted and said, "Go ahead and do the interview. I want to show Shelly my new office around the corner." Sonia looked at me like, *That's okay with me if it's okay with you.* I hesitated for a sec, and then I thought, *What harm can there be? Besides, it's Ron.* He just wanted to show off his new office. The office was just around the corner. We approached this tall office building. It looked like it was closed for the day, but he had a key to open the lobby door, so we went in. We took the elevator up and got off and came to his office. It was kind of small, but still a big move because of the single KC had. He started giving me a tour of the office.

"Wow, looks like you're moving up," I said as he told me what was what.

"I know you're gonna look out for The Mercedes Ladies now, Ron. Besides, you owe us one. You know that shit was not right what you did."

"That was a business decision I had to make," said Ron, "but I'll make it up to y'all, don't worry."

That was the end of that conversation.

"Have a seat," he said, pointing to the corner where there was nothing but a couch that turned into a bedlike piece of furniture. He said the real office furniture was coming soon. Then Ron sat beside me and started moving closer. I quickly moved away, but he kept moving toward me as I pushed him away. That's when he became forceful.

"Yo!" I yelled while trying to push him away. "What are you doing?"

I tried to get up, but he held me down. I was shocked at the behavior of this man I thought I knew. No matter how many times I said, "Stop!" he was not trying to hear me. He showed absolutely no respect for my feelings, like he could just do whatever he wanted because of who he was.

"No, Ron!" I yelled, thinking, *Shit! This man is strong. He's overpowering me.* I noticed a lamp on the table, and I went to grab it to hit him, but he just snatched it out of my hand. He started pulling my pants down.

"No, Ron!" I yelled, but it was no use.

He started fumbling with my underwear and next thing I knew, he was on top of me handling his business. I could not believe this shit was happening, especially from such a business-like type of person. When he finally finished, he got off of me without saying a word. I just pulled my shit up and left, wiping a few tears from my face. The elevator couldn't have come fast enough for me.

While walking back to the club, I felt used, angry, and stupid. How could I explain this shit to anyone? The first thing they would think was, *Why did you go up there in the first place?* I did not know whether to call this a rape. Maybe he did not take my "no" seriously. But I *did* say no—that much I knew. Damn! What was I supposed to do? Besides, who was going to believe my word against his? One thing was sure: Ron had hurt me again. Mentally wasn't enough; now it was physically, that bastard!

I met up with Sonia back at the club, and she noticed the look on my face right away. For some reason, I did not have to say anything to her. I felt she knew. But I felt so embarrassed, I made her promise never to tell anyone.

Chapter 53

Road Trip With the Diva

The following week Sonia called to ask if I wanted to take a trip to Philly. There was going to be a big music seminar called "Jack the Rapper," and everyone who was somebody was going to be there. She said it was a hundred dollars for registration fees, plus hotel and transportation fees. I was like, "Damn, Sonia. I don't have it like that. I can't afford to go."

She said, "Oh, girl, don't worry. I got you. Plus the radio station is sponsoring me to go."

The weekend came, and I was ready to go—this was going to be exciting for me. Sonia had the bus tickets for us, and she said she was registered already at the hotel, so we could share a room; plus she had special passes. We reached Philly after about three hours. The bus let us out at the Philly bus station, and then we took a cab to the hotel.

We got there and went to check in at the registration desk. Sonia found out that the radio station only paid for one. I was pissed, but clever Sonia was like, "We'll get into everything, don't worry, and the room has two beds. Girl, I got you," in a silly girl manner.

The seminar turned out to be more than I can explain. In the lobby I saw people like Joe Jackson, Jesse Jackson, James Brown, I mean, the list goes on. People I saw for years on TV were right there in front of me—this was an amazing feeling. I was overwhelmed for a moment, but I knew I had to keep my composure. I wasn't going to play myself like some groupie. Besides, Sonia and I were attracting a lot of people ourselves. People were staring us down like we were stars and shit. We were both tall, big, light-skinned, and very attractive—I must add. Plus Sonia, with her glitter purple dress, purple makeup, purple shoes, big diamond earrings, and necklace—in broad daylight—I think played a big part too. I was like, "Sonia, you dress like we are going to a ball or something."

She was like, "You know I have to dress to impress." That's Sonia. I thought it was a bit too much, but when you think about it, this was her way to draw attention to herself.

Once we got settled in our room, we got dressed up. Well, Sonia was still dressed up from the daytime, and she hooked me up with one of her expensive dresses out of her closet, so I was looking like 'em. We went downstairs to see what events were happening for the evening. Every room in the hotel was having a party going on, and we went to them all. We finessed our way into everything with no problem at the door. Sonia didn't drink or nothing. She just kept running to the mirror with her portable blow-dryer every second. I mean, homegirl was obsessed with that shit.

At one of the parties, this guy was staring me down, not in a disrespectful way, but more in a gentlemanly way. I had seen him in the lobby earlier on that day. We had eye contact for a second, but that was that. He walked over to me and introduced himself as Gregory Jones. He was an author who had just finished his book on Michael Jackson. He seemed to be quiet, very smooth, and nice. There was something about him I admired. I guess his accomplishment attracted me; plus he wasn't bad looking. We talked through the loud music and Sonia's interruptions. I was ready to leave, but before I left, he invited me to go with him the following day to a concert honoring James Brown. You know I was down for that.

Back at the room Sonia was really getting on my nerves to

the point that I wanted to kick her ass. First of all, she wanted to hog up the bathroom, blow-dry her hair about a hundred times in one night, and put on makeup on top of what she already had on just to go to sleep. It was irritating as hell. I did not know how I was gonna survive another day with her. I was not used to this primadonna/princess type of attitude of hers, so I was screaming on her ass. We argued until we fell asleep.

The next day came and I was looking forward to the concert. As planned, I met him downstairs in the lobby. The concert was great; James Brown tore the place down. I couldn't even describe it in words. Seeing him in person onstage, what? My brother Ronnie would've gone bananas; he used to imitate him to make me and my sisters laugh. He would have loved this; it was fantastic. James Brown had mad makeup on his face. It looked like you could've scraped his face and had a supply of foundation for months. It still was a hell of an experience.

After the concert, Gregory had to do a quick book signing at one of the stores in Philly, so I went with him. The book signing turned out to be good. There were a lot of people wanting him to sign their book and meet him. He wasn't the talkative type, but when he spoke, he had a very mild tone and was somewhat shy. That was cool with me. I was enjoying the moments he was showing me.

He invited me back to his room, and I thought, *Oh no, I am not falling for this shit again*. Even though he'd been nothing but a perfect gentlemen the whole evening, I wanted to make sure I was covered. So before I went up, I called Sonia back at the room and told her he wanted me to go to his room with him. She was like, "Okay, Shelly, remember what happened before with Ron."

I said, "That's why I am calling you, because I want you to wait about ten minutes. Then I want you to knock on his hotel door and say it's an emergency, and that I have to come quick. Make up some shit, Sonia, okay?"

She agreed to the plan, but I heard a little uncertainty in

her voice. I knew I should've just told him no, but he showed me such a good time that night, I didn't want to appear ungrateful. I know, I know, maybe I was not playing it smart, always worrying about the next person's feelings, but one thing was for sure, I did not trust any guy's word anymore.

Once we entered his room, this mild-mannered guy tried to make his move. He wasn't forceful with it, just real smooth. He said, "Is it all right if I kiss you?" Before I could give a yeay or nay, his lips were in position.

I said, "Ah, wait a minute. I have to go to the bathroom." I thought this would bide me time until Sonia knocked on the door. Here I was in the bathroom waiting for that knock; it was twelve minutes already since I had been in his room. I was thinking, *I know she is not blow-drying her hair or putting makeup on just to come knock on the door. Come on, Sonia.*

I finally came out of the bathroom, and I looked. His ass was laying in the bed butt naked. I guess when I excused myself to the bathroom, he thought I was going to come out ready or something. I looked in astonishment. I didn't know if he should have been embarrassed or I should be. I was like, "Ah, what the hell you doing?" Then the knock came. Damn, about time. There couldn't be better timing than that. My girl came through. Before he could answer, I was like, "Who is it?" He looked at me like, *This is my room. Why are you answering?* I did not care.

"Who is it?" I said all loud.

"It's Sonia, Shelly. I have an emergency. You need to come now."

He looked like, *I know this shit ain't happening.*

I just looked at him and shook my shoulders. "Ah, I got to go. You wanna cover up before I open the door?" Then I opened the door, and there she was, smiling away, and then I closed the door behind me. Even though she got on my nerves the whole trip, I was more than glad to see her. I wasn't about to get caught out there again.

After an exciting weekend of arguing with Sonia, a free

concert, parties, escaping a booty call, and meeting people, I was more than ready to leave Philly. Smart-ass Sonia, though, failed to tell me that she didn't have a bus ticket for me to get back. This was the topping on the cake. I was like, "Call your parents or your chauffeur to come get us, but I better get home." She finally broke down and asked her mother to use her credit cards. She could see that I was heated. During the trip back we didn't have much to say to each other.

Chapter 54

Our First Single

By the time I got back to New York, I received a call from my old friend Donald Dee. "What's up?" he said. "Where the hell you been?"

"Oh, I went with Sonia to this music seminar down in Philly," I said nonchalantly.

"*What*!" he said, sounding pissed. "And y'all niggas couldn't let me know? That shit is fucked up, both of y'all."

Of course I blamed the whole thing on Sonia.

"Oh, Donald," I said, "it was a last-minute thing, and it wasn't all that. You might have not had fun anyway."

I didn't want him to think he missed out on a wonderful event—and really, he hadn't—but he seemed to get over it easily enough.

"Well, fuck it," he said, getting to the point of his call. "I got a proposition for The Mercedes Ladies. Peep this—I am recording a single. Grandmaster Flash is going to produce it, and I want y'all to be on the track."

That shit sounded good to me.

"No question, Donald," I said point-blank. "Just let us know the time, place, and when we start."

"First, I want to meet with y'all to plan this shit right," he said. "We got to rehearse before we even think about laying it down on wax."

I had heard this before, but I was like, "Okay, Donald, no problem." I promised to get the girls together, and set up a meeting.

Rehearsals and meetings were taking place at the house. Moms let us use the living room. The rehearsals were going good for a minute, but D did not like the fact that Donald had sole control of the routines. So in the middle of the rehearsals, D and Donald were not seeing eye to eye. This led to constant arguing between them. He would get mad and start making comments about her reputation out on the streets, and they would go at it verbally.

Once we were ready for studio time and ready to start recording, D could no longer take the harsh words that Donald kept throwing her way. One night they had the blowout of all times. I mean, she called him all types of motherfuckers, and he came back with sloppy ho, "That's why niggas got your name all in the streets."

Next thing D left right in the middle of the rehearsal and vowed never to come back as long as Donald was around. She meant it. She called me to officially quit The Mercedes Ladies and said she was going to go solo. I saw she wasn't going to listen to no reasoning by me, so I told her I wished her luck. She had to do what she had to do.

That left Nettie, Camela, Lizzy, and me. Lina and Eve simply stopped coming to rehearsals, and I got tired of calling them. We continued working with Donald and Flash on the single in the studio. We were working hard to nail this single, putting in hours on top of hours. They both were very strict and hard producers. It was not an easy task working with them two. Flash, when it came to music, was a perfectionist and a genius. He would pace the studio floor back and forth with his hands behind his back. Then he would stand there with one hand on his face, in a deep-thinking position, and have the other arm wrapped around his waist. Then he closed his eyes, like he was meditating, while tapping his leg and bouncing his head up and down, making all types of expressions on his face. Then he would be silent for a minute, and then he'd run over to the studio board to do his thing.

Donald, on the other hand, was more like a mac daddy genius music producer. You know, he would be like, "Yo, peep this. You got to sing this note this way, see what I am saying? You know, like this," while demonstrating with the hand movements. "You see, you see what I am saying. Gotta nail this shit."

To me, they were both geniuses when it came to music, vocals, and producing. To be in the studio with them, you learned a lot.

The single, "Come Rock to Donald's Groove," was finally finished. We sounded hot on that track with the collaboration of Donald's vocals and Flash's production. I knew it would be a hit. It was a hot record. One night we were at home listening to the radio, and all of a sudden we heard "Come Rock to Donald's Groove, come on, clap your hands, if you're ready. Come on, clap your hands, if you're ready. Come . . . Rock to Don . . . ald's . . . Groove." We started screaming all over the house. Our shit was playing on the radio!

Moms came out of her room to see what the commotion was all about. But as soon as she heard our song coming through the radio, she could not contain herself either. By this point, the whole household was bugging out. I got on the phone to call Nettie and she was screaming too.

"They're playing our shit on the radio!"

"How crazy is that?"

"Mercedes Ladies, we're on our way!"

That was one of the most exciting moments in my life. But as soon as the celebration came to an end, it was time to get back to work.

Donald called to let us know we had some heavy rehearsals lined up. We had to prepare for some shows that had been booked to promote the single. The first show was at the Broadway International on 145th Street and Broadway. Donald came out of his pocket to get us the outfits.

"Don't worry about that," he said when we asked whether we were going to get paid for the show. "Bigger things is going to happen. Y'all in there rolling with me."

By this point in our careers, we fully understood the importance of promotion and we were all right with that. Our mindframe was, *Let's do this.*

On the day of the show, we got dressed in our fly white pantsuits. Backstage, we couldn't believe our eyes when we looked in the dressing room mirror.

"Damn, we look like superstars," I said out loud, and everybody laughed because we knew it was true.

After we saw Donald with his white linen suit, we were in star mode for real. When it was time to perform I could hear the crowd screaming as we entered the stage. We walked to our places and took our positions onstage, waiting for the beat to start.

"This shit feels good," I said to myself. But at the same time it felt funny not having Lady D performing with us. I missed her crazy ass and the energy that she used to bring at moments like this—before or even during a show. How I wished that she and Donald did not have that falling-out that made her leave. Anyway the show had to go on. We must have looked fly standing there because the crowd started screaming before the music even started. Then once that beat dropped, the place went crazy. That's when we started singing:

"Come . . . Rock . . . To. . . . Don. . . . ald's . . . Groove," we sang, putting those funky pauses between each word. "Clap your hands if you're ready / Come on, clap your hands if you're ready." That shit sounded like birds singing in the trees. Every harmony note was on point. When Donald came onstage and started his first rhyme on the song, the crowd went bananas. You could not tell me we were not on our way to stardom!

The show was a huge success. The crowd responded very well to the single, and all the other numbers we did went over big. While Donald was handling some last-minute business upstairs, the promoter walked up to congratulate me.

"The show was tight," he said. "We've got to get you back here to perform again sometime. And make sure Donald gives y'all your cut tonight. He got paid."

What made this man tell me that? Either he just wanted to show us some respect, or maybe he knew Donald when it came to money! I didn't really know. I decided not to say a word to the other girls. First I wanted to see what Donald was going to do. By the time he came back downstairs, I took him to the side where nobody could hear us.

"Donald, let me ask you something," I said as I looked him in the eye. "Did you get paid for the show?"

"Yeah, yeah," he said. "That's how I was able to pay for your outfits."

Having seen Donald in action when handling business, I knew he was full of shit. The outfits were probably already incorporated in the deal. I could just hear him telling the promoter. *Yo, I need money for the girls' outfits, besides paying them to perform.* But there was no way I could prove it, so I just looked at him like, *All right, Donald. You got us.*

When I told the girls our show money went for the outfits, they looked at me like I was nuts.

"Come on," Nettie said. "If that was the case, we could have worn jeans."

"Word," said Lizzie and Camela. "We needed that money."

But in the end, I convinced them not to sweat it.

"Let's just keep on working," I told them. "Maybe we'll get a record deal behind this."

It wasn't long before the shipment of records finally came to the office, and Donald called us to come pick up our copies. Nettie and I went to pick up the wax from the office.

"Y'all copies are in those boxes on the desk," said Donald.

I walked over to the desk and opened up a box to check out

the cover art. I looked on one side. It said *Donald's Groove by Donald Dee, produced by Grandmaster Flash*.

Okay, I told myself, *I see* their *names*. Then I flipped the record sleeve over to the other side, and there was a bunch of information about Elektra Records, the label that put it out. I looked over at Nettie in disbelief.

"Yo, Donald," I said. "Where is our name at on the single?"

"It's on there," he said. "Look!" He pointed to a block of fine print where they were thanking all different types of people. Down there in tiny letters it said, *Thanks to The Mercedes Ladies*.

"That's it?" I said in shock.

"What kind of dumb shit is that?" said Nettie.

"What did you expect?" he asked in a casual tone.

"I mean, *damn*, Donald," I said, maintaining my composure. "That's all the credit we get? We worked our asses off day and night along with you and Flash."

"At least your name was mentioned," said Donald. "Y'all gonna get what's coming to you."

After that we did not know how to feel. Part of us was mad, but we were in no position to do anything about it. That was the final cover and that record was a done deal. Anyway, it was a big step beyond anything we'd ever done before—our voices on a record and our name in print. What we did not realize was that the game was changing faster all the time. The year was 1984, and a group from Queens called Run-D.M.C. was about to blow this hip-hop culture up into a big industry.

We did three or four more shows with Donald, with nothing to show for it but a lot more promises.

"Just hold on, ladies," he would tell us. "Y'all gonna get a big payday."

Yeah, right. The only payday consisted of Donald buying us food while we hung around the studio and watched him work on other people's projects. After we got tired of that, we started fading away from Donald. I stayed in contact with him, but our relationship was never really the same again.

Donald went on to work with Ice-T and to produce his

own groups. But within a few more years, I heard he developed throat cancer. By that time he was responsible for some of the most successful groups out, including Malyra and SWV. When I heard that he was dying, it was very painful for me to endure. Regardless of everything else, that was still my homey. In his last days, I tried to reach out a few times but I never heard back.

Years later, while attending his funeral services, I reminisced about the good times we had, from that first night in Harlem World to the studio and the stage.

Rest in peace to our brother Donald Dee. You stay in our hearts forever.

Chapter 55

The Final Chapter of The Mercedes Ladies

Grandma took sick and could not care for herself, so Moms ended up having to move to Atlantic City to watch over her. Great-grandma was okay, but she was too old to take care of Grandma by herself. My sisters and I had to jump into full survival mode to take care of ourselves. I guess you could say we were well prepared for things like this from our experiences growing up. Even when we lost the apartment, we did not fold. We just had to split up and find new places to live.

The Mercedes Ladies were not really paying anybody's bills, but we weren't completely out of the music business either. D had a single called "Heart Beat" that was put out by none other than my boy Ron. I couldn't be mad at her since I never told anybody what had happened between me and him. I did worry about D a little but what could I say? She was taking her chance in the game, and I couldn't stand in the way. The song got a little radio play, and she did a couple of shows. We even went to some of her gigs to show support—after all, she still was our sister. We appreciated the fact that D never showed us anything less than full respect when she was on the solo tip. This was a good move on her part because the single did not go far, and D wasn't making no money. She was eventually dropped from the label. It's true what they say about being nice to the people you meet on the way up—you see the same ones on the way down.

I took a job at this bar in Bronx River called the Round Table. I knew one of the owners from my old block, and he always told me if I needed a job to come look him up, so I took him up on his offer. It was a popular spot that was known for selling drugs. I knew it was a risk working there, but I had to survive financially. In fact, I got D a job there too after her "Heart Beat" record fizzled out. Neither one of us knew anything about tending a bar, but this club only served straight drinks anyway, so no fancy mixing was required. The clientele inside the Round Table didn't seem to mind anyway, as long as we poured the drinks nice and strong. That way the customers were always happy, we always got good tips, and the owners never noticed. They mostly concentrated on the drug situation they had going on in there. D and I wanted nothing to do with that, and we tried to keep it that way, but drugs have a way of affecting everybody around them, like it or not.

It seemed like every damn weekend I was behind the bar there was a shoot-out inside or just outside the Round Table. Still I hung in there for a few months, until the bar got raided. It was a normal evening with sports on TV and funk on the jukebox when suddenly the front door burst open and a half dozen cops came rolling in. During the commotion, somebody threw their guns and their stash behind the bar. Of course the cops found it right away, and since I was the bartender they tried to make me take the fall. But when they had a female officer take me in the bathroom and search me, they couldn't find anything. They interrogated me for a long time about who the stuff might have belonged to. I didn't know anything, except that they had nothing on me. Hey, I was just a barmaid. In the end they took all the guys downtown to jail and let me go. I thanked God as the cops told me they better not catch me in there again.

Of course I had to get out of there, and I advised D to do the same. I wasn't trying to get locked up over someone else's mess. I'd had enough. That was my last day having anything to do with drugs, whether using, selling, or associating with them. It took me a long time to learn my lesson, but I learned it well: drugs just aren't worth all the drama and misery they can bring to your life. Especially when you know what your life is worth.

By this time my sister Lizzy had found a good job working for a big advertising company and Camela started working for a law firm downtown. See, Moms made sure those two went to a decent school called Jay Walton Thomas High School. That school trained you for secretarial jobs and stuff like that, so these young ladies were well prepared. Not everybody is so fortunate, but when you know better you do better.

Funny enough, that gig with D was the last word I heard from any of The Mercedes Ladies. DJ Nettie took a lot of civil service tests and eventually landed a job as a traffic enforcement agent. We never heard from Lina and Eva again.

While doing research for the book, I came across an old photograph of The Mercedes Young Ladies up in Club Crystal. It was taken on the same night we wore our matching gold chains. I don't know what happened to everybody else's Mercedes Ladies medallions, but I know mine ended up in the pawnshop when times got hard. It hurt me to sell it, because of all the memories we'd shared and all the history—or *herstory*—we made together. We promised each other that night that we'd be "Mercedes Ladies For Life." That's a bond from the heart that's stronger than any gold chain. Meanwhile, there are few female DJs making noise and the next generation of female MCs is messed up. Remy Ma's going on trial for attempted murder. The only female artist with a single on the radio is somebody named Lil Mama who says "My lip gloss be poppin'." I'm listening to this girl on the radio on a rainy afternoon, and I'm asking myself: "Is this what our whole hip-hop journey was about?" Well I hope she continues to grow, for her own sake, and for the sake of all the females out here.

Chapter 56

The Purpose

Back in the hospital, 2006

They took Moms upstairs to intensive care with all kinds of monitors hooked up to her. I sat there beside her bed just praying and thinking, *Mom, you can't leave me now.* The doctor came in and said to my sister Camela and me, "I am gonna be honest with you. She has a fifty-fifty chance of pulling through. It could turn for the good or bad."

Those words hit me right in the heart. I don't know how I would be able to deal with that; it was scary losing Moms. I started thinking about life, the meaning, the purpose of why we end up where we end up, the journey we go through. I thought, Damn, Moms always had to struggle. She never went after her dreams, because of the times she came through or the way it was dealt for her. Maybe she shouldn't have had so many kids. No, no, then I would not be here. But is that what life is meant to be about, struggle and then die, or can it be changed through our recognition of who we truly are? No, I got to break that cycle. I am not going to let that shit win over me.

I got off from work and went straight to the hospital; Junior was going to meet me there. I walked into her room expecting to still see her lying there. I walked over to the bed. Oh my

God, I witnessed one of God's miracles. All I could say was, "Mom . . . Mom," with tears rolling down my eyes. She was lying there with that smile of hers, and she said, "Shelly, what happened?"

I said, "You was sick, Mom, that's all."

She said, "Really? All I remember was a voice that sounded like Cooley saying, 'You gonna be all right Mom.'"

Chills ran down my arm. Remember my brother Cooley? Well, he died from AIDS over nine years ago on my birthday. I guess his spirit was with her.

She finally got well enough to get out of the hospital, and she had to stay with Junior and me until she was strong enough to travel back to Atlanta. Yes, Junior and her were still fussing, but this time he was in control only for her good. She did not like that she had to be on a strict diet and he was the enforcer. She would be on the phone talking to my sisters in Atlanta, "I can't wait to get out of New York. You know I am not used to nobody telling me what to do. Junior and Shelly are getting on my nerves, girl."

Junior and I would just laugh; we were so glad to hear that fussing.

I wondered why, after ten years, she finally visited me and all this shit happened. It must have been for some reason. You see, I had started writing my story over fifteen years ago but never followed through with it. I would jot certain things down—you know, like diary type of shit. I really didn't know what I was going to do with it. I was steady watching how the hip-hop game was growing and growing. I decided to go into managing. Hell, I knew a lot about the game to try and bring another artist through.

While pursuing the managing thing with this very talented artist I discovered from Harlem, BMDubb, I saw that things really hadn't changed much when it came to women in the industry. I would shop the demos we completed in the studio, even put a mix tape out. I was getting a lot of good feedback, setting up all kinds of meetings. It's like I thought I was right in there with this management. Hell, a hot artist, I just could not give up hip-hop; it was like hunting me. The meetings would turn out like, "I like him, but he sounds like DMX. Oh, he got the look. Uh, by the way, are you and he dating? What's up with you? Can you and me hang out?" etc. It was the old bullshit of a woman trying to be taken seriously for her work and people with power shifting it in another direction. My artist had to take on a nine-to-five; hell, you got to keep the roof over your head, but I would tell him to just keep on writing. The game looks like it's changed so dramatically now: everything became overflooded and the business shifted to the South, but I stay on the grind, you know me.

I met this guy while I was working—you know, a regular nine-to-five joint. He was doing some type of research while pursuing his degree in journalism. His name was Robert, a very nice person. We started talking about what he was in college for, and he told me he was a writer for a hip-hop magazine.

"Oh, really? Well, would you believe me if I told you I was part of the first all-female hip-hop crew?" He was shocked, and he asked me to do a story on Mercedes Ladies in his magazine.

Damn, I thought, *just when I thought the whole game was a wrap, here it comes looking for me again.*

I was ecstatic and without hesitation I said, "Of course." Well, that was just the first of the articles. From *VIBE* to *The Source* to *Stress* magazine, they just kept coming. Everyone was calling me to be on panels, appear in documentary films, or give interviews for people writing books. I always tried to say yes. After all, somebody has to represent the pain and struggles of the females who were trying to make it through.

One day the phone rang and there was an excited voice on the line. "Hello, my name is Cristina, and I find you girls' story amazing. I feel the world should know about the pioneer females who helped mold this game. We are doing a book called *Hip-Hop Divas* and we would like to feature your crew in there. Girl, y'all deserve it." I was speechless. After she hung the phone up, I was screaming.

Well, the book came out, and we were the first chapter in there. The girls were so proud. I mean, to be in a book with people like Mary J. Blige, Missy Elliott, Lauryn Hill, Lil' Kim, Foxy Brown, and Queen Latifah. Wow! And then to see my other pioneer sisters in there like Pebblee Poo, Sha Rock, and Roxanne Shante—I was overwhelmed with emotion just to see young black women finally getting the respect they earned and deserved.

Mom was so happy about her girls being in the book she told everybody. She must have called every family member all over the map, just bragging. Well, during the promotion of this book, I was introduced to the head editor of the project named Rob Kenner.

I decided to pitch to Rob that I had written down a lot of our adventures in the form of a book. He was like, "Yeah, send me a copy and let me read it." Well, I never finished it. I was just writing, so I just sent him what I had. I was thinking that if he liked it, they'd probably hire some professional writer to do it.

Well, lo and behold, that's not what happened. Yes, he loved what I had so far, but told me I had to finish it. I was like, "Okay, I'll finish it," but having to work, plus struggle through some of life's curves—it was on pause. Shit, this was hard; I was not a professional writer. Why couldn't they just have one of his writers write this while I tell the story?

But I couldn't back out. You see, I told my mother I was going to finish the story. And all of this was just a year before Moms went and got sick on me.

After my mother's heart attack, watching her lying there fighting for her life, I came to the realization that I had to finish my book. God had put me through this to make me see how precious our gifts are. There are always blessings within the struggles we go through, so in life we have to recognize the silver lining behind every dark cloud. When the bartending thing was not working out, I took a job at a hospital that was very stressful but at least nobody was going to come bust me at *work*. That job led me to meet Janet Taylor, who's a doctor at the hospital. She was amused to find out that I was in the first all-female group of hip-hop, after reading *VIBE Hip-Hop Divas*. She told me her friend, Kenard Gibbs, was the president of *VIBE* at the time. She suggested that I set up a meeting with him, and she told him about the story I was writing. I talked with him on the phone, and then he put me back in the hands of none other than Rob Kenner—what a coincidence. God was so determined to make me recognize my gift that He led me to people who believed in what I wanted to do more than I believed myself.

That's when I decided to put aside my other projects and focus on telling my story in a book form. I came to this important decision shortly before my mother was diagnosed with congestive heart failure. That's the sort of reality check that really makes you let go of the little distractions in your life and helps you reaffirm the things that are really important. Just being able to talk to my mother each day is a blessing, especially when I can share what progress I am making on the book.

One night I decided to Google the name Mercedes Ladies and I discovered that our crew's roots ran deeper than I thought.

"Junior! Check this out!" I said excitedly, calling my husband away from his Knicks game.

"What is it, Shelly?" he said, hitting the mute button on the remote.

"We go all the way back to Africa!"

"You interrupted the Knicks game to tell me that? Thank you for the knowledge of self, baby, but this is overtime."

"No, Junior, I mean The Mercedes Ladies started in Africa!"

I started reading him the article I'd found from the French newspaper *Le Monde*. It described a group of women in the West African nation of Togo (a slim little country that lies between Ghana and Benin) who signed contracts with import-export companies in Europe to ship certain types of African textiles on an exclusive basis. They made a fortune. "Nicknamed the *Nanas-Benz* (the Mercedes Ladies) after the luxury sedans they are driven around in by young chauffeurs who, so it is said, also act as gigolos when required, these modern-day Amazons, single, widowed or divorced, keep a firm hold on their own real estate, shops and Swiss bank accounts." The article went on to say that profits had fallen in recent years but that these Mercedes Ladies still account for half of the country's economy!

Even these Mercedes Ladies have a predecessor, an arms dealer named Madame Tinubu who was so powerful that she "built up an economic mini-empire and wielded decisive political influence." The paper went on to quote the African journalist and author Corine Madjo, who explained that the idea of African women as powerless victims was a lie—perpetuated by men writing their own version of history, or *his*-story. Ms. Madjo told the newspaper:

> The condition of the African woman as it has always been presented by Westerners is one big fallacy. It's wrong to say that the African woman is an inferior and doesn't take any part in decisions. Those who wrote about Africa from the 19th century on were well-off young men who brought all their class prejudices with them. The people they talked to were the village chieftains, and just because they didn't see the women, they assumed that they held no power. But in traditional African societies the women are always asked for their opinion before a decision is taken, even though they never speak in public. What's more, in traditional African society the queen mother and the first wife play a crucial political role. Nowadays the situation is very different. The men have grabbed power for themselves, and women are having to fight on every front.

All this talk of men grabbing power and women having to fight was sounding very familiar. And I'd already seen a few rap starlets driving real Benzes on TV when I had to pawn my damn Benz medallions. This research was tripping me out. The Mercedes Ladies of the Bronx could certainly learn a few lessons from Africa's Mercedes Ladies when it came to business. But it's good to know we're not alone out here.

My mother ended up back in the hospital recently. She had another heart attack, this time a silent one. But she's a strong woman, and she pulled through again. I'm starting to feel like nothing can break her down. At least I know she'll fight to the end.

When I saw her after the surgery, she said she wanted to talk to me.

"Shelly, you know what came to my mind?" she said, propped up on her hospital pillow.

"What, Mom?"

"Please finish your book," she said, then added: "Especially tell them about me," and burst out laughing.

That was all I needed as a writer—along with my husband, who has given me nothing but support, encouragement, strength, and his talent—to finish my book of a tale based on the first female hip-hop story from the hood.

Throughout our lives, everything has a purpose. For every situation—even the ones we may deem as bad—there's always a reason why we have to go through it. Whether it is to learn, to teach, or to tell—you may not see it right away, but no doubt, there's a reason.

Hey, maybe I wasn't meant to be a rapper, a singer, or an actress—that's fine with me. This girl from the hood always knew she was special. I just had to take a long journey and figure out my purpose and find it.

Afterword

It seems like you can't turn on the radio or TV these days without hearing a heated debate about how hip-hop is destroying women's self-esteem. Whether it's Don Imus, Reverend Al, or Oprah, everybody seems to have an opinion about this culture created by underprivileged kids living in the roughest inner cities of America. Yet somehow, the only voices you hear defending hip-hop culture always seem to belong to men with high-paying contracts and corporate careers to protect. And as usually happens whenever the mainstream mass media grab hold of a hot-button issue and run with it, half the story never gets told.

I have to speak. I have to add another voice to the conversation. A voice who was there in the beginning of what is now a multibillion-dollar industry known as hip-hop. Once upon a time, hip-hop was a culture, not a commodity. There were no hip-hop radio stations or hip-hop record shops or hip-hop boutiques selling the latest hip-hop fashions or hip-hop dance classes at your local health club.

All this "bitch" and "ho" madness is never going to stop until we as women start recognizing our worth. As Mercedes Ladies, we never tolerated any of that mess. Oh no! Disrespect us, or call any of us out of our names, and you'd better be ready to throw down. We demanded respect and usually got it.

I guess it was the way we were raised. Even though most of us came up from having nothing and struggling with our identities, looking back I realize that we were respected because of the way we carried ourselves. It did not matter that women of color were presented in negative ways on television. We were not considered beautiful. Our hair was considered no good. We were always the ones cleaning up someone's house if we weren't working as prostitutes. At home, most of the time we faced stressful situations with no father figures around. But coming from generations of strong women, from my great-grandmother to my grandmother to my mom, we always found a way to strive and survive. No matter what struggle they were up against, they never allowed anybody to talk to them with a lack of respect. When we walked through the neighborhood, guys could be on the corner running numbers, selling drugs, or nodding from taking drugs—still, they would stop and say, "Hello, Ms. So-and-So, how are you today? Can I help you with those bags? Can I get the door for you?"

This is the way I grew up. Women demanded respect and carried themselves in a manner to get respected, no matter what outfit they decided to put on. All this stuff about women of color being called "nappy-headed hos" or what have you, I guess it was happening somewhere behind closed doors, but in my neighborhood it simply wasn't tolerated.

And let's be real for a second, women like attention from men too. When I was growing up, if you wanted attention from the brothers of the hood, all you had to do was go outside and walk down the block with the tight jeans on, hair permed with the baby hair slick down to the sides, bangle bracelets with the matching big loop earrings hanging down. The fellas would holla at you, no doubt. "Yo, girl, what's up?" "When you gonna give me that number?" "Can I take you out?" You'd hear so many different lines coming at you, but you'd just keep on walking with your head up and a cute smile. Let's be real—that shit made you feel good. And for the most part, they never said anything disrespectful to you, if only because they knew somebody would tell your moms, your uncle, your cousin, or your brother(s), who would come looking for their ass later. You couldn't wait for the next day to slick your do even more, try on some different color earrings, perfect-fitting jeans, or in the summertime, maybe even some hot pants. Maybe you didn't look like the women on television, but you enjoyed the attention from the brothers around the block. It made you feel beautiful.

So is the love of attention a hip-hop thing or just a woman thing? Being around women of different cultural backgrounds, I've observed that women in general enjoy male attention. We like to feel beautiful and we love the feeling of being admired and desired. That's why we wear makeup and spend hours getting our hair done, or searching for clothes and shoes. To hear our man say, "Honey, you look good!" can make our day. But where did all of this disrespectful stuff come in? How did we go from women just wanting a compliment to "bitch this" and "ho that"? How did we lose the respect we used to have from the hood? What's up with all these negative stereotypes being aimed toward women of color? And why are they presented as being part of hip-hop culture?

There are so many reasons and situations I could come up with to explain why some of us are letting ourselves be exploited and disrespected. Yes, I said it—*letting* ourselves be disrespected. Of course our brothers in the rap game are somewhat to blame. They hold so much power that some of them don't know what to do with it. They have people from all walks of life listening to what they have to say, copying what they wear, and watching how they represent their sisters through their lyrics and videos. Quiet as it's kept, they also have corporations marketing and packaging their creativity to maximize profits.

Bottom line, they put the shit out there for money. Remember, a lot of these rappers come from the hood and for most of them, this is a way out. Nobody wants to hear your moral agenda if they're making money. Imagine having nothing and being able to become a millionaire just through your gift of gab. Given that kind of choice, you might be willing to say some wild stuff too.

In the beginning, hip-hop was just some rec time. It was about street respect and a way to express whatever was on your mind, from ghetto reality to some crowd-pleasing party shit. There was no real money involved, but you never heard an MC call a woman out of her name on the mic. There might be some rough dudes inside the party, but the MCs said things to make the ladies around the way feel good.

Now it's about some real money. We're talking about millions and millions of dollars, the kind of money that can feed your family and generations to follow. Hip-hop was a blessing to help a lot of people get out of poverty by any means necessary, but unfortunately those means now include mindless violence and calling our women bitches and hoes to get paid. Yes, sex sells, but who is benefiting off of it? A handful of rap stars make big money and move out of the hood to keep their families safe, but the rest of us still have to walk the streets that they continuously pump that negativity into. Crack sells too, but we don't want it in our community. The degradation of women is just as bad—it's self-destructive and it shouldn't be allowed. We as black women are the ones who need to say, "I won't tolerate my sisters being degraded. It's not fair to our daughters, or to all the ladies who are trying to do something in a positive light."

But we can't just blame our brothers in hip-hop. We need to dig a little bit deeper and get to the root of why we are being portrayed in such a distasteful way. And yes, we have to take some of the responsibility too. Ask yourself, if they did stop calling us bitches tomorrow, and stopped portraying us as big-booty-shaking chicks in their videos, would *we* stop? We need to take a look within to recognize our own worth. Some of us crave attention so much that we're not satisfied with a respectful compliment. We feel the need to take it to the next level. "Girl, I want my booty bigger." "Girl, I think I want some implants." "I want to be in that video—so what if I have to shake my ass for twelve hours for fifty dollars. Girl, I'm gonna be *seen.*" "So what he got a girl? Long as he pay me, I'll be the chick on the side." Etc., etc., etc. I hear it all the time, right out of some of our sistas' mouths. I am not just writing this on hearsay. No, I was born, raised, and still am in the hood. So I know a lot of us are not recognizing our worth. And the rest of us need to stop pointing fingers and looking down on the sisters who are trying to find their way. Why not try helping them instead, before it spills over to the next generation?

We have a lot of young women who are lost. They don't have any positive role models. They are looking at these videos, and they need a way to feel good about themselves. Their insecurity makes them take their clothes off and think, *Wow, I'm being accepted!* But somebody needs to tell these girls it's not just about exposing yourself. You can keep your clothes on and aspire to be the one making the deals and counting the money.

I know we all have dreams of making it out of the hood, but we have to start making real plans like furthering our education, starting businesses, becoming doctors, lawyers, making decisions that will enlighten our souls, not decisions that will leave us feeling empty. So many women are unhappy and we don't know why or what to do about it. Yes, some of our men are very wrong. But it's up to us to let 'em know. Until we step up and start displaying ourselves how we want to be seen, it will never end. The empty soul will continue to hunger.

We have to teach the next generation that it's okay to be

who you are. It's our duty to let them know—don't settle, don't give up, keep dreaming. And keep working to make your dreams come true. The road may seem endless, but there's something you're supposed to get from the journey. With God's strength, you can't go wrong. Trust the real hip-hop mother.